# THE CIA'S GREATEST COVERT OPERATION

# The CIA's Greatest Covert Operation

## Inside the Daring Mission to Recover a Nuclear-Armed Soviet Sub

### DAVID H. SHARP

 University Press of Kansas

Published by the University Press of Kansas (Lawrence, Kansas 66045), which was
organized by the Kansas Board of Regents and is operated and funded by Emporia State
University, Fort Hays State University, Kansas State University, Pittsburg State University,
the University of Kansas, and Wichita State University

Library of Congress Cataloging-in-Publication Data
Sharp, David H.
    The CIA's greatest covert operation : inside the daring mission to recover a nuclear-
armed Soviet sub / David H. Sharp.
        p.    cm.
    Includes bibliographical references and index.
    ISBN 978-0-7006-1834-7 (cloth : alk. paper) 1. Jennifer Project. 2. Glomar Explorer (Ship)
3. K-129 (Submarine) 4. United States. Central Intelligence Agency—History—20th
century. 5. Soviet Union. Voenno-Morskoi Flot—Submarine forces—History. 6. Submarine
disasters—Soviet Union. I. Title.
    vb31.u54s53 2012
    910.9164'9—dc23                                                    2011041677

British Library Cataloguing-in-Publication Data is available.

Printed in the United States of America
10 9 8 7 6 5 4 3 2

*There are small but great moments in history when some few have dared to do the impossible. This book is a record of one of those moments.*

# Contents

# Preface

In the summer of 1974 the CIA executed a clandestine recovery mission in the central North Pacific Ocean.[1] The recovery target was a Soviet Golf II–class submarine, *K-129*, that had sunk for unknown reasons six years earlier. The recovery vessel was named the *Hughes Glomar Explorer*. The program was code-named AZORIAN.[2]

On February 7, 1975, the *Los Angeles Times* exposed the recovery mission on the front page of its late edition. The exposé was followed within a few weeks by many more articles in nationally distributed newspapers and magazines, putting an end to any possible plans for future espionage missions with the *Explorer*.

Since that time, at least three books have been written purporting to tell the "true story" of the CIA's recovery program, and more than half a dozen books have addressed some aspects of the program and its results within their pages. None of these books—using mainly second- or thirdhand information—has portrayed an accurate and complete history of the recovery mission itself. Attempts to tell the story of the CIA's role in the development and operation of the recovery system, or the creation and execution of the complex security plan that enabled the recovery mission to be performed clandestinely, have been little more than uninformed speculation. The CIA has kept its secrets well.

AZORIAN is the most fascinating example of what has sometimes been described as the technical arrogance of the CIA's Directorate of Science and Technology during the Cold War years. The CIA has said very little about the program since it was exposed in 1975. The agency initially acknowledged only that it was the owner of the *Hughes Glomar Explorer*, and that the ship was built for the purpose of collecting intelligence. In 1992, however, the director of central intelligence (DCI), Robert Gates, acknowledged to the president of the Russian Federation, Boris Yeltsin, that the *Explorer* had been involved in a partially successful attempt to recover a portion of the *K-129* submarine. Gates also hand-delivered a visual record of the burial-at-sea ceremony for the six Soviet sailors whose bodies had been recovered along with parts of the submarine.[3] After Gates's visit to Moscow, the CIA remained silent on the subject of AZORIAN until January 2010, when special circumstances forced them to release a heavily redacted history of the program through Freedom of Information Act (FOIA) channels.

———

In the summer of 2007, after reading one more book on the *Hughes Glomar Explorer* program that was full of inaccuracies and absurd conspiracy theories, I suddenly realized four sobering facts: (1) The true story of the CIA's role in the *Glomar Explorer* program has never been accurately documented; (2) there was almost no institutional memory of the program remaining in the CIA; (3) I was one of the last remaining members of the CIA program team who had been heavily involved with all phases of the program, from concept development through operations, and all aspects of the program, including engineering, security, program management, and politics; and (4) I wasn't getting any younger. If I didn't write the story, who would be left to tell it?

I started to write. I had lots of memories about the program, as well as my personal notebooks that I maintained while on the ship from 1973 through 1975. I also had a copy of the unclassified deck logs of the *Hughes Glomar Explorer* for the entire period of the 1974 recovery mission. I thought I had enough material and memory to write the history. I was so wrong. I hadn't realized how much my memory had faded over thirty-five years. Every part of the story I wrote down brought up new questions that I couldn't answer. I realized I was going to need help.

The obvious sources for the help I needed were those program participants—both government and contractor—who had worked together to achieve such amazing results. I knew their names, but I didn't know where they lived or which ones were still alive. I had to find those guys and see if they'd be willing to help me fill in the blanks in my own memory.

My first contact was with R. Curtis Crooke, the former president of Global Marine Development Inc. I had kept in touch with Curtis over the years and knew where to find him. Curtis, in turn, got me back in touch with Sherman Wetmore, the chief Global Marine engineer on the ship during the mission, and with Oscar "Ott" Schick, the Lockheed program manager who oversaw the construction of those parts of the recovery system built by Lockheed's Ocean Systems Division. Sherm then introduced me to Michael White, a European film producer and remarkable researcher who was creating his own historical film of the AZORIAN program.

Eventually, this chain of contacts developed into a network of government and civilian friends who were able to fill in the blanks in my memory. More than that, though, they provided new information and stories that I had never known about. Especially satisfying was the opportunity to get back in touch with old friends that I hadn't heard from for many years.

By June 2008, I had a draft manuscript completed. As a former CIA employee, I'm required by law to submit any book or article that I want to publish to the agency's Publications Review Board (PRB). The PRB performs an "expedient" review—with a thirty-day goal—of a submitted manuscript and provides the author with a revised copy containing appropriate recommendations for redactions or changes that are needed to protect national security. I submitted my manuscript on June 24, 2008.

About three months later, I received a letter from the PRB requesting a meeting to discuss their concerns about the publication of my book. At the meeting, I was told that publication of a book about AZORIAN would likely "cause serious harm to national security," and that therefore *not one page* of the manuscript could be published. The PRB also informed me that I had a right to appeal the decision, in which case a senior CIA official reporting directly to the director of Central Intelligence would make a final ruling on whether *any* of my manuscript could be published.

With the help of my legal counsel, Mark Zaid, I prepared an appeal to the board's decision. The task of preparing the appeal was made significantly harder because of the board's refusal to allow Mark (who held a secret clearance) to read my manuscript. In January 2009, I submitted the appeal to the assistant deputy director of Central Intelligence (ADD/CIA).

Almost four months later—and still with no response to my appeal—I was informed that the PRB was reviewing the manuscript again to determine just what parts of the book might be publishable after all. Unfortunately, the PRB chose to redact almost all material that had not already been *officially* acknowledged by the CIA, even though the same material had been previously exposed in numerous open-source publications. Puzzlingly, the PRB also redacted material in my book about which the CIA had no knowledge. The PRB essentially took the position that even though they could not ascertain whether some of the events described in the book actually occurred, they were redacted because if they *had* occurred they would be classified. I never received a response to my first appeal, nor any explanation of the reasons for redaction of more than one-third of the words in my manuscript.

In January 2010, I submitted a second appeal to the ADD/CIA requesting permission to publish my manuscript. Five months later, I still hadn't received a response. My queries to the PRB for the status of my appeal were answered: "Your appeal is being processed."

Finally, I sent a letter to the board advising them that if I received no response within thirty days, I would be forced to consider other options available to me—including litigation. I sent copies of my appeal letter to the director and deputy director of the CIA, to Senator Barbara Mikulski (my senator from the state of Maryland and a member of the Senate Select Committee on Intelligence), and my attorney, Mark Zaid.

Within thirty days, I received a formal response from the CIA signed by the CIA's associate deputy director. Almost all of the material in the book was now approved for publication. Even more satisfying, the redactions that were sustained in the ADD/CIA's response were understandable and reasonable. I can only speculate as to why the agency had such a change of heart regarding publication of my book, but I was extremely gratified. After two years of frustration in the CIA's publications review process, I finally had a manuscript that I was permitted to send to a publisher.

With the help of many friends and shipmates, I've prepared a history that is as close to true as I can make it. That said, there are some caveats that apply.

The names of most of the CIA officers in the book are pseudonyms. Revealing the true identities of employees whose CIA affiliations have not been previously exposed would be an invasion of their personal privacy and could create security problems for them and for the agency. The names of senior CIA officers whose identities have been previously exposed in the media are real.

The names of several government agencies and commercial corporations that collaborated with the CIA on the AZORIAN program are not mentioned. For those agencies and organizations, revelation of their CIA association could be awkward. The names of contractors and government organizations that routinely and openly contract or collaborate with the CIA on other programs are included in the manuscript.

Finally, I must acknowledge that my memory is far from perfect. Even my program associates disagreed on the timing and details of some of the incidents recalled in the book. To those veterans of the AZORIAN program who may detect some errors in my story, I apologize beforehand. I'm sure there are some differences of opinion that will arise, and perhaps some outright errors will be found. I feel confident, however, that these transgressions will not materially affect the overall validity of this history.

The engineering, security, and operational histories of the AZORIAN program are impressive and historically significant. The stories of the dedicated CIA officers and contractors who persevered to pull off this remarkable mission are inspirational. Their efforts deserve to be documented definitively and accurately. That is the purpose of this book.

# The CIA's Greatest Covert Operation

# I

## Genesis

### A Soviet Submarine Is Lost—and Found

In early March 1968, for reasons still under dispute, a Soviet Golf II–class submarine with hull number PL-722 sank in about 16,700 feet of water in the central North Pacific. The sub (designated by the Soviet navy as *K-129*) was a diesel-powered boat, although it carried three nuclear missiles and two nuclear torpedoes.[1] It had an overall length of 330 feet, weighed about 2,500 tons, and normally carried a crew of eighty-three men. The *K-129* wasn't a fast boat. It could manage a speed of about fifteen to seventeen knots on the surface, and about thirteen knots submerged. That was fast enough, though, to enable it to sail from its home base near Vladivostok to a typical patrol station within a few hundred miles of Hawaii in less than ten days. With an endurance of seventy days, it could spend well over a month on station before returning back to the Kamchatka Peninsula.

The *K-129* had left its home base of Ribachiy, near Petropavlovsk on the Kamchatka Peninsula, on or about February 25. It was following a route to its likely patrol station 700–800 nautical miles northwest of Hawaii. From there it would be available for nuclear attack on U.S. targets if the Cold War suddenly became hot.[2]

But the *K-129* never reached its designated patrol station. Its covert, submerged transit toward Hawaii was interrupted by a violent and fatal incident that resulted in the loss of the submarine and all of its crew. The sub's position, when it sank, was almost exactly at the geographic coordinates 40° N, 180° W, an area of the ocean frequently traveled by Soviet submarines on routine operational patrols in the North Pacific.

When the *K-129* failed to make its scheduled communications report to its fleet command headquarters on March 7, the Soviet Pacific Fleet commands tried desperately to reestablish communications with the sub. There was no response from the *K-129*. On March 9, the Soviets concluded that their submarine had been lost. The next day, naval headquarters in Moscow approved a massive search effort to find the *K-129* and, hopefully, to rescue any survivors. Although the Soviets had no evidence to explain the loss, there were strong suspicions that a U.S. Navy ship or submarine had been involved.[3]

————

The assumption of U.S. involvement, even without any supporting evidence, was understandable if not provable. During the late 1950s and 1960s, both the United States and the Soviet Union were driven to take dangerous risks in probing each other's military might and preparedness. This jousting routine of threats, bluffing, and probing sometimes slipped over the line into actual physical conflicts. Airplanes and pilots from both sides were lost without official explanation while engaging in these tactics. In the oceans, both commercial and military ships sometimes fell victim to overzealous tracking or harassment exercises.

No services participated more actively and frighteningly in these Cold War conflicts than the submarine corps of both states. With land-based intercontinental ballistic missile (ICBM) locations having been identified and targeted by both parties, the nuclear weapons carried by submarines became the tie breaker that could potentially tip the balance of a nuclear war. In order to monitor the locations and identify the operational procedures used by these missile-carrying subs, both the United States and the USSR were willing to take major risks. These underwater cat-and-mouse games brought both countries' subs into close contact. Sometimes too close. Many near incidents and some actual collisions between submarines, or between a submarine and a surface ship, had already occurred.

At the time of the *K-129* loss, both the United States and the USSR were growing increasingly disturbed by these dangerous ocean maneuvers. Concern went beyond the accidental loss of ships and lives. These incidents could potentially turn the Cold War into World War III. The United States forcefully denied having any knowledge about the cause of the *K-129*'s loss. The Soviet Union was unconvinced.

Whatever the cause of the sinking, the Soviets understandably went into a crisis mode when they lost contact with their boat. Their concern for the possible loss of a submarine with its ninety-eight crewmen was heightened by the fact that the boat carried nuclear weapons.

They immediately sent out an armada of surface ships and submarines to search for the lost Golf II. The search was intense and covered a wide area. However, they had only an approximate idea as to where the sub's position might be and only limited search technologies to apply to the effort. Their emergency responses to the loss were essentially confined to attempting communication with the submarine using radio and acoustic signals and, failing to communicate, searching for oil slick, debris, or survivors from a boat that had presumably sunk.

Sonar was also used by both the surface ships and the submarines to attempt location of the boat on the ocean bottom. This was a hopeless task, though, since any sonar return from a sunken submarine at a depth of nearly 17,000 feet would be masked to a large degree by the acoustic returns from the ocean bottom. Eventually, the search was called off. Although certainly devastated by the loss of a submarine and its crew, the Soviets felt confident that the extreme water depth in the search area, coupled with the large size and mass of the submarine, precluded any concerns that the wreckage of the boat and its weapons might fall into the hands of a foreign intelligence service.

———

The significance of the *K-129*'s demise wasn't lost on the United States. Although confident that no U.S. naval vessel had been involved in the incident, responsible government officials recognized that the tracking and harassment tactics currently being employed by the navies of the United States and the USSR had raised the potential for the occurrence of such a fatal collision. There was genuine concern over the impact that such an incident could have on the relations between the two countries. In March 1968—while the Soviets were still searching for their lost submarine—the United States invited the Soviet Union to participate in the formulation of a bilateral Agreement on the Prevention of Incidents On and Over the High Seas.

———

The Soviets couldn't find their submarine, but the U.S. Navy thought that perhaps it could.[4] Once it was clear that a sub had been lost, acoustic analysts under the command of Captain Joseph Kelly began looking at the signals from the Navy's Sound Surveillance System (SOSUS) and the hydrophone arrays built by the U.S. Air Force Technical Applications Center (AFTAC),[5] a system of acoustic sensors used during the Cold War to detect the presence and track the routes of Soviet submarines, and to geolocate the impacts of ballistic missiles that had been test-fired by the Soviet Union. These sensors, with a range of thousands of miles, were used operationally in both the Atlantic and Pacific Oceans. All of the SOSUS and AFTAC detection systems, some of which were colocated, were operated out of U.S. Navy facilities and ships.

Analysts looking at the acoustic records for the time frame in which the K-129 was believed to have sunk were able to identify a set of signatures that were consistent with the sounds that would emanate from a sinking submarine. Using these signatures, recorded at several of the AFTAC acoustic array sites, they were able to pinpoint the location of the event to within a circle about four miles in diameter.[6]

With this discovery, the Navy planned an underwater search mission aimed at finding the lost submarine. For security reasons, the CIA has refused to allow me to publish any details of the Navy's underwater search capabilities or the results of the search mission. Knowledge of this capability was (and still is) restricted to those with appropriate clearances and a need to know.

However, other authors writing about the search for K-129 have consistently suggested that the search vehicle was the USS Halibut, one of the earliest U.S. nuclear-powered submarines.[7] The Halibut was originally designed to launch ballistic missiles, but was later modified to perform a wide range of other special missions.[8] Without confirming or denying the popular belief that the Halibut was the vessel that located the lost Soviet submarine, it was determined that the K-129 had not simply broken into many pieces when it struck the ocean bottom; much of the sub was still intact. Authors Sherry Sontag and Christopher Drew wrote, "Although severely damaged, the submarine looked basically intact. . . . Inside the first [silo] was twisted pipe where a nuclear warhead had once sat calmly waiting for holocaust. Inside the second silo, the warhead was completely gone. The third silo was intact."[9]

The U.S. government has never released any photographs of the K-129 wreckage to the public, in spite of many requests made under the Freedom of Information Act. In fact, the government currently refuses to confirm or deny that such photographs ever existed. Several authors, however, have described the sunken submarine based on first- or secondhand information.

In *The Universe Below*, William J. Broad quotes an unnamed project architect who asserted that the sunken submarine was badly broken up. However, Broad's source went on to say, "The only section deemed interesting enough for retrieval was an intact section of the bow and center structure that measured some two hundred feet in length."[10] CIA's recovery efforts were focused on recovering that section. It was referred to as the target object, or sometimes just the target.

Sherman Wetmore, who was Global Marine's chief engineer during the *Hughes Glomar Explorer* (*HGE*) mission and had personal access to photos and video recordings of the *K-129* on the bottom, also described the target object in a speech he presented to the American Society of Mechanical Engineers at a ceremony memorializing the *HGE* in 2006. Wetmore said, "[It was] generally oblong but not symmetrical; having a length of 160 feet, a width of 64 feet and a maximum height of 55 feet." As for the weight of the target object, Wetmore said, "2,000 tons was the best estimate given to us as baseline criteria."

This was exciting. If the United States could somehow gain access to that target, it could confirm the existence of nuclear missiles on the Golf II–class sub, learn what materials were used, and analyze the construction of the warheads. There were other potential intelligence prizes as well. Access to the control room in the sail—the vertical structure above the submarine hull—might permit recovery of the ship's logs, communications and cryptographic systems, codebooks, and operating manuals. This information could give the Navy the capability to monitor and read classified Soviet communications, providing a tremendous tactical advantage in the continuing Cold War task of maintaining an accurate track on the location and movements of all Soviet submarines.

With the support of the entire U.S. government chain of command, from the president down to the chief of naval operations, Admiral Thomas H. Moorer, the Navy put its most experienced underwater scientists to work on the task of devising a way to recover the secrets from the Soviet sub.[11] This team included Captain Jim Bradley, a submariner who had cut his teeth on diesel boats and was currently responsible for planning underwater espionage missions for Admiral Hyman Rickover's nuclear fleet. The team also included Dr. John Craven, a senior Navy scientist who was on the special intelligence task force responsible for finding the *K-129*.

The team, led by these two men highly experienced in submarine operations, came up with a predictable—if not necessarily practical—recommendation. They proposed to use a small mini-sub to descend to the target. The mini-sub would use much of the technology then being used by Craven for the Navy's Deep Submergence Systems Project,[12] which included development of the Deep Submergence Rescue Vehicle and the Deep Submergence Search Vehicle, the latter being designed for research and search-and-recovery missions down to a depth of 20,000 feet.[13] Under the Navy's plan, the mini-sub would plant small explosive charges on selected portions of the *K-129* sail to blow away steel plates, permitting access into the sail area. Remotely controlled appendages attached to the mini-sub would reach into those openings and recover the intelligence objects of interest, returning them to the surface for exploitation. Some tests were reportedly run to verify that the explosives technology could actually create penetrable openings in the sail without destroying the equipment or files to be recovered.

Unfortunately for Craven and Bradley, Admiral Moorer wasn't impressed with the scheme.[14] He dismissed their ideas of selective recovery of the missile warheads and the cryptographic and communications equipment.[15] He had serious reservations about the use of explosives to surgically open the submarine without destroying the valuable contents, and he questioned the ability of mini-subs at depths of nearly 17,000 feet to remove and recover intelligence artifacts as small as a codebook and as large as a nuclear warhead. Besides, he was impressed with the fact that the main section of the submarine seemed to be substantially intact. Why not, he reasoned, go after the whole thing? And, in so doing, make up in some part for the loss of the USS *Pueblo*, which had been captured by the North Koreans in 1968.

To the chagrin of Bradley and Craven, Admiral Moorer told his superiors that the Navy had no workable plan to exploit the sunken Soviet Golf II class. Moorer went on to say that, in his opinion, if a way to recover large portions of the submarine could be developed, the value to the country would be immense. Other key members of the intelligence community felt the same way. The potential intelligence coup was too valuable to just forget without looking for other ideas. They decided to go to the CIA to see if its new, ambitious team working in the area of underwater espionage could come up with a scheme for recovering the entire target.

## CIA Gets in the Game

On April 1, 1969, Deputy Director of Defense David Packard sent a letter to DCI Richard Helms asking him how his agency might propose to exploit the sunken Soviet sub.[16] Helms was understandably cautious. After all, the CIA was not noted for building ships and had only limited experience in marine engineering. Spy planes? Satellites? Yes and yes. But most of its previous ocean espionage activity had been in support of the activities of other agencies or services. Still, he passed the question down to Carl Duckett, the newly appointed deputy director for science and technology (DD/S&T).

If Richard Helms was somewhat diffident about getting into the submarine salvage area, Carl Duckett did not share that reluctance. He jumped at the opportunity to study the problem and offered to pull a team of scientists together to explore all possibilities. This was the kind of special challenge that Duckett loved.

Buoyed by Duckett's confidence and his own enthusiasm for the collection of intelligence by technical means, Helms told Packard that he believed the CIA might, indeed, be able to bring some new ideas to the exploitation challenge. He asked for two months to study the problem. Packard agreed and designated Dr. John Foster, director of defense research and engineering (DD/R&E), as his focal point for coordination.

Carl Duckett had been an unusual and controversial choice for the position of DD/S&T. Although a skilled technical manager, Carl Duckett did not even have a college degree. He had an impressive background in missile technology, though, and very good technical instincts. Carl had some other special talents as well. He had a keen memory and the ability to influence people and win them over to his cause. He made friends easily and socialized frequently with key members of Congress who could usually be relied on to support his cause—whatever it might be. Duckett was a popular manager of his own people, too. Summarizing his leadership style, he was easy to talk to, he listened well, and he always remembered a person's name.

Duckett's choice to head up the CIA project team was John Parangosky. Parangosky had great credentials as an R&D manager in the CIA, but he had no experience with any type of marine engineering or underwater operations. He had started his career working for Richard Bissell in the CIA's Plans Directorate as a senior officer at a U-2 base in the Middle East, but he later became involved with the R&D of what were then referred to as *special systems* for the collection of technical intelligence. (Prior to the formation of the National Reconnaissance Office (NRO) and the CIA's Science and Technology Directorate in the early 1960s, the U-2 operations were managed in the Plans Directorate, now called the Operations Directorate.)

In 1958 Parangosky had been placed in charge of R&D for the A-12 (or OXCART) hypersonic reconnaissance airplane, which was intended to replace the aging and increasingly vulnerable U-2 for intelligence collection over Soviet territory. In 1961, as OXCART entered the flight test phase in Nevada, Parangosky and his R&D staff also took on a major role in the development of the CORONA reconnaissance spacecraft. The CORONA program was the first major space challenge undertaken by the newly formed

National Reconnaissance Office, an organization created to coordinate the efforts of both the CIA and the Air Force in the use of overhead reconnaissance to collect strategic intelligence from behind the Iron Curtain. He was remarkably successful in all these endeavors and was regarded as something of a miracle worker.

Parangosky had another characteristic that made him a good choice for the new program. He was almost fanatically obsessed with the need for good security. He was even very sparing in the disclosure of his name. Most contractors knew him only as "JP."

Given the challenge of recovering the K-129, Duckett gave Parangosky free rein to choose six or seven engineers/scientists from the vast technical resources of the DD/S&T. I don't know what criteria Parangosky used to cherry-pick agency personnel for his special study group, but it's pretty clear that either there were no experienced marine engineers in the agency or else he just didn't place high emphasis on prior experience in ocean engineering. The initial full-time study team consisted of about seven men with very diverse backgrounds.

Dr. Earnest Ruggles was an oceanographer working for the Science and Technology Directorate's Office of Research and Development (ORD), a scientific office that investigated cutting-edge ideas and technologies. Ruggles had been working with a special group exploring the possibilities for intelligence collection from the marine environment. He'd heard that there was a new program being formed around John Parangosky. Ruggles was interested, and he asked his close friend, Dr. Jack Sparkman, if he'd be interested in moving to the new project with him.

Jack Sparkman was a senior chemical engineer from ORD. He'd never had an opportunity to work on a large program, and he was excited about the possibility. Sparkman and Ruggles both went to talk to Parangosky. Sparkman recalled that his first impression of him was that he was all business. Sparkman reflected later, "His only interest seemed to be his program—and to hell with anything else or any other part of your life!" Sparkman figured that was just the right attitude for a program manager. He and Ruggles both signed up on the spot. They hadn't even been briefed on the program yet.

Another member of the original AZORIAN team was Jack Mahoney, an innovative mechanical engineer with an impressive background in aeronautics and space systems. A natural at solving tough engineering problems, he quickly recognized a satisfying challenge when he saw it. And the mission that Parangosky described to him sounded very challenging, indeed.

Other early members of the team included Bill Rivers, a former Air Force captain and an excellent administrative officer; Alex Hausman, a highly respected physicist and mathematician; Paul Eastman, a senior member of the agency's office of security; Doug Conrad, Parangosky's deputy and a close friend of Carl Duckett; and me, an electronics engineer with mostly aircraft experience. On a part-time basis, Parangosky was also able to get the services of Frank Hillcrest, an intelligence expert on Soviet submarines.

I got hired onto the staff in typical Parangosky fashion. I was finishing my second year of graduate work at the University of Virginia—under the sponsorship of the CIA—when I received a call from him.

He said, "Dave, I've found a new job for you that you're going to love!"

I asked, "Can you give me an idea of what the job is?"

"No."

"Do I have a choice, John?"

"No."

"How much time can you give me before reporting?"

"Be here next week!"

I chafed a little about being unable to negotiate anything, but I knew Parangosky well enough to have confidence that he wouldn't bullshit me about having a job that I was "going to love." I was also sure that the job would be exciting. Working for JP was *always* exciting. I showed up the next week.

Among the nine of us, only Earnest Ruggles and Frank Hillcrest had real knowledge of any aspect of the oceans or the vessels that operated on or within them. None of us had any prior experience with actually building large systems to operate in the ocean. Looking back, we were an unlikely group to be taking on a marine engineering task that the chief of naval operations had declared "probably impossible."

Parangosky's capabilities as a program manager were obvious, but he in no way fit the stereotypical model of a successful manager of large R&D programs. To begin with, he had no formal technical education. He had some training in law, and by some accounts was a very competent violinist, but his grasp of mathematical and engineering concepts was meager. He made up for his lack of technical skills with a prodigious appetite for reading about current progress in science and engineering, and a highly developed ability to sense whom he could trust for technical guidance.

On the OXCART program, it had been Kelly Johnson, head of Lockheed's Skunk Works in Burbank, that Parangosky trusted and used for a sounding board. This is not to say that John Parangosky and Kelly Johnson had a completely smooth relationship. I witnessed many heated arguments between the two over technical and schedule issues. In the end, though, Parangosky nearly always took Johnson's advice. And, as it turned out, that was pretty smart. It was almost always good advice.

Parangosky also had a fierce temper and could be irrational in his arguments. If displeased with a contractor's performance, he'd threaten to terminate the contract, and sometimes he followed up the threat with action. His own staff often got the same treatment, some of whom were "fired" more than once. However, he almost always gave the injured party the opportunity to bring himself back into good graces. I suspect that in most cases his irrationality was intentional, to keep his staff and the contractors from ever getting complacent.

I was fired twice by John Parangosky, most memorably in 1964 when I was a young man working at Area 51 of the Nevada Test Site on the OX-CART flight test program. I was notified through Air Force channels that our planes were being tracked by USAF air defense radars during some of their test flights. That was not supposed to happen. The A-12 was a stealth aircraft, and the CIA's experts in this area believed that the radar signatures of our aircraft were too small to be tracked by either U.S. or Soviet radars. I drove out to one of the radar sites at Angel's Peak, Nevada, to see for myself. Much to my surprise, the Air Defense Command actually was tracking our hypersonic 2,000 mph aircraft, which was still so secret that few Air Force officers had even been briefed on it.

When I reported my findings to Parangosky, he said, "Don't tell me that! It's impossible. I don't want to hear it." When I pressed my case, he shouted over the telephone, "You're fired! Pack your bags and go home!" The CIA manager of the Nevada flight test facility overhead the conversation, looked at me, and shrugged. "He's the boss," he said.

Fortunately for me, my supervisor, Norm Nelson, was as hard-nosed as Parangosky. He was Kelly Johnson's right-hand man at the Area 51 test site and later distinguished himself as the program manager for the Lockheed F-117A stealth fighter and general manager of the Lockheed Skunk Works. Nelson waited a day, then he called Parangosky back and convinced him that I should get another chance. Of course, the fact that the agency's own stealth experts conceded shortly thereafter that the OXCART vehicle wasn't invisible to radar after all probably helped convince Parangosky that I wasn't a totally lost cause.[17]

---

The sensitivity of the new study effort was such that Parangosky was unwilling to brief any outsiders on his work. He knew, though, that we'd have to have at least one contractor to provide technical support to our group. He chose a small West Coast engineering company that had supported the agency on several other programs, mostly in the space arena. Although not an apparent match for the work to be done, this company had an existing contract with the CIA and a cadre of personnel with top secret security clearances. We only had two months to come up with a concept credible enough to warrant additional funding and analysis. There wasn't time to establish new contracts and clearances for a company with marine engineering credentials. We couldn't afford to waste time trying to hire experience.

That said, our contractor's engineers were an impressive set of talents. The CIA core staff and our new engineering support company made a good, cohesive, technical team. In addition, we all shared the common credential of zero experience in ocean engineering.

Our first concepts were, not surprisingly, unimpressive. One of the very early ideas called for using mini-subs to attach rocket boosters to the *K-129*, then launching the target to the surface. I realize this sounds incredibly naive (and it was), but most of the AZORIAN technical team's previous experience was in airplanes and/or satellites. As the old saying goes, "To a hammer, every problem looks like a nail." Besides, Carl Duckett had worked previously with the ballistic missile people in Huntsville, Alabama. The idea of using boosters to raise the submarine sounded perfectly reasonable to him, who was jokingly referred to as "Mr. Rocket" by some of his friends in Congress. We finally realized that even if we were able to attach the boosters and launch the target to the surface, what would we do with it then? How would we keep it on the surface? I don't want to belabor the flaws in this approach. I just want to point out how much we had to learn when we started the AZORIAN program.

Another approach, slightly more mature, called for using a submersible to attach flotation bags or pontoons to the target. Once attached to the hull, the flotation bags would be filled with enough gas to create positive buoyancy that could lift the target to the surface. The gas for the pontoons could be generated on the seafloor—either chemically or by electrolysis— or, we could pump air from a ship through a long pipe or tube to the ocean bottom. Both approaches had technical issues that would have to be solved. There was precious little information available on how to generate large quantities of gas at pressures of 7,500 pounds per square inch (psi), or what kind of compressors would be required to pump air down a three-mile-long pipe. We knew the compressors would have to operate at pressures of at least 5,000 psi, and the pipe would have to be able to withstand the same pressure. For sure, automobile radiator hose wasn't going to do the job.

Even recognizing the problems ahead, the CIA team was undaunted. They were confident they could find a workable approach for recovering the G-II sub. Dick Helms and Carl Duckett backed Parangosky and his staff all the way. In mid-July 1969, Helms briefed David Packard on the progress of the agency's effort and requested authorization to continue the work. Packard, perhaps impressed more by the enthusiasm of the program team than by the actual study results, agreed to extend the CIA's efforts. The Special Projects Staff went back to work eagerly. We were sure we could find a workable way to float the target to the surface.

Then, Frank Hillcrest (the only guy on our team at the time who really knew submarines) blew our concept to smithereens. He pointed out that we had no idea how many air bottles might still be on the target with compressed air in them. As the target was raised, this air would expand, perhaps leaking out of the tanks into the hull of the submarine. Would the air just leak out of the hull? Or would it keep expanding, contained within the hull, creating constantly increasing buoyancy that we had no way of controlling? There was a real probability that the target could go into an uncontrolled rate of ascent, breaking the surface near to (or even under) the ship. In other words, our quarry could become our hunter. And even if the submarine reached the surface without damaging the ship, what would we do with it then? Tow it home in plain view across thousands of miles of open ocean—while the Soviet navy watched? We scrapped that idea, too.

———

After a couple of weeks, a collaboration among Jack Mahoney, Jack Sparkman, and our technical support contractor resulted in a new, more comprehensive approach. Our plan was to build a large steel barge with a *keyhole* in the center that would just fit around the target object. The barge would be filled with pentane for buoyancy and weighted down with steel ballast approximating the estimated weight of the target. Pentane was selected as the buoyancy medium because it had a relatively low coefficient of expansion with pressure and with temperature. The buoyancy of the pentane would remain fairly constant at different depths and pressures. The ops concept was to tow the pentane-filled barge to the recovery site, where it would be loaded with enough additional ballast to make it negatively buoyant. Then, supported by six very large nylon cables wrapped around powered winches, the barge would be lowered to the bottom. During the final stage of lowering, the keyhole would be aligned with the target and the barge would descend the rest of the way to the bottom. Once the target was within the keyhole, it would be locked into place by an arrangement of sliding wedges. Ballast would then be jettisoned from the barge—now with the target enclosed—until it could be lifted by the nylon lowering/lifting cables. When the target had been raised to the surface, more ballast would be dropped so that the barge became positively buoyant on its own. It could then be towed, with the target concealed in the keyhole, to a secure location for exploitation.

The new concept wasn't perfect. Like our previous ideas, it had some serious technical and operational issues. For example, the volume of pentane required to fill the barge was equal to two years' worth of the total worldwide pentane production. And, we hadn't yet addressed how we would explain the strange behavior and mysterious mission of a pentane-filled barge in the middle of the North Pacific Ocean. In spite of the weaknesses in this concept, though, we thought we were on the right track. We just had to work on the details.

———

In August 1969 a high-level executive committee (referred to as the ExCom) consisting of David Packard as chairman, Dick Helms, and Dr. Lee DuBridge (science adviser to the president) approved the establishment of the structure, management, assets, personnel assignments, and intelligence objectives for a new organization that would be responsible for the submarine recovery.[18] Dr. Kissinger, the president's national security adviser, notified President Nixon of the new organization and its mission and secured his support for the operation. From that point on, the CIA's program to recover the *K-129* was managed under the auspices of the new organization whose name, activities, and even existence were very tightly controlled within the intelligence community. (This information is still considered to be very sensitive. The CIA redacted the name of the organization in its history, *Project AZORIAN,* released through FOIA channels in February 2010. Although other authors have speculated on the name and nature of this office [Richelson 2002, 195; Sontag and Drew 1998, 83; Polmar and White 2010, 59], that information is still classified.)

The support of the president and Dr. Kissinger was considered a pivotal moment for the program. There had been a lot of uncertainty about the president's reaction to the proposal. Nixon was somewhat of an enigma to DCI Richard Helms. Almost all communications between the two had been through an intermediary—either National Security Adviser Henry Kissinger or his military assistant, Colonel (later General) Al Haig. Nixon's dislike/distrust of the CIA was widely suspected throughout Washington. Reportedly, in the president's first postelection meeting with Henry Kissinger, Nixon had denounced the CIA as a group of "Ivy League liberals" who "had always opposed him politically."[19] The fact that Nixon was willing to endorse what had to be considered a high-risk espionage program against the Soviet Union—even while he was heavily engaged in negotiations with the USSR to reduce Cold War tensions by limiting the proliferation of strategic arms—showed that he was willing to take risks for the recovery of valuable intelligence, and that his confidence in the CIA was perhaps not as meager as previously assumed.

———

I want to point out that, although in hindsight the early recovery concepts of the CIA's program office failed to withstand the hard technical and operational scrutiny to which they were inevitably exposed, we were operating with precious little precedent in technology for this scale of salvage. Earlier attempts to salvage large objects (such as a large boat or ship) were almost exclusively limited to shallow water operations in which divers could attach inflatable canisters or air bags to the vessel. Our task was to raise an object weighing between 2 and 4 million pounds from a water depth of over three miles. There were no precedents. In all probability, if we had had any marine engineering experience, we would never have dared to take on the job.

In trying to develop a recovery concept, we seemed to be running into one stone wall after another, but occasionally we'd have an experience that would make us feel good. Shortly after we discarded the idea of floating the target to the surface using air-filled pontoons, Parangosky got a call from Captain Jim Bradley, who had been one of the key architects of the Navy's rejected plan to exploit the *K-129* with a mini-sub.[20] Bradley claimed that the Navy had come up with a way to recover the entire target object covertly, and that the scheme was far superior to any technique that the CIA had briefed him on to date.

Parangosky called Jack Mahoney and me into his office. "Go down and listen to those guys, see what they have to say," he told us. "Don't commit to anything—just listen—I want you to be just a bird on the wall!" (This was JP's mangled version of the expression "a fly on the wall.") Then he added, "I don't want any cowboys and Indians over this!" His orders were clear enough.

When we got to Bradley's offices, we were ushered into a secure room where a couple of his officers proceeded to brief us on their idea for covertly recovering the target. Here's the plan: Using a manned submersible, they would attach large flotation bags to the hull of the target. To the manifold for the flotation bags, the submersible would also attach the end of a long pipe hanging down from a submerged submarine near the surface. The submarine would then pump air from its ballast tanks down the pipe into the flotation bags until the target broke loose from the bottom and began to rise with positive buoyancy. That was it. No talk about controlling buoyancy or rate of ascent, or mention of any mechanical challenges related to design of the air delivery pipe. Mahoney looked at me and grinned. We'd been down *this* road before. Mahoney understood the issues better than I did, so he took the lead in the questioning.

He asked, "Do you actually have enough air in your ballast tanks to provide the necessary buoyancy?"

"Sure," they replied.

"Even at 7,500 psi, when the air will be compressed to about 1/500th of its surface volume?"

"Uh, we may have to get more air from the surface, but that won't be a problem."

"Have you thought about an air hose design? And, can you carry that much weight and volume in the submarine?"

"Sure, we could carry more than 25,000 feet of hose."

"Will your air hose withstand, say, 5,000 psi? 'Cause that's the pressure your compressors will need to pump the air down that hose. And, it's going to have to be larger in diameter than your electromechanical cable if you're going to pump all that high-pressure air down into those pontoons."

"Well, we haven't looked into all those details yet."

Then, he hit them with the killer question: "Have you thought about the amount of compressed air that might still be in pressure bottles in the sub? And what effect they might have on buoyancy and rate of ascent?"

The Navy briefers whispered among themselves for a couple of minutes and then said, "We'll get back to you when we've had a chance to do more analysis on the concept."

On the way back to headquarters, we were both in high good humor. Mahoney said, "Now, *that* was therapeutic!" And it was—even if it had been somewhat sadistic. It was refreshing to know that our CIA engineering team really *was* able to compete with the Navy in the development of marine engineering concepts.

We briefed Parangosky on the concept and our conclusions. When we'd finished, he seemed very pleased. He asked, "You didn't piss anybody off, did you?"

"Nope," said Mahoney. "We were cool."

JP just grinned.

———

It wasn't just Jack Mahoney and I who were enthusiastic about the work we were doing. In fact, the whole program office (about eight people during the first year) was head over heels in love with our program. Consider, how often in an engineering career do you get the opportunity to come up with a concept for achieving something that has never been done before? Sadly, most engineers never get the chance to create a solution out of whole cloth. Those of us on the program were blessed—and we knew it.

———

After President Nixon's approval to continue the program, we proceeded to brief all the major players involved with an operation of this type and magnitude—cabinet secretaries, directors of intelligence agencies, and chiefs of staff. We had a real road show going on trying to convince the decision makers that the recovery of a Soviet submarine would provide priceless intelligence, and that the CIA had a team that could pull off the recovery operation. Enthusiastic? Yes—and occasionally a little out of control. We all felt so personally involved in the program that we frequently stumbled over our own zeal.

One memorable example of our awkward eagerness to impress occurred while we were trying to convince one of the other intelligence agencies to support the program. We were briefing the director. I was supposed to give the electronics portion of the briefing, and Jack Mahoney was supposed to brief the mechanical engineering aspects. But we all wanted to talk all the time. And all of us wanted to talk at the same time. Mahoney had just completed his briefing, and the director asked a question. For some impossible-to-explain reason, I stumbled over a bunch of feet to the front of the room and blurted out, "I'd like to address that question!"

The director looked over at me and said, "Well?"

My mind went totally blank. I couldn't even remember what the question was, let alone what I had intended to say. All I could think of to say was, "Would you repeat the question, please?"

The entire audience broke up with laughter as I slunk back to my position in the back of the room. To my great relief, Parangosky didn't make a big deal over my faux pas. He did, however, develop some protocol for us engineers to follow during future briefings. Paraphrasing, the protocol said basically, "Give your own briefing, then get off the stage!" Point taken.

———

The presidential approval—and the continued funding implied by the approval—provided the welcome gift of a more relaxed timetable for Parangosky and his team. We started researching ocean engineering literature, ideas, and experiments that might be relevant to our tasking. Three of the most useful idea sources were the Mohole Project; the books and articles written by oceanographer Willard Bascom; and the experiments performed by the National Science Foundation with its research ship, the *Glomar Challenger*.

We first learned about Project Mohole through Willard Bascom's *A Hole in the Bottom of the Sea: The Mohole Project*. Project Mohole was a scientific endeavor to obtain a sample of the Earth's mantle by drilling through the Earth's crust to the Mohorovicic discontinuity, or "Moho." The Moho is the boundary between the relatively low-density crust of the Earth and the higher-density mantle that lies below the crust. Geologists believe that increased knowledge about the mantle could lead to a better understanding of the forces that influence continental shifts and earthquakes. The Moho is thirty to fifty kilometers deep over typical landmasses. Under the oceans, however, the Moho depth averages only about five kilometers.

In the 1950s, the idea of using a floating ocean platform to drill through the crust to the mantle was actively promoted. The idea was first proposed by Walter Munk, a member of the National Academy of Science (NAS) and the National Science Foundation (NSF), who convincingly argued that samples from the Earth's mantle would yield new and important insights into the actual composition of the Earth and how it was formed. Munk proposed drilling in a deep part of the ocean because the Earth's crust is thinnest there. Sponsored by the NSF in 1958, Project Mohole employed a specialized research ship, the *CUSS I*. Built by Global Marine—an offshore drilling company—it was funded by a consortium of oil companies (Continental, Union, Superior, and Shell) whose first initials were used for naming the ship. The NSF plan called for the *CUSS I* to drill through the crust in 11,700 feet of water off the coast of Guadalupe, Mexico. Although the program never achieved its goal of drilling into the mantle, the feasibility of drilling in deep water was convincingly proven.

We in the AZORIAN program office were especially intrigued by the positioning system the *CUSS I* had used to maintain a relatively constant position over the drilling site. (Remember, satellite navigation was still a long way off.) Global Marine anchored four floating radar reflectors in a pattern around the drilling point. Each reflector was several miles from the ship. Using the ship's radar, the operator sequentially scanned the reflectors and determined the ship's position using the distance radials from the reflectors to the ship. The *CUSS I* didn't have any side thrusters, but it had four steerable main propulsion thrusters somewhat resembling large outboard motors. The ship's operators used these steerable thrusters with manual control to maintain the position over the drilling hole. Accuracy of the position estimation was rough, since the positions of the anchored reflectors would change constantly with wind and tide. Still, Global was able to hold the ship to within a 600-foot radius. With that positioning accuracy, the maximum offset angle between the ship and the hole that was being drilled was less than three degrees. That was close enough to avoid any serious bending of the drill string and was pretty impressive technology for that time.

For the record, Project Mohole never achieved its goal of drilling through the Earth's core. The deepest hole drilled was claimed to be 601 feet. The effort was canceled in 1966, primarily because of increasing costs. But it showed us the way.

———

In addition to writing about Project Mohole, Willard Bascom wrote a number of other books, some of them related to his strong interest in looking for sunken ships and treasure. Searching for objects or ships on the ocean bottom was very challenging in the early 1960s, primarily because of the difficulty in knowing the search ship's position accurately. The first satellite navigation system, Transit, was still not fully operational. The early ground-based navigation systems (Decca, LORAN, and Omega) were often unreliable and had inconsistent accuracy. Obviously, if the position estimates for the ship were not precise, then the position estimates of the search sensors looking at the ocean bottom from the end of a long cable or drill string were totally inadequate. The problem was especially critical in deep water.

Bascom had founded a small company—Ocean Science and Engineering Inc.—in 1962, and he reportedly enjoyed some considerable success with undersea exploration for diamonds off the coast of South Africa. He had invented and patented an underwater search technique that employed a dynamically positioned drill ship and used recently developed side-looking sonar technology along with closed-circuit television cameras, magnetometers, and other sensors to search for targets in the area of interest. This technique could be used for finding old shipwrecks, or—of greater interest to the intelligence community—the nose cones of Soviet test missiles that had been launched into the sea. It was clever, and the modest cost was especially attractive for a low-budget treasure-hunting expedition.

Bascom approached the CIA in the mid-1960s with a proposal for using his patented search technique to recover Soviet boosters and nose cones from test missiles fired into the ocean.[21] He claimed that the CIA and the Air Force were extremely enthusiastic about his idea, and even gave the collection scheme a code name—Sand Dollar. Ultimately, however, the CIA dropped the program, citing—according to Bascom—insufficient funding.

Willard Bascom was an extremely innovative scientist and an engaging author. In the area of underwater search-and-recovery techniques, he was far ahead of his time.

———

The most exciting marine technology for most of the CIA team were the design and operational capability of the *Glomar Challenger*—a new, state-of-the-art 400-foot drilling ship operated by Global Marine Inc. for the National Science Foundation. It was being used in 1969 under the aegis of the NSF's Deep Sea Drilling Project, a research effort involved with collection of core samples from the ocean bottom for oceanographic and marine geology science.

What excited us about the *Challenger* wasn't the results of the research, but rather the sophisticated use of acoustic technology for dynamic station keeping. The *Challenger* was equipped with an array of four hydrophones mounted at each corner of the bottom of the ship. These hydrophones were used to receive acoustic signals from a beacon that was dropped onto the ocean bottom in the vicinity of the chosen drilling operation. The signals received by the four hydrophones were compared to measure their differential time of arrival. With this information, the position of the ship with respect to the underwater beacon could be calculated. This position estimate was fed into an automatic station keeping (ASK) system on the ship that controlled power to the *Challenger*'s main thrusters (for fore and aft control) and tunnel thrusters (for side-to-side control), allowing the ship to maintain its position over the hole without having to change its heading. The system was subject to short-term errors in its position estimates due to pitch and roll motions of the ship. However, by averaging out the signals over several wave periods, the estimation error could be driven down to less than a degree. It was claimed that the *Glomar Challenger* could maintain station over a point 10,000 feet below within a radius of less than 100 feet.

Global Marine had also developed an acoustic system that permitted the drill string to be recovered into the ship (for replacement, say, of a drill bit) and then lowered back to the bottom, actually reentering the hole that it had been withdrawn from. This was a tremendous boon for oil drillers. Until that time, a broken drill bit essentially put an end to drilling activity in a particular hole. The ability to perform such an operation in water depths greater than 10,000 feet was impressive to us. We began (somewhat naively, as it turned out) to think of Global Marine as a marine technology center analogous to, say, Lockheed Missile Systems Corporation's status as a center for satellite and missile technology. Don't misunderstand me. Global

Marine *was* the leader in the field of deepwater operations from surface ships. However, ocean technology had never received the huge government financial support that had been given to the missiles and space industry. Ocean research and marine engineering were just beginning to come to the attention of potential government sponsors.

When the *Challenger* next arrived in port, Global Marine arranged a discreet tour of the ship for several of the headquarters team. Since most of us had never set foot on any boat larger than fifty feet, we were seriously impressed. After the visit and tour of the *Challenger*, most of us agreed that Global Marine had a place in our future.

## CIA Meets Global Marine

In late 1969 John Parangosky felt it was time to run his team's recovery concepts by a marine contractor for comment and critique. After our tour of the *Challenger*, we believed Global Marine Inc. to be the most forward-thinking of the commercial contractors doing work and research in the deep ocean. We decided to approach them as a potential team member.

Our first contact was with the vice president of Global Marine, Curtis Crooke, in November 1969. Bright and charismatic, Crooke managed the technology development arm of the company. He had played important engineering and design roles in the development of the *CUSS I* (associated with the Mohole Project) and the *Glomar Challenger*.

Global Marine's first contact with the AZORIAN program was classic Parangosky. Crooke had been talking to several customers in his office when his secretary called him on the intercom. She advised him that a man had just called and said that he needed to talk to him immediately. Crooke told his secretary to tell the caller that he was in a conference and wouldn't be available until tomorrow. Five minutes later, the secretary called Crooke again: "The man says to tell you that he might be a potential customer." Crooke scratched his head and told his secretary, "Tell him to come by in an hour. I should be free then, and I'd be glad to talk to him."

Fifteen minutes later, the secretary called again and said, "That man is in the office!" Recognizing that Parangosky wasn't going to go away or sit quietly, Crooke asked his clients to come back later and told his secretary to bring Parangosky into his office. In marched JP, closely followed by his chief scientist, Alex Hausman, and our chief of security, Paul Eastman. Eastman immediately shut the door to the office securely, startling Crooke, who was unable to remember when his office door had ever been shut before.

Parangosky got right to the point. Without identifying the real mission objective, he asked Crooke if he thought it might be feasible to somehow lift 2,000 tons or so from an ocean depth of three miles or more. Crooke said he'd have to think about that. Parangosky gave him a number to call when he was ready to talk and abruptly left the office. Crooke couldn't recall Hausman or Eastman saying a single word during the meeting.

Crooke was intrigued. He relished the idea of working with the CIA in an endeavor far removed from the deep ocean drilling ships that he had been associated with for years. After getting a go-ahead from Bob Bauer, the president of Global Marine, Crooke called Parangosky and set up a meeting outside of the Washington area to get briefed on the program.

After his briefing on the real AZORIAN mission, Crooke was given a short description of the team's recovery concepts—rockets, air-filled pontoons, pentane barges, the works. He listened with interest and made some polite comments. We agreed to meet again in a couple of weeks—at headquarters this time. Crooke would be augmented with two of his best technical talents—John Graham, Global Marine's dour chief engineer and senior naval architect, and Sherman Wetmore, a taciturn but very talented marine engineer who worked for Graham.

But Parangosky wasn't about to take a chance on both Crooke and Graham visiting the Washington area—let alone the CIA—as representatives of Global Marine. Crooke tells this story about his first trip to agency headquarters in Langley:

> The CIA security officers arranged the hotel reservations for us. The reservations were made in real names, but Graham was instructed to identify himself as president of "Graham Pharmaceuticals." I was supposed to be his vice president. When John and I got to the hotel desk, we followed directions and identified ourselves as president and vice president of Graham Pharmaceuticals. The desk clerk handed us both a registration card to be filled out. When John got to the blank space for filling in "Company Affiliation," he looked over at me. I looked over at him and we both broke out laughing. Neither one of us knew how to spell "pharmaceuticals"![22]

Crooke was still encouraging in this meeting, and tolerant of the CIA team's recovery concepts. Graham and Wetmore were more honest. They obviously had no enthusiasm for any of our ideas and weren't about to humor us, even if it meant that Global Marine might lose its opportunity to work on the program. They did agree, however, to go back and do a more rigorous analysis on the CIA approaches (the pentane-filled barge still being our preferred solution).

Several weeks later, Crooke called and told us that he and Graham didn't think any of our concepts were worth further consideration. He believed they were all too complex and had little or no chance of success. Just as important, he acknowledged that the CIA concepts involved technologies with which Global Marine had no previous experience. (Nor, for that matter, did anyone else have experience with the concepts that we had developed.) Following are some of the problems that Global Marine had with our favored approach, the pentane-filled barge.

First, trying to tow a large barge with an open section through its middle (with or without part of a submarine in that open section) would be a recipe for disaster. It would be impossible to make the barge seaworthy. Second, assuming we were able to get the barge to the target site, making it negatively buoyant while transferring the lifting load to six or more large winches with huge nylon lines mounted on the towing ship, would be very tricky. Third, even trickier would be the task—after recovery of the target—of making the barge positively buoyant again without having it collide with the underside of the surface ship. Finally, although pentane is liquid at room temperature, it is a very volatile hydrocarbon and readily forms explosive mixtures with air. To provide sufficient buoyancy for the barge and target, a quantity on the order of 2 to 3 million gallons of pentane would be required. It's one thing to transport volatile, flammable liquids in a specially built tanker, but it's something else altogether to carry that much explosive potential in a barge that's going to be lowered to the ocean bottom with the real possibility of sustaining structural damage during the target capture.

Graham had convinced Crooke that the best approach would be what he referred to as a "grunt lift"—a single lifting pipe that would lower a "claw" to the bottom of the ocean to grab the target (all 4 million pounds of it) and lift the entire load back into the ship.

This idea seemed preposterous to the CIA team. We felt that John Graham had been drilling for oil too long and couldn't recognize or understand the value of new aerospace thinking. There's no question that Graham was on our shit list. He had dissed the results of our high-tech study efforts and proposed a brute force solution in their stead. After all, we asked, how large would a steel drill string have to be to support the weight of the 2,000-ton target, a claw of (probably) comparable weight, and the weight of the drill string itself? Further, how could he design a ship with a hole in the middle of it large enough to contain the part of the submarine we wanted to acquire—our target object? We compiled a list of questions and challenges to Graham's idea and set up another meeting with the Global Marine team.

We wanted to shoot down the grunt lift idea right away so we could get on with our own concepts.

Well, we had the meeting, and Graham and Crooke had an answer for almost everything we threw at them. By Graham's calculations, the pipe string (he didn't use the term "drill string" for this project) would have to have a cross section of about 160 square inches, or a diameter of slightly over 15 inches, with a 6-inch-diameter hole in its center. To contain the target after recovery, they proposed to build the ship with a 200 × 64–foot "well" with closable gates in the middle of the ship. During transit, the gates on the bottom of the ship would be closed and the well would be dry. For recovering the target into the ship, the well gates would be open. Although the idea of lifting so much weight over a distance of more than three miles directly into the hold of a ship using a single string of steel pipe seemed preposterous, the concept was really brilliant—and so much simpler than the ideas we had come up with. We and Global Marine were both aware that there were many design issues still to be resolved, such as the stability of the ship with perhaps 16 million pounds of target/claw/pipe suspended from a derrick platform about 100 feet above the main deck. Another issue would be the interactive motion dynamics of the ship, the claw, and up to three miles of steel pipe. We knew we had a long way to go. Still, we finally had a recovery concept that didn't require knowledge of such unknowable things as the number of intact air bottles in the hull of a sunken submarine.

----

Okay. We had a concept for recovering the target. However, we knew that Global Marine couldn't handle the whole system development by itself. Although they were excellent ship designers, they didn't have the expertise to take on some of the other elements of the recovery system.

The claw, for one thing. It had to be as light as possible while still having the requisite strength to pick up and contain the structurally suspect target. Global Marine's mantra was to design any ship's component with a large safety factor—and then double the thickness just to make sure it wouldn't fail. We were looking for a contractor who was skilled in making light-weight, high-tech systems.

Not surprisingly, Parangosky gravitated toward some of his old aerospace associates from previous programs he had worked on for the National Reconnaissance Office. These included McDonnell Douglas Corporation, Lockheed Missiles and Space Corporation (LMSC), and Lockheed Aircraft's Advanced Development Projects (the "Skunk Works"). Of special interest was LMSC's Ocean Systems Division (OSD), which had been working on underwater vehicles for the Navy's highly classified Deep Submergence Systems Project. Under the direction of Dr. John Craven, OSD had developed designs for the Deep Submergence Search Vehicle and the Deep Submergence Rescue Vehicle.[23] They knew the marine environment and, equally important, they knew how to apply space technology to deep-sea scenarios.

We also questioned whether Global Marine would be able to design and build on its own a highly precise station-keeping system that would enable the recovery ship to hold position over the target with an accuracy of 50 feet or so. The station-keeping system used on the *Challenger* couldn't provide that kind of positioning control in 16,700 feet of water.

The Marine Systems Division of Honeywell, located in Seattle, had done some promising experiments with what they called a long baseline station-keeping system. The system employed a single acoustic transmitter/receiver on the ship's bottom and an array of acoustic transponders on the ocean bottom. Honeywell believed that position-estimating accuracies of less than ten feet were quite possible. We encouraged Global Marine to talk to Honeywell about designing the automatic station-keeping system for the ship.

The pipe string was another system component requiring the development of new technologies. There were plenty of steel companies that could forge drilling pipe, but none of them had ever produced sections of pipe that were fifteen inches in diameter. However, some of those steel companies had experience with forging the barrels of large cannons. Furthermore, gun barrel steel looked like a good material choice for the lifting pipe. We were hopeful that the technology could be easily adapted for our requirements.

So, we had bought into Global Marine's concept for recovery of the target, and we had convinced ourselves that the required technologies to complete the mission were available. We had also identified a set of potential contractors that could supplement Global Marine's capabilities in the design and development of the recovery system. We felt relatively comfortable about the technical approach. It was time to think about legal aspects, cover stories, security problems, and all the other operational issues that make espionage such an interesting business.

## Go-Ahead

At this point, the CIA had a technical concept for recovering the submarine. However, we hadn't even begun to work out a security plan that would enable us to perform a *covert* recovery of a submarine with an *overt* operation in the middle of the Pacific Ocean. We were confident that there was a way to do it—we just had to figure out what that way was.

Another issue that had to be addressed was the legality of the proposed recovery operation. Commercial salvage laws don't apply to so-called ships of state—ships belonging to a sovereign government. A ship of state still belongs to its government, even if it has sunk. The CIA's General Counsel was concerned that the proposed recovery operation might be seen by the Soviets as nothing less than piracy.

There were some mitigating arguments, however. On August 16, 1928, the Russian Admiralty in Leningrad advised the British Admiralty that a sunken British submarine, *L-55*, had been raised in the Baltic.[24] Apparently, the *L-55* had been sunk (presumably by the Russians) nine years earlier in Kaporsk Bay when the British were helping the White Russians against the Bolsheviks after World War I. The bodies of the *L-55* crew were returned to the British Admiralty for interment, but the Russians refurbished the submarine and put it back into service for the Soviet navy for another twenty years.

The Russian episode did not make the CIA's planned recovery of the *K-129* legal, but it did give the agency some assurance that the Soviets might find it difficult to protest strongly on moral grounds. The legal issues did not overly concern DCI Richard Helms. He advised Duckett and Parangosky to proceed with the program.

Helms was becoming increasingly enthusiastic about AZORIAN. He had always been a strong supporter of the agency's reconnaissance aircraft and satellite programs, and he consistently urged the Directorate of Science and Technology to push the envelope of what was possible. Once persuaded that the submarine recovery was technically feasible, he became a strong advocate. Helms presented regular progress briefings to the ExCom of the National Security Council to keep them up to speed on the progress being made. With his low-key style, Helms was a very persuasive briefer.[25]

Of course, the agency's enthusiasm for heavy lift was not shared by everyone. Some Navy officials were shocked and outraged. In particular, John Craven and Captain Jim Bradley were very outspoken opponents. Bradley reportedly said, "Oh, no, Jesus Christ almighty! You people are in a tank! That's a pipe dream!"[26] Director of Naval Intelligence, Rear Admiral Frederic "Fritz" Harlfinger, believed the CIA's plan was crazy and impossible. They all clearly recognized that funds going into the AZORIAN program would be funds that the Navy's undersea intelligence operations were *not* going to get.

The Navy didn't unanimously reject the CIA's approach, however. Admiral Thomas Moorer, the chief of naval operations, reportedly favored the CIA plan. Moorer liked the idea of trying to recover as much of the *K-129* as possible, and he was impressed with the boldness of the concept.[27] Senator John Stennis, chairman of the Armed Services Committee, was also a supporter, as was Senator Margaret Chafee, the minority chair. Secretary of Defense Melvin Laird wasn't enthusiastic about the program, but he went along with it, rationalizing that the recovery system could potentially be used in the future to rescue the crews of sunken American submarines.

———

On October 30, 1970, Helms briefed the ExCom on the heavy lift recovery concept jointly developed by CIA and its contractor team. There were strong advocates both for and against proceeding with the program. Dr. John Foster, the DD/R&E, was very enthusiastic about the potential intelligence value if the *K-129* could be recovered. Dr. David Packard, the deputy secretary of defense, was less enthusiastic. Funding was a big issue in his mind. Ultimately, the ExCom agreed that AZORIAN should proceed at a cautious pace until technical feasibility could be more convincingly demonstrated and program costs could be more realistically projected.[28] This was a huge step for the CIA and the program office. With the ExCom approval, we could begin awarding contracts for design and development—not just for low-level concept studies.

A major program milestone had been passed. Now the CIA was going to have to work out a security plan that would enable the covert recovery of the *K-129* while operating in plain view of the whole world.

# 2

## The Magic Trick

There is a small class of espionage programs whose operational success is totally dependent upon maintaining total mission secrecy. For this class of programs, compromise of the mission dictates its cancellation. This heavy dependence on the continued covertness of a mission is less common than might be thought. Other black programs, such as the B-2 bomber or the typical intelligence-collecting satellites of the National Reconnaissance Office, use very tight security precautions in order to gain a tactical advantage. By *delaying* exposure of a program and its mission, adversaries have less time to analyze their vulnerability to the system and develop countermeasures against it. Eventual exposure of the mission is assumed, though, and the system must retain at least some of its effectiveness even after it is compromised.

For the *Hughes Glomar Explorer* program, any compromise of the mission would have forced cancellation of the recovery attempt. The CIA knew that the Soviet Union would not stand idly by while a U.S. ship was attempting to salvage one of their nuclear-armed submarines. Because of the absolute dependence on retaining covertness, the security planning for AZORIAN was given unprecedented attention by the CIA. The manpower, dollars, and personal hardships invested in this effort would have been unthinkable for most programs.

### The Magician's Tools

Okay. The CIA had a concept for recovery of the submarine, and we had a contractor team and approval to proceed with the program.

Now the program office had to figure out how it was going to pull off the stunt in full view of anyone who cared to watch. We had to come up with a program protection plan.

A program protection (PP) plan includes all the methods and techniques that go into ensuring that the security objectives of a program are met. Although various PP planners break out the necessary features of a plan in different ways, the following security disciplines must be addressed for all classified programs.[1]

- Threat assessment identifies the possible threats to the compromise of Critical Program Information (CPI) and assesses the vulnerability of the CPI to each of those threats. Threat assessment is essentially a counterintelligence effort.
- Traditional security provides for physical protection of documents, investigation of personnel who will have access to sensitive aspects of the program, and communications methods that permit information to be securely passed between individuals and contractors.
- Operations security (OPSEC) provides for the protection of certain events or activities (often referred to as "observables") associated with a classified program that might reveal sensitive facts about the nature of the effort.[2] For example, government sponsors of classified programs frequently need to use OPSEC to conceal visits of program office engineers and managers to the offices of contractors not openly associated with the government sponsor.
- Perceptions management (PM) is the science of managing the perceptions that outsiders have about a classified program. PM frequently employs a cover story—a credible and benign explanation to explain program observables. PM also includes observables control—hiding observables that are not consistent with the cover story while featuring those observables that are consistent with the desired perceptions. In some cases, PM might involve the *creation* of observables to support a cover story. The creation of untrue observables and the public dissemination of false information about a program are often referred to as disinformation.

Parangosky and his security staff walked a narrow line in developing the program protection plan for AZORIAN. The issue of whether or not to use disinformation to reinforce the credibility of the Deep Ocean Mining Program (DOMP) cover story was studied extensively prior to authorizing any use of it. The harm (to individuals, corporations, organizations, or governments) that could result from the use of disinformation had to be weighed against the need for using it to protect the security of the program. These are tough decisions for any manager of a classified program.

———

John Parangosky had carefully avoided signing any formal agreements with contractors up to this point in order to avoid an observable CIA contractual relationship. He was one of those very rare program managers who fully recognized that the cover story for a classified program should be developed prior to showing any observables, because every observable exposed at the beginning of a program limits the options for cover stories.

The possibility that the recovery operation might have to be performed under commercial cover (i.e., no apparent government involvement) had been considered early on. Of course, the option of allowing the CIA to be openly associated with the program was clearly off the table. Parangosky hoped that commercial cover wouldn't be necessary. It would add a new measure of difficulty to a security challenge that was already daunting.

Under a commercial cover, the need to conceal government involvement would seriously handicap the communications between the headquarters staff and the contractors. Several options for technical exchange were available, but none of them were attractive. The CIA staff members could simply avoid exposure to uncleared contractors, seriously limiting their effectiveness, or they could ostensibly quit their government jobs and go to work for a contractor—not very credible for longtime CIA employees. Or, they could change their personal identities and assume an alias. None of these options is easy. Pulling off a commercial cover requires a discipline that is hard to indoctrinate into a program team and even harder to enforce. The larger the contract, the harder it is to manage a program with commercial cover. Small contracts have fewer observables and fewer people with access to those observables. A large program—one costing hundreds of millions of dollars—presents very special problems. I am aware of only a few truly large government development programs that have successfully used a commercial cover.

## Picking the Best Lie

The AZORIAN program office looked at all the possible cover missions that might be used to explain the presence of a large ship in the area of the target. Parangosky established a cover division (also referred to as the Commercial Operations Division) within the program office to perform the necessary research and analysis.[3] (By this time, summer of 1970, the AZORIAN program office had expanded significantly—it was no longer just a group of eight or nine engineers.) Some of the options considered were deep-sea drilling, scientific research, treasure hunting (salvage), and ocean mining.

The idea of using deep-sea drilling as a cover story for the AZORIAN mission had some real traction. After all, the National Science Foundation (NSF) and Global Marine had been using the *Glomar Challenger* for deep-sea drilling experiments for a number of years. Those experiments held the promise of opening up large portions of the open ocean to oil exploration and production. The idea of the NSF, say, sponsoring a larger ship (i.e., the *Explorer*) to continue and expand this activity didn't seem too far-fetched. The problem was that, except for the A-frame derrick in the middle of the ship, the *Explorer* wasn't going to look anything like a drilling ship. Oil drilling ships only need a small moon pool under the derrick to permit drill string to pass through. There was no credible way to explain (or hide) the 199-foot-long well in the middle of the *HGE* intended to hold the claw and a large portion of a Soviet submarine.

There were other problems, too. The pipe string on the *HGE* was way too large to pass as drill string, and there was no explanation for the large docking legs—to be used for raising the capture vehicle (CV) and target into the ship—on either end of the well. Deep-sea drilling experiments were a reasonable thing for the NSF to be doing in the open ocean, but the *HGE*'s design and appearance didn't match up to the job. Almost overlooked in our efforts to rationalize the Deep Sea Drilling Project as a mission cover was the fact that there were no known oil deposits in the area of the target site!

———

The program office also thought about the NSF and Global Marine teaming up to continue the earlier experiments to drill through the Mohorovicic Discontinuity—a continuation of Project Mohole—to learn more about the inner core of the Earth. After all, they had worked together on Mohole from 1958 through 1966 with the Global Marine ship *CUSS I*. That ship worked off the coast of Guadalupe, Mexico, in 11,700 feet of water. Arguably, it would make sense to drill in the North Pacific in 17,000 feet of water because the Earth's crust should be thinner in the deeper water. Of course, this idea failed for the same reason that deep-sea drilling to find oil failed. The *HGE* just wasn't a credible ship design to be doing that job.

———

Treasure hunting as a cover story was not a completely crazy idea. Willard Bascom, one of the NSF's main contributors to the Mohole Project, had also written extensively about recovering ships and treasure from the oceans. His company, Ocean Science and Engineering (OSE), was heavily involved in undersea exploration and recovery of diamonds. Reportedly, OSE had recovered 20 million carats of diamonds for the De Beers diamond company in the oceans off South Africa. OSE was also involved in the development of a mechanical arm that was attached to a 243-foot salvage ship, the *Alcoa Seaprobe*, built by Alcoa for the express purpose of ocean research and recovery of objects from ocean depths up to 1,000 feet. The *Seaprobe* greatly resembled a drill ship, with a large pipe-handling derrick amidships for lowering the search sensors and recovery mechanisms.

The tough question for using treasure hunting as a cover was "Why such a massive effort?" The *Explorer* was going to have a weight about sixteen times that of the *Seaprobe*. Why? What kind of "treasure" would it be recovering? The likely answer would be *ships*—not *artifacts*. And that was the fatal flaw in the cover story. The only known sunken ship in the area we wanted to operate in was a Soviet submarine. In this case, the cover story would have been *too* close to the truth.

————

At the same time the CIA was looking for a suitable cover story for AZORIAN, there was a growing commercial interest in the economic potential of ocean mining. Large areas of the ocean bottom are covered with clumps of minerals that have formed together as nodules. These nodules (referred to as *manganese* nodules) vary in diameter from fractions of an inch to perhaps seven to eight inches. They're composed primarily of manganese (about 25–30 percent), but they also have significant concentrations of nickel, copper, cobalt, iron, silicon, and aluminum—the nickel, cobalt, and copper having the highest economic value. Commercial recovery of these nodules had been considered since their discovery in the nineteenth century, but the technology wasn't available to make the effort economically viable. During the 1960s, international consortia had been exploring the world oceans to measure the distribution density and quality (concentrations of the most valuable elements) of manganese nodules lying on the seafloor. Fortuitously, one of the attractive nodule mining areas just happened to be in the central North Pacific—in the general vicinity of the *K-129*'s resting place.

So, ocean mining looked like a credible thing to be doing in the North Pacific. But would an ocean mining system look anything like the *Hughes Glomar Explorer*? At first blush, it didn't look like a good match. Most of the consortia talking up ocean mining planned on using a scheme that vacuumed the nodules up from the ocean bottom into a bottom-crawling processor. The bottom crawler would then grind the nodules into a slurry that could be pumped up through a hollow pipe into the hold of the mining ship. Although the huge well in the *Explorer* could pass as a storage hold, there was no good explanation for the sliding gates that permitted the well to be flooded. There were also no apparent justifications for the 15.5-inch-diameter lifting pipe that was capable of supporting about 17 million pounds, the gimbaled derrick, or the massive truss structure docking legs.

Since the appearance of the boat didn't match up to the most popular concept for nodule recovery, we attempted to come up with our own scheme—one that would be consistent with the capabilities and appearance of our boat. Our homegrown ocean mining concept called for a large machine—or mining vehicle—to be lowered to the ocean bottom. The mining vehicle would be moved across the bottom, collecting nodules and storing them in a hopper built into the miner. When the miner was full of nodules, it would be hoisted into the ship's well. The massive hopper would be returned to a port for offloading and subsequent processing of the nodules.

The ship and our mining concept were a pretty good match. The well of the *HGE* would be a logical place to store a very large mining machine that could be lowered to the seafloor when the well gates were opened. The outsized lifting pipe was consistent with the need to lift a container loaded with heavy nodules, and the gimbaled derrick was a logical solution for minimizing the stresses on the pipe during recovery of the miner and its payload. The docking legs would be used to engage the mining machine and stabilize it before lifting it into the open well of the ship. Essentially, the operations would mirror our recovery procedures—with the claw replaced by a mining machine.

Did this mining concept make as much sense as the vacuum approach favored by the mining consortia? Probably not. Experienced ocean mining engineers would probably think the design was flawed—but would it be credible, in spite of being flawed? To explore the technical credibility of our ideas, we asked Global Marine to bring some ocean mining consultants onboard. One of those consultants was Manfred Krutein, a former German U-boat crew member who had immigrated to America in 1960 and become involved in the still-nascent ocean mining industry.[4] Much to our relief, Krutein thought our concept of raising the nodules from the ocean bottom to the ship in a large hopper might sell. He wasn't ecstatic about our idea, but he didn't call it ridiculous either. We began to think that the cover story might just work.

Ocean mining as a cover seemed to hold together from the standpoint of credibility, but John Parangosky wasn't sold at all. He had a major problem with one aspect of the plan: We'd have to use a commercial cover. There was no way we could explain the involvement of the U.S. government in an ocean mining venture. Government involvement in the program would have to be totally invisible, and Parangosky wasn't ready to take on the cost and inconvenience of hiding all government presence. He insisted that we continue looking for an alternative cover story that would impose fewer requirements for operations security.

Parangosky asked me to chair a panel of program office personnel tasked to come up with a consensus on an optimum cover story. The panel included a couple of engineers, but mostly members of the Commercial Operations Division and the security staff. We secluded ourselves in a secure conference facility near Warrenton, Virginia, for several days while we hashed over all the pros and cons of our various options still under consideration.

At the end of three days, we still had no consensus. I personally favored the ocean mining concept, but some others felt that it would be too difficult to execute. We had run out of time, though, and since I was the panel chairman, I elected to recommend the ocean mining cover—with the exceptions of the other panel members noted in the final report.

I presented the panel's report to Parangosky, but he was unimpressed. He wanted more time to "think it over." I reminded him that we had explored every option we could think of, and none of them (in my opinion) were superior to ocean mining. I further suggested that time was passing quickly, and that he should make a decision. Mistake. Parangosky was blunt. He told me (actually, more like shouted at me), "You people think I'm indecisive! I'm *not* indecisive! I'm decisive! When I appear to be indecisive, it's because I'm being *decisively* indecisive to make sure you get your facts right!" I retreated quickly, decisively choosing not to extend the conversation.

Eventually, however, Parangosky approved the ocean mining cover story. And once he made that commitment, woe to anyone who tried to second-guess the decision. When nitpickers would express their doubts, Parangosky would shout, "Look at yourselves! You're stomping on ants while the elephants go thundering by! Get on with it!" And so the Deep Ocean Mining Program (DOMP) was born.

### Who's the Front Man?

Okay. Now we had a cover story that appeared to be viable. Unfortunately, the ocean mining concept only made sense for commercial companies to undertake. For credibility, the ostensible sponsor of the mining operation had to be a corporation. That meant that there could be no visible association between the government and our contractor team members. This condition was obviously a security challenge, but it also created contracting and legal problems. The military and intelligence arms of the government frequently write contracts for black procurements that protect the identity of the specific government sponsor, but not the fact that the sponsor is an agency of the government. The details and statements-of-work of these acquisitions are classified by the sponsor and are only visible to people actually cleared and briefed on the program. Shareholders are told that the company has secured a government contract whose details are classified. The information given to the shareholders is true—they are not being misled. This type of black procurement doesn't cause a problem. Over many years, procedures and protocols for this type of contracting have been worked out among the government, private industry, and the government oversight agencies.

On the other hand, for a government agency to write a contract that protects both the work to be performed and the fact of any government involvement is quite another story. What can the contractor management say to its stockholders? Who can the contractor report the customer to be? And what can he report about the nature of the work? He can't say that it's classified—only the government has authority to classify information. If the contractor refuses to name a customer and won't release any information on the nature of the ongoing work, the shareholders will, rightfully, demand information on what the corporate officers and board of directors are doing with the company that those same shareholders have invested in. And you can be sure that the Securities Exchange Commission will back up their demands.

The logical conclusion was that we needed a prime contractor that was privately—not publicly—owned. The CIA could write a single black contract with this company, invisible to anyone except the CIA and the company officers, to act as a contracting proxy for the CIA. The prime could then write (under its own name) white contracts with the other participating contractors for the ostensible development of the multiple segments of an ocean mining system. These nonsensitive white contracts could be shared with the stockholders of the various corporations, but the association with the government would be invisible to them.

In addition to being privately owned, the prime contractor would have to meet two tough criteria. First, the company had to be large enough to credibly take on a financial venture of this magnitude. Second, the company's business interests had to make it a likely candidate to be engaged in ocean mining. These criteria didn't leave a large field of candidates. Of the companies meeting those criteria, Hughes Tool Company appeared to be one of the most promising options.

Hughes Tool was solely owned by Howard Hughes and had plenty of money to invest in speculative new ventures. Hughes had a well-deserved reputation for being willing to take a chance on developing new and exciting technologies and businesses. The Hughes Aircraft Company, which he founded in 1939, had become one of the largest aircraft and aerospace corporations by the 1950s. His development of a huge wooden seaplane (often irreverently referred to as the "Spruce Goose") during World War II had established him as a fearless entrepreneur willing to take chances. Under the Hughes Tool Company aegis, Howard Hughes also held controlling interest in Trans World Airlines from 1939 through 1966. In the late 1960s, Hughes diversified his holdings by purchasing a number of Las Vegas casinos, including the Sands, the Castaways, the Frontier, and the Desert Inn.

Although the Hughes Tool Company was not actively engaged in mining activities, it was the largest supplier of drilling bits—the design for the two-cone roller cutter bit had been completed and patented by Howard Hughes's father in 1909—to companies involved in both land- and sea-based oil exploration. The drilling bit business, however, was just a small part of Howard Hughes's enterprises. In 1970, when the CIA was looking for someone to be the ostensible sponsor of an ocean mining program, the most active part of the Hughes empire was the casino gaming businesses in Las Vegas.

There were some issues to consider with regard to doing business with Howard Hughes. His longtime business associate, Robert Maheu, had been publicly identified as the go-between when Attorney General Robert Kennedy allegedly sought to use the Mafia to assassinate Fidel Castro. Hughes's other lieutenants, in charge of the Nevada holdings, were also somewhat tainted by their association with Las Vegas gaming interests. On the other hand, the CIA reasoned, their activities in Las Vegas had probably taught them discipline with regard to any public discussion about their business interests, suggesting they'd probably be good security risks. These Las Vegas property managers, sometimes known as Hughes's Mormon Mafia, were Chester Davis, Raymond Holliday, and Bill Gay. They controlled all access to Howard Hughes. They were the men whom the CIA would have to contact to determine if Hughes could be persuaded to take on a patriotic job for the country that would probably yield him little profit.

After a quick background check, a meeting was set up with several representatives from the Hughes Tool Company. Because of what we'd heard about the Nevada managers, we were somewhat surprised to find that they were gracious, articulate, and serious. Best of all, they were genuinely interested in working with the CIA on a major espionage program. Over the space of a few weeks, the details of a plan were all worked out. Here's the concept:

The CIA would have a secret contractual relationship with the Hughes Tool Company through which all the money for the AZORIAN contracts would flow. Hughes Tool would be the customer of record for contracts with the chosen contractor team. Only a few people in Hughes would know that the CIA was involved and was providing all the money for the operation. To explain its operations, Hughes Tool would announce a plan to explore the economic feasibility of ocean mining for the nickel, copper, and cobalt found in manganese nodules. The program would be called the Deep Ocean Mining Program, or DOMP.

To support the DOMP, Hughes would create a program office near the Los Angeles international airport. This office, operating under the Hughes aegis, would accommodate the eighty-five or so engineers, security officers, and operations planners who would actually be responsible for managing the sea trials, system integration, and preparation for the mission.

The task of coordinating all of the Hughes activities in support of AZO-RIAN was assigned to Paul Reeve, a senior Hughes Tool Company officer and close confidant of Howard Hughes. Reeve's responsibilities extended across both the classified program aspects of AZORIAN and the unclassified public implementation of the DOMP cover story. His title was general manager, Ocean Mining Division of Hughes Tool Company.

Paul Reeve had an uncanny ability to maintain his composure, humor, and effectiveness in all situations—when things were going good, and (as was often the case) when things were going badly. He was a remarkable man, universally respected and admired by everyone on the program.

———

There's been a lot of speculation over the years about Howard Hughes's physical condition and appearance during the years that Hughes Tool was involved with the CIA on the AZORIAN program. Just for the record, I attended several precontractual meetings with the Hughes representatives, but I never met, saw, or heard Howard Hughes. To my knowledge, no one from the CIA (including John Parangosky) ever saw or spoke to Howard Hughes.[5] Most of us assumed that his health had already deteriorated to the point that he was unwilling or unable to meet "outsiders." I don't know what authorities had been delegated by Hughes to his Nevada managers— they were very discreet regarding those details—but it was clear that when the Mormon Mafia spoke, they spoke for Howard Hughes. It appeared to me that Raymond Holliday was probably the individual who had the closest relationship with Hughes.

## Roles and Responsibilities

Having established Hughes Tool Company as the sponsor for the DOMP, the CIA started defining responsibilities for the chosen team of contractors. Global Marine would be responsible for design and construction of a ship (the surface ship) capable of lowering and raising 17,000 feet of lifting pipe with a claw and a 4-million-pound payload at the end of the pipe. Global Marine would also be responsible for operating the ship while at sea and would provide a "mining" crew for maintenance and operation of the ship systems associated with the recovery operations. To enhance security, Global Marine formed a new corporation under Vice President Curtis Crooke that would be solely responsible for Global Marine's AZORIAN activities. The new corporation was named Global Marine Development Inc., and Curtis Crooke was named president.

Lockheed would be responsible for design and construction of the claw (formally designated the capture vehicle), which, after being lowered to the ocean bottom on the end of the lifting pipe, would grasp the *K-129* target so that it could be raised into the well of the surface ship. Lockheed would also be responsible for design, construction, and delivery of a large submersible barge (the transfer barge) that would serve the dual functions of providing a closed facility for construction of the capture vehicle and a means for transporting it to a suitable ocean location where the claw could be transferred from the barge into the surface ship.[6]

–––––––

Hughes Tool Company would be more than just the prime contractor. Hughes's long experience in the oil fields motivated the company to take on a key segment of the development program. Hughes Tool requested, and got, the responsibility for design and acquisition of the lifting pipe.

Global Marine moved out quickly to subcontract with Honeywell Marine Systems in Seattle for the development of an automatic station-keeping capability that would permit the *HGE* to maintain its position over the target within a twenty-foot radius. Lockheed also contracted with Honeywell to support the design and development of the claw's optical and acoustic sensor suite. These sensors would be used to search for the target and to position the claw during the capture operations on the bottom.

Now, we knew that the interfaces between the multiple segments of the recovery system were going to be difficult to identify, define, document, and control. To make configuration control easier, we wanted to have one of our contractors coordinate all these interfaces—to act as a systems integrator. The problem was that Global, Lockheed, Honeywell, and Hughes did not really understand each other's fields of expertise very well. Honeywell and Lockheed could "talk the same language"—and Global Marine and Hughes shared common backgrounds in drilling technology—but Global Marine and Lockheed not only couldn't talk the same language, but also had an uncanny ability to ruffle each other's feathers whenever they tried. So, in spite of dire warnings from the managers of other large CIA programs, it was decided that the government program office would have to take responsibility for systems integration.

Unfortunately, none of us in the program office, except for John Parangosky, really had much experience with the management of large system acquisitions. The systems engineering disciplines that nowadays are so ingrained into government program offices working on, for example, satellite systems were not present in our AZORIAN program office team. Parangosky was going to have to do a lot of training and indoctrination of his own people. Furthermore, the commercial cover really constrained the degree to which government engineers could be present in some of the contractor's plants. CIA engineers at Lockheed, or even Honeywell, could be explained. Both contractors had a history of doing classified work for the government. CIA personnel in Global Marine or Hughes Tool? Don't even think about it.

### Keep a Low Profile

Back in the early 1970s there were not many options for transmitting classified communications. Secure Teletype was available for short messages. For transmission of long documents, the most common mode of transmission was hand-delivery by special couriers. Large defense contractors such as LMSC and Honeywell had secure communications systems provided by the government. Global Marine, however, had no classified government contracts (that I knew about) and no capability for sending or receiving enciphered cable traffic. To get around this problem, Global Marine set up a DOMP program office in one of the Tishman office buildings in the vicinity of the Los Angeles International Airport. One of the technical analysis contractors that had been hired by Global Marine to support the program,

Mechanics Research Inc. (MRI), was located in the same building and had fully encrypted communications capability for their classified contracts with government space programs. Messages from headquarters to Global Marine were sent to MRI and then delivered "down the hall" to Global Marine. The arrangement was somewhat inconvenient but workable.

The availability of secure voice communications systems was still pretty rare in the 1970s. Although the HY-2 secure telephone systems were available at some of the largest government contractors, the intelligibility, voice recognition, and reliability left a lot to be desired. It was for good reason that the HY-2 systems were usually referred to as the "bubble phones." Except for internal CIA communications within the agency's own buildings, secure voice was not used at all during the early phases of the AZORIAN program.

The headquarters security staff strongly discouraged communications with the contractors over unsecure telephone lines, and telephone calls from CIA buildings to the contractors were absolutely forbidden in order to foil any hostile traffic monitoring that might link the program office with one of the contractors. When a telephone conversation was absolutely necessary (in order to, say, coordinate an impromptu visit), the AZORIAN engineers had to visit one of the many pay phones in the Tysons Corner (Virginia) business area near the program office. Then, while standing out on the street with traffic noise all around, they had to try to avoid saying anything that might explicitly identify the program or the subject they were taking about. Needless to say, there were a lot of misunderstandings ("Oh! So *that's* what you meant!").

Since secure voice communications were not an option, most of the technical exchanges between the contractor team and the program office were formally scheduled meetings held in various third-party conference rooms. Most often, these conference rooms were part of a large hotel complex that might be located in the Washington, Los Angeles, or San Francisco area. The government security team would rent the conference rooms using a cover corporation as the ostensible sponsor. No one had to sign in at the desk, so the names and affiliations of the contractors and government employees were never "on record." Prior to the meeting, a security team would perform an electromagnetic sweep of the conference area to ensure there were no hidden microphones, and then they would maintain watch over all the entrances to ensure that no unauthorized people showed up in the meeting. Obviously, this wasn't a perfect solution—there was still substantial security risk involved—but it was the best that we could do. A lot of business got transacted during those monthly, daylong meetings.

Even having the monthly technical interchanges outside of the contractor's facilities didn't satisfy Parangosky's security worries. He was concerned that foreign intelligence analysts monitoring the airline, hotel, or car rental lists might notice the same names showing up frequently in just a few cities and tie those names back to the CIA. Trying to cut down the personnel observables, JP required the program engineers to rigorously justify each planned trip to Los Angeles, Seattle, or San Francisco. The trouble was, almost all of the trips were justifiable. Communication between the program office engineers and the contractors was critically important.

Every couple of weeks, at least a half dozen or so of the engineers would hop on a plane to the West Coast on a Sunday evening. These flights, leaving about 5 p.m. from Washington's Dulles Airport, were offered by American, United, and TWA airlines. After a week of meetings at one or more of the contractors, the same engineers would hop on one of the Friday "noon balloons" and return to the East Coast.

All this travel may sound tiring, but remember that the early 1970s were the years of elegance in jet travel. Most of the coast-to-coast flights were on the Boeing 747s. Standard equipment was a stand-up lounge with a piano and perhaps two dozen comfortable seats for sipping drinks and schmoozing with the flight attendants. And, there was a lot of schmoozing going on. Since so many of the engineers had their personal favorite airline, and took the same flights over and over, the flight attendants recognized them all. Familiarity naturally led to curiosity, and we engineers were frequently asked about what kind of jobs we held that required such frequent travel. What were we going to say? "I work for the federal government"? Anyone who used that old federal government line was instantly pegged as someone who worked for one of the intelligence agencies. To avoid that embarrassment, most of us had more convincing cover stories provided to us for use in just such situations.

These stories lacked color, though. They were bland and uninteresting and didn't pique the interest of the gorgeous flight attendants. (Back in the 1970s, *all* flight attendants were gorgeous.) Some of our people improvised. One of our team members told the TWA flight attendants that he was a "porn star." This assured him lots of attention at the piano bar and plenty of free drinks from the stewardesses. He used this story consistently—except when he was flying United Airlines. On the United flights, he was a crop duster pilot. He assured me that both stories were equally effective for increasing the quality of his schmoozing.

To placate Parangosky, one of the security officers came up with a plan for reducing the profile of the CIA engineers while on the road. This security officer, Robert James, was somehow able to convince one of the agency's principal contractors to underwrite negotiated agreements with one of the major car rental companies and one of the larger hotel chains that were unlike anything I'd ever heard of. Under this plan, which became known as the "James M.O." (short for "James modus operandi"), desk clerks for the car rental agency and hotel chain in Los Angeles, San Francisco, and Seattle were instructed to give a car key, or room key, to anyone arriving at the desk and claiming to be "Bob James"—without asking any questions or requesting any ID. Under the terms of the agreement, our associate contractor agreed to pay all such charges claimed by the rental car and hotel chains. No questions asked.

As one might imagine, there were a number of incidents that occurred while using the James M.O. On one occasion, there were five CIA engineers lined up at the car rental desk along with a handful of other customers. The first CIA engineer in line identified himself as Bob James and was given a key immediately—no paperwork, no required I.D., just a signature reading "Robert James." Then the second guy in line (also CIA) announced that *he* was Bob James.

At this time, the harassed clerk who was just trying to save time shouted out to everyone in the line, "Are there are any more Bob James in the line?" Three guys immediately raised their hand. The clerk shook her head and said, "How can you all be Bob James?"

One of the bogus Jameses, a member of our Commercial Operations Division with a great sense of humor, responded, "We're actually an acrobatic team—'The Flying James Boys.' Perhaps you've heard of us?"

The clerk did a double-take on some of the more corpulent members of our team, shook her head, and handed out keys while we all signed our names as "Robert James."

On another trip, to a different city, when I walked out to the lot to pick up the car I'd just rented using the James M.O., I noticed there were no license tags anywhere on the car. I went back into the lobby to ask the clerk about the mistake. "No mistake," she said. "I thought you spooky guys would probably prefer a car with no plates."

And so it went. I think the James M.O. may have been one of the most unusual tradecrafts ever used by a CIA program. I have no idea whether it actually lowered—or raised—the profile of the AZORIAN engineers. But it surely was convenient. And it was a lot of fun.

Even the flexibility offered by the James M.O. had its limitations, however. In some cases, Parangosky preferred to have some of the engineers he knew and trusted actually working directly with the contractors. Of course, he couldn't assign career CIA employees to a contractor like Lockheed or Global Marine. Their agency affiliation was too visible.

However, JP had a way around this limitation. Over the years, while managing a number of large programs for the agency, he had accumulated a list of talented engineering consultants whom he trusted. These consultants had sometimes been hired by the agency as contract employees, but they had never showed up as CIA careerists. Parangosky could bring them into a program with little concern that their agency association would be compromised.

Norman E. Nelson had worked for Parangosky on the OXCART program while ostensibly working for Kelly Johnson's Skunk Works. When the AZORIAN program came around, Parangosky encouraged Paul Reeve—the head of Hughes's DOMP—to hire Nelson as an employee. Nelson soon became a key member of the DOMP team.

In another case, Global Marine was having a difficult time dealing with the sophisticated electronics systems that were so prevalent throughout the program. I felt they needed a skilled technical manager to build up a staff in that area. I had met Donovan J. White in 1963 while working on the OX-CART program at Area 51. At the time, White had been the manager of an instrumentation support team working out of EG&G in Las Vegas. I believed White could help us, so I talked to Parangosky about how best to use him. Parangosky told Crooke that we were going to bring White into the program, either as our employee assigned to oversee Global Marine's electronics efforts, or as Global Marine's employee. The choice was Crooke's. He hired White. In a short time, he was promoted to the position of VP for electronics.

Mostly, these infiltrations of JP's trusted technical cadre into the contractors' workforces worked out just fine. They were all competent engineers who actively supported the contractors they were assigned to. Sometimes their advocacy on behalf of their employer even exceeded what we in the program office might have preferred. The net effect, though, was an increase in the contractors' capabilities and improved technical communications.

## A Security System Named JENNIFER

Security procedures and practices for the AZORIAN program were defined by the JENNIFER Security System. Incorporated in this security system was the JENNIFER Control System for classified documents. All of the classified program documents, whether delivered by cable or diplomatic pouch, were given a number so they could be registered for future reference. The registration number included the code name of the originating contractor or government office, a unique identifying number, and the date of origination. The documents were filed in standard five-drawer safes with combination locks. A master list, including only the originator, document number, and subject, was also filed to facilitate search and access. This was the typical document registration system used by the agency before the 1980s. Similar systems were used on the U-2 program, the OXCART program, and the CORONA program. Remember, all of these programs existed before the convenience of data storage on computer hard drives. We didn't even have computers in the offices. We did have copying machines (all Xerox, for the most part) and we had lots of secretaries who had time to do the copying, filing, and searching.

The name of the security system, JENNIFER, had special significance. It was named after the daughter of the chief of AZORIAN security, Paul Eastman, who had supervised the creation of the security ground rules for the program. Eastman's young daughter, Jennifer, had recently and tragically died. The name was given to the security system in her memory. (JENNIFER was never the code name for the submarine recovery program, even though numerous authors throughout the years have identified that name with the mission. The program name was AZORIAN from the very beginning.)

The JENNIFER control system worked very well for us throughout the lifetime of the program. Classified documents were well protected and controlled. We did, however, have some unusual problems with registration and control of *unclassified* documents. Much of the documentation for the AZORIAN acquisition was actually unclassified. All the work done at Sun Shipyard (the builder of the *Hughes Glomar Explorer*) was unclassified, as was the work done by Western Gear, and much of the work done by Global Marine. Any documents that were consistent with the ocean mining cover story could be handled as unclassified.

It was difficult to know, however, just how much information should be released without classification. For example, physical interface details between the *HGE* and the mining machine (white-world talk for capture vehicle) could be treated as unclassified. Even so, we were concerned that analysis of a large number of these unclassified documents describing the interfaces between the ship and the mining machine might give away too much information—information that might cause someone to question the DOMP cover story. For the most part, however, the control of these white-world documents was handled without incident—thanks in large part to our sizable team of security officers who oversaw all aspects of the AZORIAN paper trail.

## The Headquarters Proxy

The operations security and tradecraft techniques described above were effective—if not convenient—during that period when the system components were actually being fabricated at the various contractor plants. On July 23, 1973, however, Sun Shipyard in Pennsylvania completed their work on the *Hughes Glomar Explorer* and formally delivered the ship to Global Marine. The next day, the *HGE* set sail to the West Coast. Its destination was Pier E in Long Beach, California, not too far from the storage location of Hughes's Spruce Goose. By September, the program focus would shift from system acquisition to sea trials and integrated system testing. All of that would be taking place on the West Coast—2,500 miles from CIA headquarters in Langley.

Parangosky had already committed the government to manage the trials and integrated testing, and he knew that the job couldn't be managed by CIA engineers commuting from the East Coast. He needed a West Coast program office (WCPO) that could act as a commercial proxy for the headquarters staff.

The Deep Ocean Mining Program provided the cover story for the new WCPO under the aegis of the newly organized Summa Corporation. (Hughes sold his Tool Division in 1972 and placed all of his remaining business interests under the name of the Summa Corporation.) Summa established a suite of offices in a Hughes building located on the corner of Imperial Boulevard and Sepulveda Boulevard—very close, and convenient, to the Los Angeles airport. The Summa offices were located on the fifth and sixth floors of the building, with the only entrance on the fifth floor. (The stairwell connecting the two floors, internal to the office suite, was built covertly.) The name on the fifth-floor door read simply, "Summa Corporation," although it was understood by the other users of the building that these offices were really the headquarters of the Summa Corporation's DOMP. In reality, the Summa DOMP office in Los Angeles was a West Coast extension of the CIA's AZORIAN program office.

The Summa office had been set up in 1972 but played a minor role in the program before the beginning of the system integration phase. Once the *HGE* had transited from Philadelphia to Long Beach, however, the Summa office became the center of the systems engineering effort.

The WCPO housed about eighty-five engineers, analysts, security personnel, and administrative support people. Most of the staff were bona fide employees of the contractors employed to support the system integration job. They came primarily from Global Marine, Lockheed, and Mechanics Research. Only a small handful of people were CIA career employees, and they all worked under alias identities. All of the WCPO personnel could travel to any contractor, using the cover of the DOMP, without attracting unusual attention.

A young man named Steven Craig was both the chief of security and the office manager for the WCPO. Craig and his staff had a remarkable talent for getting things done quickly and effectively. Usually, he was able to operate within government guidelines. Sometimes not. Craig was perfect for the WCPO because he could employ whatever techniques were called for to accomplish a job without implicating the headquarters staff in those actions. If he screwed up (i.e., got caught), he took the heat. Steve followed the old maxim "Better to ask forgiveness than permission."

Communications for the WCPO presented some special challenges. We needed to be able to exchange secure Teletype messages with headquarters, but the existence of government-supplied secure communications hardware in the Summa DOMP offices wasn't an option. The solution was to set up an office for a legitimate government organization—complete with the latest and best secure communications capabilities—on the sixth floor of the Hughes building, directly adjacent to the WCPO space.

During nonworking hours, the government side of the common wall between the WCPO and government offices was part of a locked and vaulted area containing communications and cryptographic machines. First thing every morning, the government vault would be opened, allowing easy access between the government office and the WCPO facilities, and providing the WCPO with secure Teletype and telephone for communications with AZORIAN headquarters in Langley.

This access between the legitimate government office and the WCPO, known as the Harvey Wallbanger entrance, was also routinely used to permit some high-profile government officials to enter the WCPO offices without risk of being observed and identified with Summa's DOMP. Harvey Wallbanger (also the name of a vodka cocktail that was very popular during the 1970s) was just one more of the creative and effective techniques devised by the AZORIAN security team, enabling government management of the program without exposing a government presence.

The Harvey Wallbanger entrance had its limitations, though. It wasn't considered secure enough to permit visits to the program office by the highest-level CIA officials, like CIA director Bill Colby or Carl Duckett.

When Carl wanted to meet with the program people on the West Coast, he'd rent a suite at one of the luxury hotels near LAX and the WCPO and hold the meeting there. The suite would be swept for hidden audio devices by our security team prior to the meeting, and the attendees would arrive individually at staggered times. The meetings usually lasted all day, with long discussions on both the technical and political aspects of the program. Duckett was on a first-name basis with everyone in the room. He never forgot a name, he always asked about the individual concerns of each man, and he always ended the meeting by expressing his appreciation for the personal inconveniences that some people were experiencing as part of the job.

Parangosky used the Harvey Wallbanger entrance often, but he never felt comfortable with it. He was extremely security conscious and perhaps just a little paranoid. On one occasion, he was being escorted through the Harvey Wallbanger hole-in-the-wall when he noticed a window washer working on the sixth floor of an adjacent building perhaps 100 yards away. Parangosky ducked back into the government office and refused to enter the Summa offices until all the windows of the WCPO had been covered.

———

There were extraordinary security precautions for AZORIAN within the CIA headquarters building as well. Both Carl Duckett and John Parangosky knew that normal security procedures would not provide the required program protection. Although CIA personnel are disciplined in the practice of protecting secrets, Duckett and Parangosky didn't want to take any unnecessary chances.

To protect the nature and mission of the program, the AZORIAN program office was organized as a Special Projects Staff (SPS), reporting directly to Duckett, the deputy director for science and technology.[7] There were no cover stories to explain the charter or mission of the SPS. It was simply listed as "off limits." No questions were answered. If you didn't have the necessary clearances, you were told nothing.

To further protect the mission of the program office, SPS was set up as a self-sufficient organization with its own dedicated administrative, security, contracting, and engineering personnel. There were few part-timers. Rather than depend on support-as-needed from the large centralized CIA offices for contracting, finance, security, etc., Duckett insisted on dedicated personnel from each of those offices. In most cases, the directors of the centralized offices were not even briefed on the work that their employees were doing for Parangosky. Yes, there was resistance and resentment from those managers with a vested interest in the matrix-type program management concept, but Duckett and Parangosky didn't budge. The AZORIAN program office was a self-contained organization.

One additional point should be emphasized in this discussion of program protection, and that is the critical contribution of the security staff to successful achievement of the program protection goals. AZORIAN had a huge security presence in the program office. Fully 10–15 percent of the employees in the headquarters program office and the WCPO were involved in some form of program protection for AZORIAN. Recognizing the vital importance of comprehensive security protection, Parangosky's meetings—on whatever subject—were always open to the chief or deputy chief of the security staff. Security had a voice in *every* activity. That relationship was vital to the success of the program protection plan.

Soviet Golf II–class submarine, similar to the *K-129*. (Courtesy of the U.S. Navy.)

The *Hughes Glomar Explorer*, the ship built by the CIA to recover the *K-129*. (Courtesy of the Central Intelligence Agency.)

Carl Duckett, director
of the CIA's Directorate of
Science and Technology.
(Courtesy of the National
Reconnaissance Office.)

John Parangosky,
program manager of
the CIA's Special Projects
Staff, the program office
for AZORIAN. (Courtesy
of the National
Reconnaissance Office.)

The *Glomar Challenger,* the ship that convinced the CIA
that Global Marine had the necessary technology to build
the recovery ship. (Courtesy of the National Science
Foundation.)

Curtis Crooke was the first Global Marine officer
approached by the CIA for AZORIAN. In order to
enhance security, Global Marine spun off a new
corporation, Global Marine Development Inc., to
manage construction of the *Hughes Glomar Explorer.*
Crooke was the new corporation's first president.
(Courtesy of Curtis Crooke.)

John Graham, Global Marine's chief engineer and senior
naval architect, with his wife, Nell, at the launching of the
*HGE* from Sun Shipyard in Philadelphia in 1973. (Author's
Private Collection.)

Sherm Wetmore, one of John Graham's senior engineers
and the director of the Global Marine engineering team
during the recovery mission. (Courtesy of Sherm
Wetmore.)

The *Glomar II*, the small drill ship used to survey the target site in 1970. (Courtesy of Anchorage Museum.)

Leon Blurton, Global Marine drilling super-intendent. Blurton participated actively in every phase of the AZORIAN program. (Author's Private Collection.)

The *Gidrograf*—a Soviet trawler converted for use as an intelligence collection ship—followed and harassed the *Glomar II* during all of the 1970 nodule survey missions. (Author's Private Collection.)

Dave Sharp in the small mission director office on the *Glomar II*. (Author's Private Collection.)

Windsock at the top of the *Glomar II* derrick after three weeks and seven gales at sea, December 1970. (Author's Private Collection.)

The *Glomar II* pipe rack from the top of the ship's derrick. (Author's Private Collection.)

Inside the well of the *Hughes Glomar Explorer,* 200 feet long by 74 feet wide. The keyhole of the docking leg can be seen at the far end. Water on the well floor had to be continuously pumped out because of seal leaks that developed during the first West Coast sea trials in January 1974. (Author's Private Collection.)

Centerline elevator raises a pipe double to the main deck level, where it is grasped by the transfer crane. (Author's Private Collection.)

The transfer crane loads the double on the transfer cart. (Author's Private Collection.)

The transfer cart moves the double to the rig floor. (Author's Private Collection.)

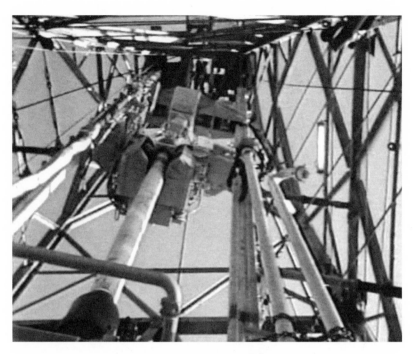

The double is raised into a vertical position in the derrick by the elevator subspinner. (Author's Private Collection.)

The subspinner lowers the double into the top of the pipe string. (Author's Private Collection.)

The heavy lift control room was used to operate the heavy lift system, the well gates, the heave compensator, and the docking legs. (Author's Private Collection.)

The control center. All capture vehicle operations, as well as positioning of the *HGE*, were controlled from here during the target capture operations. (Author's Private Collection.)

Almost 600 sections of pipe string on the Pier E dock in Long Beach. (Author's Private Collection.)

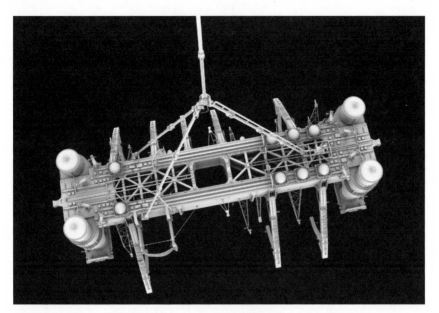

Looking down on the topside of the capture vehicle. (CGI Illustration Michael White ©2011.)

Looking up at the underside of the capture vehicle. Note the cookie cutters at the base of the breakout legs. (CGI Illustration Michael White ©2011.)

The capture vehicle in the partially flooded well of the *HGE*. Note the electronics pressure spheres and, in the foreground, one of the seawater hydraulic thrusters. (Author's Private Collection.)

The *HMB-1* tied up at Lockheed's facility in Redwood City. (Author's Private Collection.)

The interior of the Hughes mining barge, *HMB-1*. The construction area for the claw was 276 feet long and 77 feet wide. (Author's Private Collection.)

Global Marine engineer Randy Michaelson, apparently ridiculing author Dave Sharp onboard the *Explorer*. (Author's Private Collection.)

The *Explorer* and the *HMB-1* in Isthmus Cove off Catalina Island. (Author's Private Collection.)

$3$

# Living the Lie

## Making Do with the *Glomar II*

By the summer of 1970, with the ops concept for the *K-129* recovery having been resolved, we were beginning to get a better handle on just how the surface ship, the capture vehicle, and the lifting pipe were going to have to work together to acquire the target on the ocean bottom and lift it to the surface. We knew that the submarine was settled into the bottom, and that a strong suction force would have to be overcome in order to actually break it loose from the mud and silt before lifting could begin. What we did *not* know was the actual slope of the ocean floor in the immediate area of the target, nor did we have any information on the composition and density of the ocean bottom on which the target was lying. Furthermore, we didn't have full confidence that our estimates on the size and configuration of the target were sufficiently accurate to commit to a final design for the claw.

All of this information was vital to the design of the capture vehicle and the required dimensions of the well in the *HGE*. There was also some remaining uncertainty about the exact geographic location of the target. We didn't want to be cruising back and forth in a 618-foot ship during the recovery mission trying to find an elusive target on the ocean bottom, with over three miles, and 12 million pounds, of pipe and capture vehicle hanging from the derrick. Somehow, we had to get out to the target site and collect the needed additional data.

Clearly, if we were going to collect the information from the target site overtly, we had to have a credible explanation for a ship being out there. We decided to use the ocean mining cover story and collect the needed data during an ostensible survey of a half dozen or so potentially valuable mining sites in the North Pacific. One of those sites, of course, would be the target site.

Tying the target site dat-collection mission into ocean mining made perfect sense. Global Marine had already acknowledged that it was involved with feasibility studies for ocean mining, even though their customer had not yet been publicly disclosed. The ocean mining community would be unlikely to question the legitimacy of Global Marine surveys to determine the quantity and quality of manganese nodules in different areas of the North Pacific Ocean. With the obviously large investment that Global Marine's unknown customer was apparently making, it was natural to assume that the company had some a priori ideas on the best areas for mining the ocean. It also made sense that the customer would want to begin the exploration of potentially profitable mining areas while completing the design and construction of the prototype mining system.

From the CIA's perspective, exploration for nodules in the North Pacific—in the same general area that the *HGE* would be operating four years hence—seemed like an ideal solution to its problems. It would help reinforce the ocean mining cover story. And, at the same time, it would provide the opportunity to get the vital information needed about the size and shape of the target object and the nature of the ocean bottom on which it was resting.

———

Global Marine had an oil drilling ship, the *Glomar II,* that could be made available for the DOMP survey. Designed by John Graham, the ship had originally been built as an A-frame barge without engines. After construction—and the receipt of a four- to five-year contract from Shell Oil for drilling in Cook Inlet, Alaska—engines and propulsion shafts were added so the ship could propel itself from one drilling location to another. The *Glomar II* would drill in Alaska during the summer months and return to California to drill during the winter.

The ship, launched in 1964, was originally named the *CUSS II.* The name was changed when Global Marine found that the word "cuss" was very offensive in the Arabic language. Good taste and good business sense dictated changing the name to *Glomar II.*

The ship was about 268 feet long with a 20 × 20–foot hole—called the moon pool—located directly beneath the derrick to permit passage of the drill string into the ocean. Graham had designed a truncated bow into the original barge to make room for the forward anchor winches used for mooring over a drilling site. The blunt bow was retained even after the propulsion system was added. It didn't cause any problems while the ship was moored and only slowed the boat slightly in light to normal seaways.

Just how the *Glomar II* would perform in the open ocean and heavier seas remained to be seen. In wintertime the seas around the target site can get ugly. In December and January, one could expect gale-force winds every three days or so, on average. The sooner the *Glomar II* could get started, the better its chances of a successful mission (and a credible cover story) would be.

The plan was to build a platform that would be lowered on the drill string through the ship's moon pool. The platform would incorporate a mechanism for taking eight-foot-long core samples from the sea bottom. The platform would also be instrumented with a profiling sonar to measure slope in the vicinity of the target and a calibrated camera to get some "ground truth" photography of the target.

For the job of building the sensor platform and preparing the ship, Global Marine selected one of its senior drilling superintendents, Leon Blurton, as program manager. The company would also provide the captain, ship's crew (for running the ship), and a pipe-handling crew. The CIA had to provide a mission director and the needed equipment and expertise to enable secure communications between the ship and headquarters.

There were no obvious choices for the CIA crew—none of us had any real marine experience—but we did have some wonderfully enthusiastic volunteers. Dr. Jack Sparkman (aka "Red Jack") and Dr. Earnest Ruggles signed on immediately to direct the *Glomar II* survey mission. Close friends, Ruggles and Sparkman possessed an enthusiasm for the operational side of things probably unmatched by any of our team members. Together they had already volunteered for and completed several relatively unattractive assignments like, for example, a trip to fog-shrouded Adak—about 800 miles from the target site—to assess sea state conditions and pier facilities. Part of this drive may have come from the fact that AZORIAN was an assignment that actually gave them the opportunity to *build* something. Many engineers in the agency spend their entire careers working primarily on technical research and analysis of intelligence rather than design and construction of an operational system. AZORIAN was different. Most of their enthusiasm, though, was probably due to just plain old exuberance. They loved the program and wanted to do everything they could to make it successful. So, Red Jack Sparkman and Earnest Ruggles, accompanied by a security officer and a communications specialist, were selected to be the first of our AZORIAN team to actually "go to sea."

The *Glomar II* mission was not expected to be a picnic. Although it was a commercial ship, the Soviets conventionally considered any U.S. ship—even an unarmed commercial one—as a legitimate target for harassment in the open ocean. We fully expected that kind of behavior. What might happen beyond that, if the Soviets got wind of our true mission, was the subject of lots of speculation. As a precaution against being identified through photographic analysis, Sparkman and his team concealed their appearance as well as possible with long hair (long enough to cover the ears, which are an excellent personal identifier), facial hair, and alias identities.

It was essential, of course, that we have secure two-way communications between headquarters and the *Glomar II*. The program office would have to be able to advise the ship to abort if there were any indications that the Soviets were suspicious, and Sparkman had to be able to send secure messages to Langley to keep them informed on the progress and status of the *Glomar II* operations.

Radio communications from headquarters to the ship were relatively straightforward. Encrypted messages could be sent from the continental United States without revealing the identity of the intended recipient. Identical codebooks on the ship and at headquarters would permit decipherment of the encrypted Morse code messages received by the ship.

Arranging for secure encrypted communications from the ship to headquarters, however, was no simple task. We assumed that the *Glomar II*'s radio signals might be monitored by the Soviets, and commercial drilling ships never enciphered their messages to the shore. The use of encryption devices would have been totally inconsistent with Global Marine's normal operations. All radio communications from the ship would have to look like typical unenciphered messages to the white world—and to the Soviets. The only available solution on such short notice was to use a type of steganography (secret writing) known as innocent text. Innocent text, or IT, has been used for hundreds of years in many variations.

Sparkman was trained to write nonsensitive ship-to-shore cables in which a secret message was embedded. In practice, Sparkman first composed the secret message he wanted to send. Then, using a onetime pad and a (relatively) simple algorithm, the secret message was converted into apparently random letters that could be inserted into the text of the cable without being noticeable. Only the holder of an identical onetime pad could convert the string of random letters back into an intelligible message by using the reverse algorithm. This all sounds simple enough, but problems can arise when the algorithm forces the sender to use words in the innocent text message beginning with letters like "Q" or "X." It takes training and practice to become proficient in the composition of IT messages that don't read awkwardly. A poorly constructed IT message could create suspicion in the mind of anyone monitoring the *Glomar II*'s messages.

———

Sparkman and his team met the *Glomar II* in Oahu, Hawaii, in October 1970. Manfred Krutein, the ocean mining expert hired by Global Marine, was already in town as the "mission coordinator" to enhance the cover for the mission. The CIA, properly paranoid, sent a team of a dozen or so agents to Hawaii to "nose around" and look for any indications that Sparkman and his team were being followed or targeted by anyone. No indications of special interest were found, and the CIA security cadre felt confident that the Soviets were not suspicious of any U.S. government involvement. Parangosky gave the go-ahead for the mission to proceed.

When the ship had been provisioned, the *Glomar II* set out to explore for nodules. Of course, the real mission objective was to go to the target site and collect the desired data about the *K-129* and the topography of the ocean bottom in the vicinity. However, proceeding directly to that location—about 1,800 miles from Hawaii—would have looked very strange to anyone monitoring the *Glomar II* operations. So, in order to be more consistent with the cover mission, Sparkman and his crew planned to stop at three or four locations on the way to the target, spending a few days at each site ostensibly doing nodule surveys. Ultimately, they'd reach the 40N, 180W target site and collect the information that was needed. The sensor platform carried by the *Glomar II* had cameras, closed-circuit TV, sonar, and core sampling equipment. The platform was disrespectfully nicknamed "The Dork."

———

The first survey stop for Sparkman and the *Glomar II* was totally unplanned. Only two days after leaving port, the senior CIA project officer in charge of the operations in Honolulu realized that he'd sent Sparkman and his crew off to the target site without the underwater navigation charts that they'd need to find the sunken submarine. The geographic coordinates of the target had been refined to within a radius of 2,000 to 3,000 feet, but that much uncertainty would still require the *Glomar II*, with its limited sensor suite, to search an area on the ocean bottom of nearly one square mile—a very time-consuming effort with no guarantee of success.

What Sparkman needed were the charts showing the location of the underwater transponders that had been previously deployed in the target area by the Navy vessel that had initially located the *K-129*. The position of the target was mapped precisely to these transponders. The *Glomar*, with its acoustic position estimation system, could locate itself to within a couple of hundred feet of an operating transponder. The CIA was banking on the fact that at least two or three of those transponders deployed in 1968 would still be operable in 1970.

The tricky question was, how were the charts going to be delivered? The ship was already about 200 miles offshore when it was discovered that the needed charts were still in Oahu. Going back to Hawaii was a nonstarter because the weather was already marginal and it was only going to get worse as the calendar progressed.

Of course, the Navy could have been prevailed upon to send a small, fast boat out to the ship to deliver the charts, but Navy involvement with the commercial *Glomar II* was an unacceptable choice. It would be completely inconsistent with the commercial ocean mining cover story. Another alternative was to fly the charts to the ship with a small aircraft, dropping the charts in a buoyant, waterproof container near the ship where they could be recovered. This option was discarded too because of the very real chance of losing the deployed charts in high-sea conditions. The CIA team on the beach had a real dilemma.

The CIA project manager on the beach asked Manfred Krutein, Global Marine's mission coordinator, to look into the possibility of flying a helicopter out to the ship. The *Glomar II* had a helipad, and a helicopter would theoretically be able to deliver the charts safely to the ship without fear of loss. It seemed like a good idea.

Krutein made a number of calls and finally found a commercial helicopter operator experienced in landings and takeoffs from a rolling ship. He was eager to take on the delivery mission until he learned that the ship was 200 miles offshore. The range of his helicopter was only 200 miles, and there was no aviation gas on the *Glomar II* to refill the chopper for the trip back home. But the charter pilot had an idea. He suggested to Krutein that he might be able to carry an extra 50-gallon drum of gas in the helicopter if Krutein would be willing to squeeze himself and his classified charts alongside the barrel during the flight. Krutein agreed to the plan and hoped the pilot's navigation skills were good enough for him to fly directly to the ship with no search required. Since the helicopter had only a 200-mile range, there was no room for navigation error.

The chopper took off at 0500 the next morning, Krutein sharing his seat with a drum of aviation gas and an inflatable life raft that the CIA had thoughtfully provided in case the pilot's range calculations or navigation skills were off. The pilot flew first to Kauai, where he topped up the tank for the ocean leg. Then they took off and flew almost straight north, hoping that the *Glomar II* would be exactly where it said it was.

The ship's position estimate was right on. And that was a good thing, because the ship was sighted just before the tank ran dry. The helicopter landed without incident and with only slight embarrassment to its crew, who found it difficult to hide their knocking knees as they walked across the helipad to meet the waiting Sparkman. Krutein delivered the charts and the aviation gas was pumped from the oil drum into the helicopter. The return trip was eventful (bad weather) but without calamity. The *Glomar II*, with the transponder position charts, proceeded on its voyage to the target site.

Parangosky found out about the episode after the fact—and he was furious. It was bad enough that the agency's project officer on the island had failed to put the charts onboard before the *Glomar*'s departure, but the use of the helicopter for a mission that could very well have ended badly—leading to almost certain compromise of the program by the time authorities had completed their investigation—was, in Parangosky's mind, inexcusable. The punishment was quick and unforgiving. The career of the senior agent would never recover.

———

Shortly after resuming its mission, the *Glomar II* was intercepted by a Soviet ship, the *Gidrograf*, confirming our worry that the Soviets would be very interested in anything going on in this part of the ocean. The *Gidrograf* was a trawler design, but it was being used as an AGI—an intelligence collection ship. It was about 156 feet long and, like many Soviet ships of that day, was not particularly clean. There was a lot of rust on the hull—it looked like it had been at sea for a long time.

The *Glomar II* continued on its nodule survey with the *Gidrograf* staying close by. When the drill ship would hold station to sample the bottom nodules, the *Gidrograf* would drift down-current and recover all the plastic bags of garbage or other refuse dumped off our ship, presumably looking for any information that might have intelligence value. (Dumping garbage off the ship in plastic bags seems very environmentally unfriendly nowadays. I'm not sure how it was viewed by environmentalists back in 1970, but that was how the garbage was disposed of.) After several survey stops, the *Glomar II* and its Soviet shadow reached the target site, where they were joined by another Soviet ship, a submarine rescue vessel, the *CC-23*. Once Sparkman and his crew reached the target site they were continuously observed at close distance by both ships. The *CC-23* was the more aggressive of the two and blatantly harassed the *Glomar II* on a regular basis.

In spite of the harassment, Sparkman and his team prepared the sensor platform for descent. The first order of business, once the platform had been lowered to the bottom, was to find the target and record its precise geographical coordinates. Once the submarine had been found, the *Glomar II* would move around the target area using the sonar to map the contours of the bottom while using the cameras and closed-circuit TV to image the target. Finally, the core samples would be recovered from the soil that the submarine was lying on. It was a simple plan, but even the most basic operations can be excruciatingly troublesome when attempted in the open ocean—under intense surveillance.

Hampered by both the Soviet interference and the extreme weather, Sparkman's mission encountered serious trouble. During the survey operations, the "Dork" ran into the bottom and was lost. Although good calibrated photographic coverage of the target had been obtained, along with bottom topography measurements, the team was not able to collect the critical core samples from the ocean bottom. These core samples would have provided information needed to predict the loads that would be experienced by the claw as its arms were forced through the soil and under the submarine. The core samples were also needed to predict the suction that would have to be overcome to break the target loose from the seafloor. It was a serious loss, but the most important material—the calibrated imagery of the *K-129* wreckage and the precise bottom slope information—had been collected successfully. We had enough information to complete the design of the *Hughes Glomar Explorer* and the claw with confidence that the pieces would, in the end, all fit together.

———

The harassment by the two Soviet ships had been a surprise to Sparkman and his CIA team, who didn't realize that the aggressive behavior between Soviet and U.S. ships on the high seas wasn't restricted to military vessels. Commercial ships were fair game, too. Although the United States had proposed in March 1968 that the United States and the Soviet Union negotiate an agreement to prevent such dangerous actions, the USSR had not yet responded favorably to the suggestion.[1]

The Global Marine skipper and his crew were not at all surprised by the Soviet actions, however. They'd encountered this kind of aggressive behavior many times when their ships were operating in the open oceans. Occasionally, the two Soviet observers would back off to a distance of a mile or so. Interestingly, their decision to distance themselves would usually be followed by an overflight of a U.S. Navy P-3 maritime surveillance aircraft. How did the Soviets know that the Navy plane was coming? Sparkman couldn't figure it out, but the correlation was too consistent to be coincidental. (The CIA didn't find out about the treachery of John Anthony Walker until years later. Walker was a former U.S. Navy chief warrant officer and communications specialist who spied for the Soviet Union from 1967 until his arrest in 1985. Because of Walker's treachery, it is believed that the Soviets were able to read all of the Navy's classified documents and transmissions during the years in which Project AZORIAN was active.)

When Sparkman left the target site to return to Hawaii, the *CC-23* left for other duties. The *Gidrograf*, however, continued to tag along with the *Glomar II* as it headed back to port. And it was a slow trip. The *Glomar II* had not been designed for operating in the type of sea conditions it was now experiencing. The ship was marginally powered in the first place, and with its truncated bow and the prevalent sea states it was only capable of three to five knots. The *Gidrograf* was enduring a very uncomfortable ride as it followed Sparkman and his drill ship. The Soviet ship was both shorter and narrower than the *Glomar II*, and it was experiencing much higher roll angles than the wide-bodied drill ship. Going so slowly just made matters worse for the trawler. Steaming along at three to five knots was almost like standing still. With so little forward speed, the *Gidrograf* might just as well have been lying in the trough of the waves. After a couple of agonizing days, they signaled with flashing lights to Sparkman and the *Glomar II*, "Do you need a tow? We can make 12 knots."

Sparkman declined the offer, but later admitted, "I still regret we did not send back a 'cold recruitment' pitch inviting them to meet us in Honolulu for wine, women and song."

––––––

Shortly after the arrival of the *Glomar II* back in Hawaii, Global Marine's mission coordinator (and sometime helicopter copilot) in Honolulu, Manfred Krutein, received a call from Global Marine corporate headquarters instructing him to arrange a press conference and a banquet at the Ilikai Hotel in Honolulu for December 8.[2] The purpose of the planned event was to make the first public announcement of Howard Hughes's involvement in the DOMP. Curtis Crooke took the stage first and introduced Raymond Holliday, Hughes's personal representative, who announced that Howard Hughes himself was the sponsor of the Global Marine survey activities. This was exciting news for the ocean mining community, and it took a lot of pressure off the Global Marine managers, who would no longer have to evade questions about the identity of their secret sponsor.

## The *Glomar II* Rides Again

The fact that the *Gidrograf* followed the *Glomar II* all the way back to port in Honolulu bothered John Parangosky and his counterintelligence specialists a great deal. They were concerned that the continued Soviet interest in the *Glomar II* might have been an indication that they had expected something more to happen. After all, although the mission had taken six to seven weeks, the *Glomar II* had only surveyed several nodule sites. The limited time spent at the sites was not consistent with all the time, effort, and expense that had gone into preparation of the ship and its 2,500-mile cruise from California to its staging base in Hawaii. If the ship had returned to Los Angeles, the transit time from California to Hawaii and back would have been longer than the survey time spent searching for high-grade nodules.

In order to maintain the credibility of the DOMP cover operations, Parangosky decided that the *Glomar II* should stay in Honolulu and prepare for another survey mission as soon as possible. The new survey sites would be in a direction *away* from the target site. Parangosky wanted to reinforce the ocean mining cover story and at the same time diminish any Soviet suspicions that might have been raised by the *Glomar's* operations in the general vicinity where the Soviets believed their submarine had been lost.

The sensor platform for finding and photographing the target hadn't survived the first survey mission, but Global Marine believed they could design and build a completely mechanical mechanism that could pick up credible quantities of nodules for analysis and future "show and tell" within the ocean mining community. Leon Blurton, Global Marine's program manager for the first survey mission, was tasked with the job of designing and building the new nodule collector in the space of a couple of weeks.

Blurton was a barrel-chested man with tons of experience in the Texas oil patch and years of experience working for Global Marine in their offshore drilling activities. He wasn't an engineer, but he was extremely resourceful and knew what would—and wouldn't—work in a ship's environment. His nodule collector resembled a downward-looking clamshell with an actuating rod extending beneath the jaws. When the drill string was lowered to the bottom, the resistance met by the actuator would cause the clamshell to close and lock, trapping a big scoop of bottom sediment—and, hopefully, manganese nodules—in the jaws for recovery into the ship. Of course, this would be a time-consuming and inefficient mechanism for sampling the bottom of the ocean, but all Parangosky was trying to do was persuade the Soviets that we were really collecting nodules. We'd hide the clamshell mechanism from the sight of any nearby Soviet ships so they wouldn't see the primitive collection methods being used.

Having devised a plan, Parangosky had to find a CIA mission director for the second *Glomar II* survey. This mission was even less attractive than the initial one. First of all, it was pretty certain that the *Gidrograf* was going to be present—it was still hanging around the port, apparently waiting to see if the DOMP survey was going to continue—and the weather was going to be a lot worse. In December, the *average* wave height in that part of the Pacific southwest of Hawaii is about fifteen feet, and gale-force winds come through on average about every two to three days. Forty- to fifty-foot seas are not uncommon. Jack Sparkman and Earnest Ruggles had had enough time at sea to suit them for a while, and—not surprisingly—nobody else wanted to step up to the plate.

Parangosky asked each of the AZORIAN team members to come into his office for a private interview. When my turn came, and when asked how I felt about heading up the second *Glomar II* survey mission, I told him, "John, I really don't want to go. I've never been to sea on a ship, and have no experience in marine engineering. Also, I'm right in the middle of trying to complete the research for my doctoral dissertation. Furthermore, I *know* that I'm highly susceptible to seasickness. Bottom line, John, I'd prefer you consider me for the mission director job only as a last resort."

Parangosky said, "Okay. I understand how you feel. I'll get back to you."

I felt pretty good as I walked out of JP's office. I thought I'd dodged a big bullet.

Later that same day, I was greeted by Bill Rivers—one of our team members—in the hallway with a hearty, "Congratulations, mission director!"

Suspicious, I asked, "What are you talking about?"

He replied, "The word's out. You won the competition to see who would head up the second survey!"

I couldn't believe my ears. I hadn't volunteered for the mission. There must have been some mistake.

I immediately went back to Parangosky's office and knocked on the door. He called out, "Come in, Dave. I've been expecting you." When I entered his office, he said, "I knew you'd be here soon. Congratulations on your new assignment!"

I said, "John, there must be some confusion. You *know* that I didn't want that job. How come I'm the new mission director?"

He grinned and said, "You were the only one I interviewed who didn't say '*absolutely* no!!' So, you won the job."

Working for John Parangosky could be full of surprises. JP added, "Don't worry about getting seasick. Just go talk to Flick. He'll set you up."

———

"Flick" was Dr. Don Flickinger, a retired Air Force general with a degree in medicine and a long CIA relationship. Associated with the selection of the Mercury astronauts while he was working at the Lovelace Clinic in Albuquerque, Flick was hired by the CIA in the early 1960s to establish the screening tests for the OXCART pilots. When he retired from the Air Force in 1961 he was used by the CIA as a consultant for all manner of things, including the selection of personnel for special assignments. I had known Flick since 1963, when I was working on the OXCART program at the Nevada Test Site's Area 51. He was a good friend, and I had complete trust in him.

When I told Flick about my susceptibility to motion sickness, he thought a little bit, scratched his head, and said, "I've got just the thing. I'll give you two bottles of pills. The first bottle will contain Phenergan, a powerful antinausea pill that's frequently used for 'morning sickness.' The second bottle will contain an amphetamine to counteract the extreme drowsiness that can accompany the use of Phenergan. Take one of each. I guarantee you that these pills will bring you back from the brink of terminal vomiting in 15 minutes!

"However," he added, "don't take them unless you really, truly need them. Both pills can affect your judgment, and the effects of the combination can be unpredictable!" Great. I had magic pills that would defeat seasickness, but I didn't know what the side effects might be.

So, along with a communications technician and a security officer, I showed up at the pier in Hawaii early in December and met Leon Blurton and the ship's captain, an elderly and gentlemanly sailor who was going to retire after this assignment. The new all-mechanical nodule collector wasn't completed yet, and some other repairs to the ship were still ongoing. It looked like we wouldn't sail for another week.

That meant I'd have to spend a whole week in Honolulu—staying at the Ilikai Hotel—before going to sea. What tough duty! Every morning I'd get up and have fresh pineapple for breakfast on the outdoor patio. After an extra cup of coffee, I'd take a taxi to the ship and spend some time learning about the ship's systems and getting to know the Global Marine crew. Around five o'clock, I'd return to the hotel and make plans for dinner and entertainment that night. It was a hard life, but I didn't complain.

Finally, the ship was ready. I checked out of the Ilikai and moved onto the *Glomar II*. The captain planned to sail at midnight. What I witnessed just before midnight made an impression on me I'll never forget. That was the arrival of the *Glomar II* drilling crew. They came in as singles, with girlfriends, and in groups. They came by foot, in taxis, and in friends' cars. They were mostly from Texas, Louisiana, and Mississippi. But, they all had one thing pretty much in common that night. They were drunk as skunks when they arrived at the ship. In some cases, they had to be carried onto the ship and into their bunks. They knew that they'd have to be getting up and working a twelve-hour shift in not too many hours. The idea of working in the hot sun with the hangovers that many of them were sure to have overwhelmed me. Just the thought of it made me sick to my stomach.

When the ship left port, I sat on the helicopter pad with some friends looking at the sky—and getting a little nervous. The stars seemed to be moving slowly around in my field of view. I soon realized that I was on a rolling ship for the first time in my life, and Dr. Don's seasickness remedy might be getting an early test. I decided to turn in before I felt worse.

One of the friends accompanying me on this voyage was my old buddy from the days on the OXCART program, Donovan J. White—now working for Global Marine. White had been hired into Global Marine on my recommendation, and I felt that he owed me one. Besides, misery loves company. I had asked Crooke if he'd let White go on the mission, and (God love him) he agreed. Neither White nor I had ever been to sea.

———

When I went out on deck the next morning, the first thing I saw was the *Gidrograf* riding close alongside. I couldn't believe it. The Soviet AGI was far too close for comfort. It seemed so overtly aggressive. What were they planning to do? Attack us? Ram us? Surely this kind of behavior was not permissible under international maritime law! As the government mission director, I felt that I had to do something about this outrage. Showing my maturity and experience, I went to Leon Blurton, the drilling superintendent, and asked, "Jeez, Leon! What are we going to do?"

Blurton just laughed, along with the captain who had wandered by, and said, "No need to worry. But just watch—our side has some tricks, too!" Within an hour, as if on cue, a Navy P-3 aircraft flew over the horizon. Either the *Gidrograf* wasn't alerted by their headquarters about the approaching aircraft or it just didn't care. It was still in full harassment mode, close in to the *Glomar II*. The P-3 seemed to welcome the opportunity to provide some harassment of its own. It flew directly at the AGI, climbing to clear the ship only just before what appeared to be an imminent collision. This was repeated a number of times until the *Gidrograf* nonchalantly withdrew from its close formation with our ship to a respectable distance of maybe 500 yards. After a while, the P-3 disappeared back over the horizon as well. Games had been played between the United States and the Soviets. Both sides had yanked the other's chain. Honor having been satisfied, the two ships proceeded together (but not *so much* together) to the first site for nodule sampling. This was my first experience with the ocean etiquette practiced by U.S. and Soviet ships during the Cold War period.

During the next couple of weeks, we continued steaming in the area southeast of Hawaii, stopping every few days at a new nodule sampling site. The ever-faithful *Gidrograf* followed along and waited patiently while we lowered drill string and went through the motions of recovering nodules for analysis. Occasionally, she would cut close across our bow on a near-collision course, trying, I suppose, to see if they could alarm the captain of the *Glomar II*. If that was their aim, they failed completely. Our captain would just chuckle. "There's nothing to worry about," he said. "They're good sailors. They know what they're doing. They're just playing some games!" I wished that I could be that sanguine.

One moonless night during a sampling operation, while we were examining our collected nodules around the moon pool under floodlights, some of the crew began to get the feeling that we weren't alone. It must have been a change in the sound of the waves or a change in the wind—there was certainly nothing that we could see, being pretty much blinded by the floodlights in the moon pool. Then we got a call from the ship's bridge—the *Gidrograf* was lying directly alongside of us, no more than fifty feet away, with all lights out. Apparently, they wanted to get a better look at the operation. We didn't want to seem alarmed, so we just went on with the nodule sorting, occasionally saying something stupid like "Wow! Good nodules! Hughes is going to like this!" I don't know what the Soviet crew saw—or heard or understood—but after a half hour or so, they drifted away into the blackness of the night.

The *Gidrograf* and its crew were actually beginning to earn a grudging respect from me. This whole voyage was no fun for either them or us. The weather was terrible—gales came through about every three days—so we tried to do our sampling operations during the lulls after each storm. With wave heights up to thirty to forty feet, the *Glomar II* was rocking and rolling all over the place, and to all appearances, the *Gidrograf* was probably having it worse than we were. We were rolling up to thirty degrees, and to my eye it looked like the *Gidrograf* was rolling, perhaps, forty or forty-five degrees. They had to be miserable, but they stuck it out. They weren't going home until we did.

The rolling of the *Glomar II* also created an issue between Leon Blurton and me. Between sampling operations, the drilling crew was leaving a lot of the drill string sections standing upright inside the derrick. This procedure speeded up the process of raising or lowering the string because the sections didn't have to be placed back on the pipe rack on the main deck of the ship. One afternoon, I happened to be reading the stability specifications for the ship. These specs talk about the "roll angle of no recovery," which, simply put, is the roll angle that you'd sure as hell better not exceed if you wanted the ship to come back upright again. The specs were pretty explicit about not stacking any drill string inside the derrick if roll angles were becoming excessive. Of course, *any* roll angle greater than about ten degrees seemed excessive to me. Anyway, I suggested to Leon that we ought to take the drill string out of the derrick and store it on the pipe rack. Leon didn't think there was any stability problem (I'm sure he was right), but he deferred to my request and stowed the drill string on the rack. But he was mumbling under his breath. I was pretty sure that, somehow, I'd pay for my advice on ship stability before the mission was over.

———

I should mention that all of these ship rolling motions were having the predictable effect on my stomach. After a couple of days at sea, I began to get nauseous. Even so, I was still able to function until about the third day. At that point, my options were to stay in bed and wish I were dead or take the Flick-prescribed magic pills for seasickness. It really wasn't a contest. I was concerned about my judgment being impaired by the pills (as Dr. Don had suggested it might be), but I figured that a functional mission director with impaired judgment was better than no mission director at all. With some misgivings, I took the pills. Amazingly, within fifteen minutes I was convinced that I was going to live. Within half an hour, I felt good enough to get up and go to the mess hall and get something to eat.

And that's the way it went for the rest of the mission. I'd last for about three days, getting more and more nauseous. Then I'd take the magic pills and be good for another three days. I never felt good enough to eat the wonderful, rich, Cajun-style (the Global Marine crew called it "Coon-Ass"–style) dinners that were prepared by the ship's Creole cook, however. On land, I'd have loved those meals, but I was afraid to chance it at sea. I subsisted, instead, on apples and cheese and crackers. The cook would watch me munching those crackers and just shake his head.

One morning he announced to the whole mess hall, "Dave, you're eating so much cheese that you're going to have to swallow a mouse to chew a path through to your asshole!" I guessed he might be right. I hadn't had to use the ship's head in days. Not that there was much incentive to use the ship's head. The toilets in the head were plumbed directly to the ocean. Along with the extreme rolling motions, the ship would lift off the crest of a wave and then slam back down into the trough. This created a seawater douche about two feet high coming up out of the toilets on the main deck. The big waves were coming in about every twelve to fifteen seconds, so using the ship's facilities during the gales required a pretty finely developed sense of timing. If you were constipated? Forget it.

One day during one of these rock-and-roll episodes on the ship, I was standing on the main deck next to the moon pool. I estimated the height of the waves at about twenty to thirty feet, and I was reflecting on the fact that most of the time the horizon consisted of the crest of the next wave. Lots of spray and foam were flying off the crests and over the rail of the ship. While I was standing there looking at the wild sea, the wind blew the top of one of the waves right across the rail onto the main deck. I felt something hit me in the chest. When I looked down, there was a sort of transparent-pinkish, gelatinous blob oozing down my chest. It must have been tough weather for jellyfish. As I wiped the slimy mess off my jacket, I thought it was probably time for me to get to higher ground. I thought it might also be time for me to take another dose of Dr. Don's magic seasick pills.

There were other diversions on the ship, too. The captain (who, as I mentioned earlier, was on his last cruise before retirement—and a good thing, too) had a fetish about painting the handrails on all the ship's ladders. He would head out on deck pretty much every day with a can of black paint and a small brush. You never knew which handrails were freshly painted until you went up that ladder. Then, of course, it was too late. By the end of the mission, most of the *Glomar II* crew had become pretty proficient at climbing ladders without using the handrails—no small feat when you're in the middle of a gale.

Appropriately enough, the captain was also the acting ship's doctor. (The *Glomar II* hadn't needed an onboard ship's doctor while working in the Santa Barbara Channel, and no one thought to augment the crew with one for this mission.) But, to give the captain his due, he did a fine job of setting the bones of a seaman who broke his arm when an especially violent ship roll hurled him into a bulkhead. Unfortunately, the captain also gave the seaman ten times the recommended dosage of morphine for the pain—damned near killed him.

As for the degraded judgment that Flick feared I might encounter while taking the magic seasick pills, he was right. I don't know if he foresaw the enhanced creativity that those same pills bestowed upon the taker, though. I sometimes found myself spending an inordinate amount of time creating interesting innocent text messages to send ashore. Any of the CIA communications security guys will tell you that writing poetry in innocent text is extremely hard—I became a master at it. Even John Parangosky (I've been told) acknowledged, upon receiving a Christmas poem (in IT, of course) from the ship during the annual headquarters Christmas party, that whatever my limitations as a mission director and engineer might be, I was one hell of an innocent text writer.

I blew all the goodwill I had built up about a week later, however. Christmas had come and gone. I stayed out of the mess hall during that time. The captain had placed a small Christmas tree there, and watching the branches of that tree rise up and down as the ship heaved down and up produced instant nausea for me. Finally, the *Gidrograf* had enough. One sunny day, the Soviet crew tooted their horn, waved, and headed over the horizon back to Vladivostok. With no more reason to remain at sea as a decoy, I exercised both my creativity and poor judgment by writing an innocent text message to headquarters: "Weather sux. Heading home." I'm told the message was not well received. I didn't care. We were heading back to terra firma, and I vowed I'd never go to sea again.

———

On the way back to Hawaii, Leon Blurton started giving me a hard time about never having climbed the ladder up to the top of the derrick (which was, to remind you, about ten stories above the main deck).

"You're not a real sailor until you've climbed the derrick!" he said.

I figured this might be my last chance to be a "real sailor," so I told him, "Sure, I've been planning on doing that! Not right now, though. Later." My hope was that "later" would bring some better weather, fewer waves, and less ship motion.

In a day or so, the weather did let up a little, and with our course back to Hawaii, the *Glomar II* was taking the waves right on the bow. This minimized the ship's rolling motion. I figured it was the right time to climb the derrick. I didn't tell anyone my intentions, but I headed off to the base of the derrick after breakfast with a Polaroid camera—so I could prove I'd made it to the top.

The only access to the top was a metal-runged ladder that was welded to the outside of the A-frame derrick. Reminding myself, "Don't look down. Just keep on climbing," I started up. It actually wasn't so bad since the ship's roll was minimal. I reached the top with a great sense of relief and took some pictures. I got a good shot of the ship's windsock (which had been torn to tatters by the gales) at the very top of the derrick, and a shot of the pipe rack down on the main deck. Feeling pretty damned good about myself, I started back down the ladder.

After descending about ten to twenty feet, I began to sense that something was wrong. The horizon seemed to be moving around a lot and I was beginning to feel a little dizzy. I looked back at the stern of the ship to see if that horizon was also moving—and then I realized what was happening. Leon had suspected I was going to make "the climb." He had collected the whole *Glomar II* crew up on the ship's helicopter pad to watch as the captain changed course ninety degrees so that the ship was riding in the trough of the waves. No wonder the horizon was moving. The ship was rolling back and forth like a rubber duck in a bathtub. Leon and the crew were all down there laughing their asses off while I was getting cramps in my fingers from trying to hold on tighter and tighter to the galvanized rungs of the ladder. Eventually, when I got closer to the main deck, the captain resumed course and we headed on to Hawaii. Everyone had enjoyed my situation immensely. Leon always said that they only played that trick on me because they "liked me." Sure. Years later, Leon was still telling the story at parties and meetings. He'd say, "Ol' Dave was gripping those ladder rungs so tight his fingerprints were etched permanently into the galvanize!"

Leon became one of my dearest friends at Global Marine. I still wonder how that could ever have come to be.

## The *Seascope*—from Minesweeper to Miner

In the spring of 1972 the *Hughes Glomar Explorer* was still over a year away from launch, and the last nodule exploration mission of the DOMP had been over a year earlier with the second *Glomar II* mission southwest of Hawaii. Manfred Krutein, Global Marine's ocean mining expert, had reported that some members of the mining community were expressing surprise that Howard Hughes and the Summa Corporation hadn't shown any further interest in nodule surveys.

Parangosky's Commercial Operations Division (COD) had tried to create a steady stream of ocean mining observables that might show up in trade publications or newspapers. They had even arranged to have a scaled-down mining machine built by a small company with past agency affiliations in Los Angeles. Summa had publicly announced that this mining machine was going to be used for experiments, and we hoped that media coverage of these reported activities would convince the industry that Hughes and his Summa Corporation were still progressing at full speed with the DOMP. Unfortunately, the experimental mining machine and the occasional news release from Summa—most of them written by the COD—didn't impress everyone.

This news hit John Parangosky like a ton of bricks. He demanded that the WCPO come up with an immediate plan to "show a presence" of Summa Corporation and the DOMP. He believed that if we didn't do something quickly—either issue a news report, or better yet, do something *newsworthy*—the Soviets might begin to question the cover story. He wanted results in thirty days or less.

Walt Logan, the director of the COD, met with Global Marine and some retired Navy and Coast Guard personnel who were working in the WCPO. The idea of issuing a news bulletin on the DOMP didn't look very encouraging. The problem was that we didn't have anything to report. We would have had to make up the whole progress report, using facts and figures that wouldn't withstand careful scrutiny by the ocean mining community. We might end up escalating the mildly curious speculation about the DOMP into open skepticism.

Given the circumstances, the COD decided that we should sponsor another nodule exploration mission. The exploration wouldn't have to be done in the North Pacific—or any other remote ocean area. It could be done just off the coast of California. The important thing was to create plenty of publicity before, during, and after the exploration mission. So long as the newspapers reported heavily on the ocean exploration activity by Howard Hughes and his Summa Corporation, it wouldn't particularly matter whether we had any real success in collecting high-grade manganese nodules. So it was decided. Howard Hughes and his DOMP were going to do a survey for manganese nodules off the coast of California—and right away. Now, all we needed was a ship that could be leased, prepared, provisioned, and made ready to sail within a few months.

Our retired Navy and Coast Guard people from the WCPO took to the ports between San Diego and San Francisco looking for a seaworthy vessel at least 200 feet long that could be outfitted with some special equipment for dredging up manganese nodules. After a couple of weeks of searching, they identified an old Navy minesweeper—the *Seascope*—that met most of the requirements.

The *Seascope* had been removed from government service years ago, and time hadn't treated it particularly well. The ship was covered with rust and looked thoroughly disreputable. However, it seemed to be in pretty good mechanical shape. With a rigorous inspection and repair of the mechanical and electrical systems, the addition of some nodule collection gear, and lots of cosmetic enhancement, the *Seascope* could be made ready to sail with the Summa pennant proudly flying from the flag mast.

The ship was leased, and within a few weeks the mechanical and electrical work had been completed. The refurbishment team was getting ready to begin a thorough cleanup of the boat when Parangosky ran out of patience.

He told us, "We can't wait any longer! We've got to get out there and show a Summa presence immediately! Be ready to sail in a week!"

The refurbishment team knew that the ship couldn't be properly cleaned and painted in that short time—but they also knew that John Parangosky meant business. One way or another, the ship would have to sail in seven days.

The team took the only avenue open to them. The paint would have to be applied right on top of the rust and dirt and whatever else was lying around on the decks. The chosen color was white. The command to the painters was to finish the job in four days. A squad of painters armed with spray guns descended on the ship and started the job. In four days, it was completed. No visible rust. From fifty yards, the *Seascope* looked pretty decent. From that distance, you couldn't see the overspray on the portholes, stanchions, and lifeboats. Not until you were onboard the ship could you observe the overspray on the dirt piles or the dead rats in the corners. The rats were still there, right where they had died (of natural and unnatural causes), except that now they were white.

With appropriate publicity and fanfare, the *Seascope* headed out to sea to explore the ocean bottom offshore of Los Angeles for manganese nodules. And they found quite a few. To be sure, they were not large or high-quality, but they were manganese nodules. The *Seascope* returned to port after a few weeks at sea with a couple of tons of nodules. Walt Logan had a few hundred of the smaller ones encased in clear plastic cubes about one inch high. These were distributed to contractors working in the ocean mining business as souvenirs from Howard Hughes's Deep Ocean Mining Program.

# 4

## Final Design

### The Big Picture

The operations concept for the AZORIAN recovery system was deceptively simple. "Grunt Lift," John Graham called it. The basic idea was to lower a remotely controlled claw down to the bottom of the ocean, capture that part of the *K-129* that we wanted to recover, and raise the claw, with the target object in its grasp, up through three miles of water into the well of the ship. Once the target was in the well, the well gates closed, and the seawater pumped out, the *Explorer* would start steaming toward a secure location where the exploitation of the target for intelligence information could be completed.

That sounds simple enough. The difficulty with implementation of the concept only becomes apparent when you stop to realize that the target object the CIA was trying to acquire weighed an estimated 4 million pounds. The claw weighed another 4 million pounds. The lifting pipe itself—all three miles of it—accounted for another 8 million pounds. That's a total of about 16 million pounds—8,000 tons—that had to be raised by a hydraulic lifting device operating in the ship's derrick.

There was a fourth element of the recovery system in addition to the surface ship, the claw, and the lifting pipe. That element was the transfer barge, or *HMB-1*. The barge served a dual purpose. While tied up at a Lockheed wharf in Redwood City, California, the *HMB-1* served as the construction site for the capture vehicle. When it was necessary to transfer the claw into, or out of, the well of the *Explorer*, the barge would be towed to a location near Catalina Island, where it would rendezvous with the ship and effect the transfer.

Nothing like this had ever been attempted before. The theory of the technical design was well understood, but the sheer size of the systems forced the designers to go consistently into unexplored territory. Except for a few supporters, the U.S. Navy hierarchy ridiculed the idea that the CIA would be able to build such a recovery system. The idea was so absurd that the Soviet navy, even after having been alerted to a possible U.S. attempt to recover their lost submarine, rejected the idea as impossible. (In a 2007 interview with Michael White, Soviet vice admiral Viktor Dygalo disclosed that the Soviet ambassador to the United States—Anatoly Dobrynin—had somehow gotten word that the CIA was planning to attempt a recovery of the *K-129* and had warned the Soviet navy high command. The senior officers, however, rejected the warning. They believed that the water depth in the central North Pacific and the heavy weight of the *K-129* submarine would combine to make such an attempt technically impossible.)

The CIA persisted, perhaps partly because the program office engineers had almost no marine engineering experience that might give them insights into the difficulty of that which they were proposing. They believed that if it was possible to lift a missile nose cone weighing a few tons from the ocean bottom, then it ought to be possible to lift a 2,000-ton portion of a submarine. It was just a matter of scale.

The operations concept was a very basic and simple solution to the task of recovering part of a Soviet submarine. The difficulty with implementing the concept stemmed from the sheer size and weight of the structure to be recovered. No one had ever attempted to lift such a large object from such a great depth. There were no precedents. For good reasons, many naval architecture experts have proclaimed the *Hughes Glomar Explorer* recovery system to be the greatest marine engineering accomplishment of the twentieth century.

## The Heavy Lifter—*Hughes Glomar Explorer*

By any standard, the most impressive part of the AZORIAN recovery system was the *Hughes Glomar Explorer*. The *Explorer* was huge. It weighed 10,000 tons more than the battleship *Missouri* and was wider by eight feet. It incorporated so many unique and revolutionary engineering features that even today it continues to amaze marine engineers and naval architects. In 2006 the *Explorer* was declared a National Historic Mechanical Engineering Landmark by the American Society of Mechanical Engineers.

The hull of the *HGE* was 618 feet long, with a beam of 116 feet and a displacement of about 55,000 long tons. In the center of the ship was a large storage well measuring 199 feet long, 74 feet wide, and 65 feet high. This well had to contain the capture vehicle prior to recovery operations, and house it and the target after the recovery had been completed. The bottom of the well was fitted with two sliding well gates that met in the middle of the hull. These steel gates, nine feet thick, were fitted into slotted guides running longitudinally under the hull on either side of the well. Opening the gates allowed the capture vehicle to be deployed or recovered out of or into the ship's well. When the capture vehicle was secure within the well, the gates could be closed and the seawater pumped out, leaving the well dry for target exploitation and for transiting from one location to another.

———

The most prominent feature of the *Glomar Explorer* was the huge derrick structure extending almost 240 feet above the surface of the ocean—as high as a twenty-four-story building. About one-third of the way up the derrick was the work platform, called the rig floor. It was from the rig floor that all the raising and lowering operations of the claw were controlled. During descent, sixty-foot sections of lifting pipe were raised from the pipe storage room to the top of the derrick and then lowered and screwed into the top section of the pipe string that was being continuously lowered into the ocean.

The muscle in the *HGE* for raising and lowering the pipe string and capture vehicle (with or without the target) was provided by the heavy lift system. This massive hydraulic system, designed and built by the Western Gear Corporation of Everett, Washington, had the capacity to raise or lower up to 14 million pounds of lifting pipe and load from its operating location at the rig floor.

The power for the heavy lift system was generated by forty-eight hydraulic pumps operating at pressures of up to 3,000 psi. The room containing the high-pressure pumps was not a place in which one wanted to spend any length of time. The noise of those pumps operating at full speed and pressure was deafening, and the vibration was teeth-jarring. The technicians manning the pump room were able to retreat to a glass-enclosed room that provided some acoustic protection while still allowing them to visually monitor the pumps. It also provided them some protection from flying shrapnel—produced by the occasional exploding pump succumbing to the combined stresses of extreme internal pressures, high speeds, and heavy vibration.

The rig floor had to be stabilized to prevent any bending or dynamic loads from getting into the lifting pipe. Although the hollow lifting pipe sections were designed to support up to 14 million pounds of capture vehicle, target object, and pipe—as a reference, 14 million pounds is just about the combined weight of 350 Greyhound buses—the pipe string was the most fragile link in the recovery system. At maximum load, every square inch of the pipe was supporting almost 110,000 pounds. Any additional stresses imposed on the pipe from roll, pitch, or heave motions of the ship could potentially cause it to break.

Pipe breakage was an ultimate nightmare for the designers and the crew. It would mean the loss of the capture vehicle (with or without the target), putting an end to any further recovery operations. Equally significant— especially to the crew—the predicted failure mode in the event of pipe breakage was truly cataclysmic. Although the analysis of failure modes was limited by the computer processing power available at the time, we knew that a failed pipe section—and the sudden loss of load—would cause the lifting pipe to behave like a huge steel spring. The upper portion of the string would suddenly contract and the stored energy would cause the pipe to shoot up into the top of the derrick. When gravity eventually brought the pipe down again, it was predicted that the wing walls of the hull on either side of the ship's well would most likely be stressed to failure. The ship would essentially be broken in half.

Recognition of this failure mode resulted in frequent utilization of the watertight doors located fore and aft of the docking well. Contingency planning called for shutting all the watertight doors whenever roll conditions or mechanical failures threatened the integrity of the pipe string. Crew members had to decide whether they wanted to float with the bow or with the stern. Most jokingly said they preferred the stern since the ship's galley and mess room were there, but no one seriously thought that either end of the ship would stay afloat very long.

———

To eliminate increased pipe stresses from roll, pitch, and heave, Global Marine designed the rig floor to be a "floating" platform, isolated from ship motions by a system of gimbals and a heave compensator. It was designed to stay level, with minimal vertical motion, no matter how the *HGE* itself might be rolling, pitching, or heaving.

To isolate the pipe string from the effects of ship roll and pitch, the entire rig floor and derrick were supported by a gigantic pair of gimbals. One gimbal isolated the rig floor from the ship's roll motions; the other gimbal isolated the pitch motions. The gimbals had to support the weight of the heavy lift cylinders, the rig floor, the derrick, the lifting pipe, the capture vehicle, and the target—well over 20 million pounds. When the *HGE* was built, the gimbal bearings were the largest such bearings ever built. They still are.

————

To minimize the vertical motions of the rig floor, Global Marine mounted the entire gimbal system and rig floor on two colossal spring/shock absorbers—the heave compensator system. These sixty-five-inch-diameter air springs were located on the centerline of the ship and had a vertical travel of plus or minus seven and a half feet. They could support up to 20 million pounds.

For a ship as large and heavy as the *HGE,* it may not be immediately apparent why it was necessary to minimize vertical motions of the rig floor. After all, acceleration forces from heave motion were almost too small to feel. The problem was that the vertical motion could, at certain combinations of wave period and pipe string length, cause the capture vehicle (CV) to go into a resonant condition as though it were hanging from the end of a large rubber band. Under these conditions, the CV could experience vertical oscillatory motion several times greater than the heave motion of the ship itself. This situation could produce significantly higher stresses in the pipe string. It could alsomake it extremely difficult to "land" the CV safely on the ocean bottom.

The heave compensator was simply another large spring in series with the pipe string. By adjusting the spring stiffness, we could tune the combined spring rate of the heave compensator and pipe string to preclude a resonant condition. The spring stiffness of the heave compensator was changed by adding, or removing, bottles of compressed air from the plenum. A maximum volume of 4,600 cubic feet of air, contained in 144 pressurized bottles, was available. More bottles on line *softened* the spring, while fewer bottles on line *stiffened* it. The spring rate of the heave compensator was adjusted so that it minimized the vertical motion of the CV.

————

With all this discussion about random waves and the need to isolate the motions of the lifting pipe and CV from the dynamic motions of the ship, you might begin to wonder how that swinging claw was ever retrieved from the ocean back into the well of the ship. That maneuver was called docking, and it was enabled by the two large truss structures—the docking legs—located at the forward and aft ends of the well.

The docking legs were constructed by the Marathon-LeTourneau Corporation in Houston from modified sections of the same triangular legs used for the jack-up rigs of offshore oil drilling. Rack-and-pinion gears on the docking legs permitted them to be raised and lowered with a total travel of about 140 feet. The legs could also be hydraulically tilted through a range of about seven degrees, corresponding to a fore and aft motion at the bottom of the fully deployed legs of about thirteen feet.

At the base of each docking leg was a large opening about twelve feet across. The lower part of this opening sloped down from either side at a 45-degree angle to a smaller vertical slot about forty-eight inches wide. The large twelve-foot opening and the smaller slot below it greatly resembled a keyhole. The capture vehicle had a large support pin of forty-eight-inch diameter on each end of its structure. When the CV was in the well, these support pins rested in the slots at the base of the docking leg keyhole. The total weight of the claw was supported by the docking legs.

When the capture vehicle was lowered from—or recovered into—the well of the ship, there was a transition period in which the dynamic motions of the CV with respect to the ship changed completely. When the CV was in the well, it was tied rigidly to the *HGE* by the docking legs that supported it at either end. The CV's six hydrodynamic motions (roll, pitch, heave, surge, sway, and yaw) were locked into those of the ship. However, when the CV was hanging on the pipe string well below the ship, its six degrees of motion were largely decoupled from those of the ship. The transition from one set of hydrodynamic conditions to the other was a very critical—and often unnerving—operation.

Obviously, it wouldn't be smart to make this transition in the well of the ship. The capture vehicle was a tight fit within the well of the *HGE*. And, since it weighed about 4 million pounds, any relative motion between it and the ship would be guaranteed to create some horrendous impacts on the ship's wing walls. The transition had to be made well below the vulnerable parts of the ship, and preferably well below the surface of the ocean in order to minimize the effects of wave action on the CV. The docking legs allowed us to transition the CV from its own hydrodynamic motions to those of the *HGE* (or vice versa), with the CV about 110 feet beneath the ship.

––––––

Although keeping the ship precisely over the target during descent and ascent was not critical, it was vitally important that the *HGE* be able to maintain its position very accurately during the capture operations on the ocean bottom. Even though the CV had eight powerful hydraulic thrusters on its deck to control its motion while positioning over the target, the combined weight of the claw and the pipe string was so great that the available thruster power was only sufficient to move the CV about 50 feet from a position directly below the ship. To accurately control the X-Y position of the CV within the ±1-foot limit demanded by the capture operations, the HGE had to be able to maintain its surface position directly over the target with an accuracy of ±20 feet. This meant that we had to know the precise position of the ship on the surface of the water within about ±10 feet—a very tall order.

Although the LORAN worldwide navigation aid system and satellite navigation systems were available during the construction phase of the HGE, they didn't provide the position estimation accuracy or update frequency required to meet that ±10-foot requirement. LORAN had an accuracy between 0.1 and 0.25 miles, depending on the geometry and the distance of the transmitters being received—not good enough for positioning the ship over the target. Furthermore, weather phenomena and ionospheric disturbances could prevent reception for significant periods of time. The satellite navigation systems available at the time were more accurate, but they only passed over a given point on the globe perhaps once every twenty minutes. In that twenty minutes, the ship might drift well off of its desired position. And GPS (oh, how much simpler station keeping could have been!) was still a concept under development. (The first GPS satellite didn't launch until 1978, and the full operational capability was first realized in 1993.)

When the design of the HGE was started, the Glomar Challenger had already demonstrated the feasibility of dynamic positioning in the open ocean using a single beacon on the ocean floor and an array of four hydrophones mounted on the bottom of the ship. By comparing the relative phase angles of the received beacon signals at each hydrophone, it was possible to measure just how far offset the ship was from the beacon. This was called the short baseline acoustic positioning system. However, this concept couldn't provide the required position estimation accuracy for the HGE at the target site, which was almost 17,000 feet deep.

Another station-keeping system design had been studied and proposed by Dr. Hank Van Calcar and others from the Honeywell Corporation in Seattle.[1] The idea was to deploy an array of transponders on the ocean bottom, with a single transmitter and receiver located on the hull of the ship. In operation, the transmitter on the ship's hull would send a single pulse downward. Each of the deployed transponders on the ocean bottom would receive the pulse and transmit a return pulse, with a frequency unique to that transponder, upward to the ship. The receive sensor on the ship's hull would detect the transponder pulses and, by noting the elapsed time between transmission of the ship's interrogation pulse and each transponder's return pulse, determine the distance to the transponder located on the ocean bottom. By measuring these distances for each of the transponders, an accurate estimate of the ship's position with respect to the bottom array could be made. This system was referred to as the long baseline system. It was minimally affected by roll and pitch motions of the ship, and the distance between the transponders on the bottom could be increased when working in deeper water, permitting more accurate position estimates. The long baseline system was able to exceed the required ±10-foot accuracy for position estimation. The design was selected and integrated into the automatic station-keeping system of the *HGE*.

The ship used its two main propulsion units, augmented by three electrically powered side thrusters in the bow and two in the stern, to hold the ship in the desired position. In actual practice, the *HGE* was consistently able to maintain its position within a ten-foot radius.

---

Curtis Crooke, president of Global Marine Development Inc., and John Graham, chief engineer and senior naval architect of Global Marine, share most of the credit for the conceptual design of the ship. Credit for the remarkable feat of taking the *Explorer* from a basic concept to a finished design in little more than two years' time belongs largely to Sun Shipbuilding and Dry Dock Company in Chester, Pennsylvania.

However, neither Global Marine nor Sun Ship would have been able to meet such a schedule without the army of aerospace analysts and engineers that the CIA had put at Graham's disposal. These analysts—most of them from Mechanics Research Inc. in Los Angeles and Lockheed Missiles and Space Corporation in Sunnyvale—were able to provide computer-aided design capabilities that were simply not available at Global Marine or any other commercial shipbuilder at that time. Without their support, the design and construction of the *HGE* could never have been completed in such a short time. Graham had as many as seven companies working simultaneously on the drawings and specifications required before construction could begin. Program direction to Sun Ship came almost entirely from Global Marine and its subcontractors. Because of the commercial cover story and the need to suppress knowledge of any government involvement, the CIA had no significant hands-on role in the construction phase.

The AZORIAN program office had one member, a naval architect by the name of Fred Glassman, who was able to occasionally accompany John Graham to meetings with Sun Shipbuilding. Fred was a relatively recent hire into the agency, and his association with the CIA was still considered to be relatively unknown. Even so, Glassman kept a very low profile in all of these meetings. The rest of us in the program office never saw the ship until it had completed its trip from the East Coast, around the tip of South America, to Pier E in Long Beach, California. Even John Parangosky only saw the ship once while under construction. He and the chief of his engineering division drove to an overlook site about two miles from Sun shipyard and viewed the ship under construction through binoculars.

Parangosky absolutely hated the fact that he couldn't be involved in the day-to-day decision making during the ship's construction, but he was very aware of the high profile he had from years of exposure in high-visibility CIA programs. John Graham, however, was quite happy with the arrangement. He and Parangosky determined early on that their personalities weren't exactly "simpatico." Being insulated from direct oversight by a customer very inclined toward hands-on management probably speeded up the program significantly—and added at least two years to Graham's life.

## Three-Mile Gun Barrel—the Lifting Pipe

The lifting pipe was the most critical link of the whole recovery system. No failures could be tolerated. Pipe breakage meant mission failure—and perhaps the loss of the ship itself. When the CIA negotiated the prime contract for AZORIAN with Hughes Tool Company, the contractor expressed a strong interest in taking the responsibility for development and manufacture of the lifting pipe. That made a lot of sense, from the standpoint of both Hughes Tool's oil patch experience and the support for the DOMP cover story that would result from their involvement in the program. The CIA approved the idea. I don't believe anyone on the program ever anticipated what a tough development problem that was going to be.

The design of the pipe string was relatively straightforward. Hughes knew that they'd have to select a material that had high-tensile strength but was not brittle or subject to corrosion-induced stress fractures. The perfect answer seemed to be 4330V Mod, a steel used for large military gun and cannon barrels.

In order to minimize the overall weight of the pipe string, it was manufactured with six different diameters. The largest diameter (15.5 inches) was used at the top of the fully deployed pipe string and had to support the heaviest loads. The smallest diameter (12.75 inches) was used for the pipe sections closest to the CV. Each thirty-foot pipe section had a pin tool joint on one end and a box tool joint on the other so they could be screwed together. During pipe-running operations, the flat shoulder of the box joint was supported by the heavy lift yokes. All sections of pipe had a uniform hollow center with a six-inch diameter through which water could be pumped to power the hydraulic systems on the CV. The pipe string, joined into sixty-foot doubles, was stored below the main deck just aft of the well.

---

The pipe-handling system managed the transfer of the pipe doubles between the storage hold and the top of the derrick from where they could be added to, or removed from, the pipe string. Because these heavy (up to twenty tons each) doubles were being moved around on a rolling ship, the pipe-handling machinery had to be very strong and the machinery's grasp of the doubles had to be very sure. A pipe section breaking loose and falling onto the deck could have been potentially catastrophic. The sequence of operations for getting those doubles from the pipe storage room to the top of the pipe string involved six different machines.

First, a double of the desired diameter was selected, moved to the center of the pipe storage hold, and placed on a centerline elevator by a pair of bridge cranes. The centerline elevator lifted the double above the level of the main deck so that it could be picked up by the transfer crane. The transfer crane grasped the double by its center tool joint and placed it on the transfer cart. The transfer cart, which rode on the transfer boom railway, carried the pipe up to the rig floor. The box end of the double was grabbed by the elevator/subspinner and lifted to the top of the derrick in a vertical orientation. The pipe double was then lowered while the automatic roughneck guided the pin end of the tool joint directly over the box end of the top pipe in the deployed string. The subspinner began to rotate the pipe as the pin end of the double was lowered into the box end and the connection was made. Finally, the subspinner then applied 50,000 pound-feet of torque to lock the joint tightly. Through this whole process, the pipe string was being lowered at a continuous rate of up to eighteen feet a minute on a ship with continuous roll, pitch, and heave motions.

## The Capture Vehicle, Clementine

In January 1972, the Hughes Tool Company issued a press release announcing that the Ocean Systems Division of Lockheed Missiles and Space Corporation (LMSC) in Sunnyvale, California, had been selected as a participant in the Deep Ocean Mining Program. J. R. Lesch, senior vice president and general manager of Hughes Tool Company, stated that "Lockheed has been engaged to design and construct a mining support dry dock, and to

design, fabricate and test mining machinery and associated equipment required in Hughes's prototype ocean mining program. The dry dock is currently under construction at the National Steel and Shipbuilding Company
in San Diego, California."

The mining support dry dock that the Hughes press release referred to
was subsequently named the Hughes Mining Barge, or *HMB-1*. The mining
machinery referred to in the announcement was, of course, the CV—or
claw—that would grasp the submarine, break it loose from the ocean bottom, and support it while it was being raised to the surface and into the well
of the *HGE*.

This press release, intended to advertise Hughes's progress on the DOMP,
was actually a little bit behind the times. Lockheed had already been working on the design and construction of the *HMB-1* and the CV since late 1969.

LMSC had good credentials for this job. When the CIA was looking for a
company with the ability to construct a remote-controlled device to capture
a large portion of a sunken Soviet submarine, Lockheed stood out. LMSC's
Ocean Systems Division was working at that time on a couple of black
deep-sea submergence programs under the direction of the Navy's John
Craven. Both of these programs, the Deep Submergence Rescue Vehicle
and the Deep Submergence Surveillance Vehicle, used special steels to create maximum strength with minimum weight, both critically essential for
the design of the claw.

The president of LMSC's Ocean Systems Division was Jim Wenzel, an
old friend of John Parangosky's. Parangosky had talked to Wenzel early
in 1969 during the AZORIAN concept development phase, liked what he
heard, and asked for a proposal. Wenzel was eager to work on the program,
but none of his people were cleared for it. He didn't even have a cleared
secretary who could type the proposal. Parangosky was unimpressed with
Wenzel's plight and refused to grant any clearances until he was confident
that Lockheed was up to the job. Wenzel ended up writing the proposal by
hand and delivering it personally to Parangosky. The proposal was accepted,
and Lockheed went to work immediately on concept designs for the claw.

Lockheed's first design was, to put it bluntly, a disaster. The concept em-
bodied the type of structure that one might expect from a high-tech missiles
and space company rather than from a company that was working on deep-
sea submergence vehicles. It was a space-frame with hundreds of structural segments welded together. It resembled a large birdcage. The desired
strength and stiffness may have been achieved, but the light weight was not.
Furthermore, the estimated cost of construction was way out of line with
the CIA's expectations. Parangosky was very dissatisfied and went to his old

friend Kelly Johnson, president of the Lockheed Skunk Works in Burbank, for assistance. Kelly agreed that the design was too complex for the intended application and sent one of his most experienced mechanical engineers, Henry Coombs, to work with the LMSC team on a new approach.

The collaboration of LMSC and the Skunk Works resulted in a greatly simplified concept. The space-frame structure was thrown out and replaced with a single massive weldment as the spine, or strongback, of the capture vehicle. HY-100 steel was specified in order to reduce cost and simplify the construction. (Simplifying the welded construction was of considerable importance, since the strongback was at that time the largest known HY-100 weldment in the world.) The simplicity of the new concept gave Lockheed the time they needed to focus on the more intricate and sophisticated design features of the CV. The product they ultimately came up with was incredibly versatile and effective, even though the mechanical design was basic and straightforward.

The Lockheed engineers and technicians were extremely proud of the final design of the capture vehicle and thought that it deserved a more respectful name than the forbidding-sounding "capture vehicle." They informally began to refer to it as "Clementine," in memory of the classic song that went:

> In a cavern, in a canyon,
> Excavating for a mine,
> Dwelt a miner, forty-niner,
> And his daughter, Clementine.

The capture vehicle was essentially a remotely controlled claw that was specifically designed to capture and retrieve that portion of the *K-129* wreckage that we called the target object. Of course, the capture vehicle was far more complex than just a set of articulated tines and fingers resembling a claw. The design also incorporated a full sensor suite of closed-circuit TV cameras and sonars to locate the target and guide the capture operations. It included a total of ten propeller thrusters to enable precise positioning of the capture vehicle, as well as its own ASK system to enable those thrusters to hold the CV in the correct position during the final descent over the target. Finally, it included four cylindrical breakout legs—one on each corner—that supported the CV while it was on the bottom. These breakout legs were adjustable in length, enabling fine-tuning of the CV's pitch and roll attitudes while settling over the target to the capture position. After the target was grasped by the articulated tines and fingers, the breakout legs were hydraulically extended to overcome the strong suction forces resisting removal of the partially buried submarine from the bottom ooze.

Electrical power for the electronic systems on the capture vehicle was delivered by two armored electromechanical (EM) cables about 2.5 inches in diameter. These cables had to be manually strapped to the pipe string by the divers as the CV was lowered to the bottom. (An automatic cable-tying machine had been designed and built for tricing the EM cable to the pipe, but it was never successfully tested.)

Hydraulic power for the positioning thrusters, tines, and breakout legs was delivered to the CV by seawater pumped from the rig floor of the ship through the six-inch-diameter hole in the center of the pipe sections. A lubricity additive was injected into the seawater to reduce friction between the moving parts of the hydraulic systems. Water pressures as high as 2,000 psi were required to operate the thrusters and to drive the tines down through the mud and up under the target object. The breakout legs used lower water pressures of about 50 psi.

––––––

Because of its massive size, the strongback was constructed in a separate steel building very close to the Redwood City slough, where the *HMB-1* construction barge would be moored. When the strongback was completed and ready to be moved into the barge, an unexpected problem arose. There wasn't enough room to get the huge weldment out of the building and pointed in the right direction for transfer to the *HMB-1*. The Lockheed engineers and welders tried every maneuver sequence they could think of, but they just couldn't get the strongback around the corner of the building's door and onto the road leading to the slough.

Finally, they called for help from an experienced and famous steel rigger in the Bay Area named Tex Bean. Bean looked at the problem and concluded, "Hell, you guys have been trying to solve this problem from the wrong end!" Tex directed his crew to remove all the bolts that were securing the steel building to the concrete footings around the perimeter. Then, with an improvised bridle and a gigantic crane, he simply lifted the entire building about twenty feet into the air. The strongback was then easily moved out to the roadway, and the building was lowered back onto its foundations. Tex Bean was a master at thinking outside the box.

––––––

The capture vehicle was an impressive piece of machinery. It measured approximately 180 feet long, 58 feet wide, and 54 feet high. It weighed almost

2,200 tons, dry. The CV was so massive, and the spaces in which it usually resided—in the well of the ship or in the *HMB-1*—were so confining, that it was difficult to capture the dramatic impact of the structure with a camera. Some of the televised "histories" of the AZORIAN program have used some interesting artist's concepts for the CV, but none of those depictions have ever captured the gigantic majesty of that single-purpose claw.

## Now You See It, Now You Don't—the *HMB-1*

In addition to the capture vehicle, Lockheed's Ocean Systems Division was responsible for building the submersible dry dock. Officially designated the transfer barge, it was known in the white world as the Hughes Mining Barge Number 1, or *HMB-1*. It was built to serve two critical functions. First, it provided a secure facility in which the capture vehicle could be built. Second, it provided a means for transporting the capture vehicle to a rendezvous point where the CV could be transferred into the well of the *HGE*. There were no precedents to guide LMSC in the design of the *HMB-1*. By the time they put together all the functions that the vessel had to perform, they realized that it was going to be a very complicated and critical segment of the AZORIAN recovery concept.

Consider some of the requirements that were heaped on the designers: The interior of the barge had to be large enough for construction of the capture vehicle. Further, it had to be completely enclosed for security reasons and weather-tight to permit construction to continue through all seasons. It had to be seaworthy and capable of being towed by a tug in the open ocean to and from the site where it would rendezvous with the *HGE*.

The transfer of the capture vehicle from the *HMB-1* to the *HGE* was always executed at Isthmus Cove, off Catalina Island. When the barge reached the site, it was slowly submerged to the ocean bottom—a depth of about 160 feet—and the telescopic roof was opened. The *HGE* was then moved over the barge and precisely located with a four-point anchor moor until the docking legs were positioned directly over the support pins at each end of the capture vehicle. The docking legs were lowered into the open barge, closing on the fore and aft support pins, and the claw was slowly raised from the *HMB-1* into the well of the ship. The gates on the bottom of the ship's hull were closed and the well was pumped dry. The ship could then proceed on its mission with the capture vehicle located in a secure and dry environment where it could be worked on and prepared for the recovery operation. The *HMB-1* would be refloated and towed back to Redwood City.

Lockheed went to Larry Glosten, a highly respected and innovative naval architect in Seattle, for the design. Glosten was given a fifteen-month schedule for design and delivery of the barge. After completion of the drawings, construction responsibility was given to the National Steel and Shipbuilding Company (NASSCO), located in San Diego. Remarkably, NASSCO was able to complete the construction in nine months, and the barge was taken out for sea trials in April 1972. When finished, the *HMB-1* measured 324 feet long by 107 feet wide. The height to the top of its telescoping roof was 90 feet. The interior of the barge—the capture vehicle construction area—measured 276 feet in length and about 77 feet in width.

A series of practice dives in water as deep as 185 feet were completed off Coronado Island and later Isthmus Cove off Catalina Island. The *HMB-1* was delivered to Lockheed's Redwood City facility in May 1972. At that time, construction of the already-designed capture vehicle could begin.

The construction site was given extensive security protection. Physically isolated from the main LMSC facilities in Sunnyvale, it was surrounded by chain-link fencing (with both Lockheed and Summa Corporation signs) and guards. Unlike the *Explorer*, which could be built in plain sight at the Sun shipyard as part of Howard Hughes's DOMP, the capture vehicle, if seen, would have been very clearly identified as a giant salvage system.

The intensive security was not hard to explain to the public, though. Obviously, the mining vehicle (the system ostensibly being built in the *HMB-1*) was the heart of the Hughes concept for deep ocean mining. It made sense that he would want to keep any knowledge of the concept or its detailed design from his potential competitors.

Fortunately, the appearance and design of the *HMB-1* were consistent with the DOMP cover story. The only variation from the cover was the work going on inside the barge. No special efforts had to be made to conceal the barge from external visual inspection during construction, sea trials, or even the subsequent CV transfer operations. Although large and ungainly in appearance, the *HMB-1* was a remarkably sophisticated and effective engineering design. It was a reliable workhorse whose useful life extended well beyond the AZORIAN program.[2]

# 5

# Getting Ready

## Who's in Charge?

When Sun Shipyard in Philadelphia finally delivered the *Hughes Glomar Explorer* to Global Marine in July 1973, Parangosky knew that the CIA was already running out of time. We had less than a year to get the ship to the West Coast, complete testing of the recovery system, and train the mission crew.

On July 6 Parangosky gathered his project team at the secret program office near Tysons Corner, Virginia, and told us, "Up to this point, the Engineering Division has been carrying the ball. Now that sea trials are about to begin, I'm going to make a change. You, Ops Division, will now carry the ball for the AZORIAN program! And you, Engineering Division, are going to sit on the sidelines like a Trojan horse, contemplating your navels!"

A few of us were inclined to ruminate over how to act like a Trojan horse sitting on the sidelines contemplating its navel. No one was much in the mind for humor, though. You didn't joke with John Parangosky in a setting like this.

So far, the direction of the AZORIAN program had been dominated by the engineers, many of whom found it difficult to stop tinkering with the design. Under a normal project schedule, the engineering team would manage the system testing until the design was final and bug-free. At that point, the operations team and the mission crew would take over control of the ship and operation of the recovery system. Parangosky couldn't wait. He wanted to turn ship management responsibility over to the operations people right away so *they* could control the final engineering configurations and be fully trained to operate the ship and manage the recovery of the sub the following summer.

Part of the reason for the hurry was the danger posed by the sea itself. Parangosky was very sensitive to the risk of attempting the dangerous deep-sea recovery operation in the higher wind and wave conditions that would prevail after the summer months. He warned us, "We only have nine months left to complete all the system integration and sea trials. We're going to have to kaleidoscope time!" (No one dared ask if he meant we needed to *telescope* time.)

I knew this transition was coming. With the delivery of the ship to the West Coast, the design phase would be over soon enough. The new point people on Project AZORIAN would be the operations types responsible for turning a design into a working system. They'd have engineering support, of course, but that would come primarily from the contractor engineers with previous experience in operating ship systems at sea. As a member of the headquarters design team—2,500 miles away from the testing action— I'd be observing from the backseat. I hated that. My complete immersion in the AZORIAN program had been sustaining me through some very tough emotional times.

———

My first marriage had gone on the rocks early in 1973. Working on covert programs for the CIA can be tough on a marriage. For more than ten years I'd been assigned to highly classified black programs that required frequent travel. During that entire time, I was seldom home for more than three or four nights a week, and my wife couldn't even be told what I was working on. Perhaps I could have saved the marriage by getting a normal job—outside the CIA—but I didn't. To make things even worse, I'd been working on my doctoral dissertation—mostly at night—for three years. These activities didn't leave much time for family life. On January 1, 1973, my wife and I agreed that it would be better for both of us if I moved out.

I rented a small garden apartment close to work. My only priorities were my weekend visits with my two children (a ten-year-old son and a seven-year-old daughter), my determination to complete and defend my doctoral dissertation, and my job. The apartment was no palace. To say it was sparsely furnished would be an understatement. I slept on a mattress on the floor of my bedroom. The living room contained a foldout couch that my kids used when they spent the night. I had an audio system and a faux leather chair that my wife had given me as a birthday present.

The dining room was special, though. It had as its sole furnishing my true pride and joy—the fuselage, tail assembly, and landing gear of a Pitts Special aerobatic biplane. It was an ongoing work in progress. I'd been building it for a couple of years. It was just a steel tube frame with no fabric cover, but it did have a cockpit and a seat—and a white silk scarf. When I had company over, the favored spot to sit was always the cockpit of the Pitts Special. Sitting in that airplane with a martini in my hand, the silk scarf around my neck, and the audio system thumping out "Take It Easy" by the Eagles (remember that line, "Looking for a lover who won't blow my cover"?) gave me a real shot in the arm. The dash, the excitement—it was the feeling I had always expected life in the CIA to provide me. Occasionally it did (even without the martini and silk scarf) when I had an opportunity to work with special people like the U-2 and OXCART pilots, and now-legendary airplane and ship designers like Kelly Johnson and John Graham.

———

I knew I didn't want to be a Trojan horse sitting on the sideline contemplating my navel. When Parangosky offered me the job of director of the West Coast program office—known in the white world as the office of Summa Corporation's Deep Ocean Mining Program—I was thrilled. The West Coast office would be managing the sea trials and integrated system testing, and I'd be involved up to my eyeballs.

There was little to hold me on the East Coast except for my two children, whom I'd been able to visit on weekends. I had successfully defended my doctoral dissertation at the University of Virginia, so school wasn't an impediment. I hesitated to accept the job only because the little bit of family life I had left might disappear completely. Parangosky assured me, though, that I'd still have plenty of opportunity to see my children while working on the West Coast. In fact, I'd be coming back every weekend to report to headquarters. (No secure conference calls in those days.) That meant I'd be able to keep my Virginia apartment as a weekend home and an airplane hangar. I accepted the reassignment and moved out to Los Angeles in the fall of 1973. Since no identifiable CIA employees were permitted in the Summa offices (except for occasional headquarters visitors who came in through the Harvey Wallbanger entrance), I got a new identity along with my new job.

———

Going to live in Los Angeles with a different identity was not without its perks. Since my cover story was that I was a private contractor selected by Summa to be the manager of the DOMP program office, my lifestyle had to reflect that position. I was told to talk to finance about my living arrangements. Our finance officer, Joe A., was an old friend I'd known since our time together on the U-2 program back in 1961. I had really been impressed by Fisherman's Village, a waterside community in Marina del Rey that was only a couple of miles from the Summa offices. There was a furnished apartment available with a patio opening right on the main channel of the marina. I thought it would be perfect for me.

The only problem was the cost. Joe said that the rent for my apartment choice would cost too much—way too much—at least $200 per month too much. We negotiated back and forth for a while, and then Joe said, "Look, we'll pay the rent, but only if you agree to cover all the costs for dinnerware, silver, and any other extras." Maybe Joe was thinking about the costs of fine china and sterling silver. I was thinking about plastic dishes (remember MELMAC?) and those stainless-steel knives and forks with the fake wood handles that were so ubiquitous in the 1970s. You could buy a set of dishes and stainless at any department store in L.A. for fifty dollars.

I said, "Joe, you've got a deal."

Joe just grinned. The old boy network that the CIA was so infamous for in those days was truly alive and well.

Joe sent a cable out to the West Coast office instructing Steve Craig (chief of security and office manager of the WCPO) to acquire a suitable car for me. Craig met me at the airport with a new Datsun 260Z sports car. Suitable, indeed. I was beginning to like my new self.

## The Voyage to Pier E

On July 23, 1973, the *Hughes Glomar Explorer* was delivered from Sun shipyard to Global Marine. Ted Atkinson, the president of Sun Ship, still hadn't been briefed on the program. When Atkinson was told that Global Marine intended to sail the ship to the West Coast the day after delivery, he told Curtis Crooke, "Look, Curtis, you can't take that ship away from here until we've been paid! Global Marine still owes us a lot of money!"

Crooke told him, "Ted, the ship is going to sail tomorrow. Your issue on payment isn't with Global Marine, it's with the U.S. government. The ship doesn't belong to us—it belongs to the CIA." Needless to say, Ted Atkinson was briefed immediately on the AZORIAN program. He was understandably upset about being kept in the dark for so long, but he agreed to let the ship sail.

It was going to be a long trip. Because the beam of the *HGE* was too large to go through the Panama Canal, it would have to sail completely around South

America through the Strait of Magellan in order to reach its new home port of Long Beach, California. Originally, the *Explorer* design called for a beam of 106 feet, which would have permitted the ship to go through the Panama Canal. However, more refined target shape and size estimates based on collected information from the *Glomar II* mission dictated an increased width for the well of the ship. In order to retain the structural integrity of the wing walls, Graham was forced to increase the beam by ten feet.

There were no mission-sensitive features on the ship at this time, and the Global Marine crew members in charge of the ship were mostly uncleared. There were no anticipated security issues. The voyage was simply a transfer of the new ocean mining ship from the East Coast shipyard to its future base of operations in California. The Global Marine captain was in full charge of the ship, but the government—to protect its interest in the *HGE*—also had three officers from the program office aboard.

These officers were under cover so their government affiliation wouldn't be compromised, but they didn't look like the typical Global Marine crew. They had short hair and wore casual clothes. The Global Marine crew let their hair grow long (this was 1973) and uniformly wore Levis or some other brand of denim working clothes.

Brent Sparrow was also onboard representing the CIA security office. Brent had retired from the Los Angeles Police Department before being hired into the security staff of the WCPO. He'd been on every kind of LAPD detail, from narcotics and arms shipment interdiction to walking a beat. He could adapt to any environment, and he fit into the Global Marine crew like he'd been born in an oil patch.

The ship stopped in Bermuda, long enough to refuel and drop off some of the shipyard personnel. On August 13, the *HGE* departed Bermuda and set sail for Long Beach—by way of Cape Horn with a planned stop in Valparaiso, Chile, for crew change.

After a few days at sea, Brent Sparrow overheard some discussions among the Global Marine crew speculating on the "passengers" who were living in prime quarters but had no apparent responsibilities. These passengers were, of course, the three program office reps accompanying the ship on its trip from the East Coast to the West Coast. The crew couldn't figure these guys out. They clearly didn't work for Western Gear, Honeywell, or any of the other Global Marine subcontractors. Furthermore, they seemed to be, well, just *different*. The three stayed mostly to themselves and, although they'd talk to some of the crew, they never said anything about themselves or their backgrounds. Brent decided he'd have to take some action. He called for a private meeting in his room with the three officers and laid it out to them.

He told them that they'd have to start *blending* with the crew and try to look and act more like men who had spent some time at sea.

He told them, "You don't have to slouch, but I don't want to see you walking down the deck like you've got a broomstick up your ass! Furthermore, when you're just standing around, don't just stand there and observe. Smoke a cigarette—pick your teeth—spit—something! Look natural!"

Brent went on to tell them that, most important, they had to change the way they talked. Their dialect was all wrong, and the crew was noticing it. Brent gave them a list of common words and phrases used by Global Marine ship's crew and coached them in the correct pronunciation. For example, "divorce" should be pronounced "dee'-vorce." (There's a lot of talk about dee'-vorce among Global Marine drilling personnel who spend half of their lives at sea.) Also, "shit" had to be pronounced "shee'-it." The coaching worked. By the time the ship had rounded the Strait of Magellan, the men from headquarters had gained a level of acceptance from the crew. Part of that acceptance may have come from the many opportunities the officers were given to vehemently exclaim "shee'-it!" during the challenging passage around the tip of South America. Although the *Explorer* was a large and heavy boat, its flat bottom provided an exciting and uncomfortable ride through the traditionally rough seas of the southern oceans. Brent Sparrow described the passage as "unforgettable." He added, "And that's a good thing, so I won't ever be tempted to do it again!"

On September 11, 1973, the *Hughes Glomar Explorer* was approaching the port of Valparaiso, Chile. The ship would refuel and take on provisions, and a new Global Marine crew would be waiting to take over for the remainder of the voyage. As the ship approached the outer harbor, the crew was surprised to hear gunfire in the background. The loud explosions continued while the ship was anchoring. No explanations were given over the ship-to-shore radio. Once the ship was anchored, the word was received that the Chilean military had executed a coup against the government of President Salvador Allende. President Allende was reported to be dead, apparently by his own hand.

There were no instructions from Washington. In fact, any word at all from Washington would have been suspicious. The *HGE* was operating under control of Global Marine—not the U.S. government. Furthermore, there were no provisions for secure communications onboard. Any attempt by the government to contact the ship would likely have been overheard by the Chileans and would have been deeply suspicious. Not knowing what to expect, the Global Marine captain had no choice but to wait and see how events were going to unfold.

He didn't have long to wait. A Chilean submarine approached the *HGE* with clear intentions to board the ship. Having no reason (or means) to deny the submarine captain's request to board, the Global Marine crew assisted them in securing the sub to the *Explorer* and waited nervously while the Chileans climbed the improvised boarding ladder. Once onboard, the Chileans saluted the captain. Next, they saluted every crew member in sight. Even the *Glomar* cooks came out on deck to see what was going on. The Chileans saluted them, too.

With the help of translators, the *HGE* captain explained that the ship was there only to take on provisions and change crews. The Chilean military was completely cooperative and did what they could to expedite the process. There were no further problems. The crew transfer was completed and, with some relief, the *Hughes Glomar Explorer* left Valparaiso and continued on its journey to Pier E in Long Beach.

––––––

Although the crew of the *Hughes Glomar Explorer* knew nothing about it when they arrived in Valparaiso for supplies, the CIA had in fact been covertly influencing Chilean politics for over ten years. After the Cuban revolution in 1959, the United States became very concerned about the possible export of communism to other South American states—including Chile. Agency support to the noncommunist political parties in Chile had started in 1962 under President Kennedy, with $200,000 being provided to the Christian Democratic Party. These efforts to defeat communist leaders in Chile were successful until the 1970 election, when the two previous conservative administrations were vying against each other *and* Salvador Allende and the communists. Allende, with supporting funds from both Moscow and Havana—and a poorly funded U.S. countereffort—scored an upset victory to win the presidency with only 36 percent of the vote.

President Nixon was furious, blaming DCI Dick Helms and the CIA for failing to keep him informed about the possibility of a socialist president being elected in South America.[1] But there was still some slight hope that Allende could be kept from assuming the presidency. In Chile, if no candidate receives a majority the congress is left with the responsibility to choose the winner. The congressional vote was scheduled just about fifty days after the election. In President Nixon's mind, that might be sufficient time to get the Chilean military to intervene in the election process—to prevent Allende from taking office.

On September 15 Nixon called Helms into the Oval Office for a meeting with very restricted attendance. Besides Helms, only the president, Henry

Kissinger, and Attorney General John Mitchell were present. The president essentially directed the CIA to intervene covertly in Chilean politics—money was no object—in an attempt to get the Chilean military to intervene in the election. In effect, Nixon was directing the CIA to instigate a coup in Chile. Helms had about thirty-eight days before the congressional runoff.

The agency made a valiant attempt to satisfy the president's directive, but there was not enough time. The CIA's attempts to keep a socialist government out of Chile failed. President Allende was sworn into office on November 3, 1970.

After Allende took office the agency continued to provide active support—all funded through third-country intermediaries—for Chilean political parties, magazines, radio stations, and student groups aimed at ensuring that Allende would not be reelected in 1976. In September 1973, however—with no CIA collusion—the Chilean military engineered a coup of its own. President Allende was killed (or killed himself) during the overthrow. CIA involvement in the coup was denied by the U.S. government.[2]

Years later, as details of the alleged CIA involvement in the Allende overthrow began to surface and the CIA ownership of the *Explorer* was admitted, many analysts and conspiracy theorists determined that the ship was somehow linked into the coup. After all, they reasoned, how could it be just coincidence that a CIA-owned ship arrived in Valparaiso on the day that the Allende government was overthrown? In fact, it was just that—a remarkable coincidence.

## Going Black

Once the *Hughes Glomar Explorer* made it to Pier E in Long Beach, the real problems of systems integration and testing started in earnest. We only had about nine months before the start of the mission, and only cursory testing of any of the major subsystems had been accomplished. We knew the ship's propulsion system worked—almost everything else still had to be tested and integrated.

The first activity was to convert the ship from a white to a black configuration. This conversion included the loading of twenty steel vans that would be used for activities inconsistent with the ocean mining cover story. Two of those vans housed the Lockheed-built control center. The control center contained all the controls and monitors for remote operation of the capture vehicle during its recovery operations. Most of the other vans were intended to support the target exploitation activities, such as cleaning, decontamination, and storage of radioactive materials recovered from the target. Other vans were set up as dressing rooms and decontamination rooms for those men who would actually be working in the ship's well on the radioactive remains of the *K-129*.

Two other black additions were a secure communications facility and a weather van. The *Explorer*, like the *Glomar II*, would have to rely on high-frequency radio for communications with the mainland and with headquarters. To make the communications more reliable, however, the *HGE* had a much more powerful transmitter installed, along with a large directional antenna measuring about thirty feet across. We also installed a capability to transmit and receive secure encrypted messages. Although we had to rely on Morse code and secret writing techniques for the *Glomar II* survey missions, we concluded that the use of obviously encrypted ship-to-shore messages would not be inconsistent with the DOMP cover story. Howard Hughes was known to be an obsessively private person, and we believed that the use of encrypted communications would be in keeping with his personality—especially for the highly proprietary DOMP experiments.

This assumption also permitted us to use a Teletype message format, instead of the Morse code used by the *Glomar II*. The speed advantages were significant. Whereas a ship's radio operator using Morse code might be able to transmit about four innocent text (IT) words per minute (*after* someone had constructed an IT message), the *Explorer* radio operator would be able to transmit about sixty words per minute using the Teletype format. Equally important, there was no need to manually convert the plain text message into IT before transmission. This was a major advantage. Converting a twenty-five-word secret message into an IT format—using one-time pads, dictionaries, thesauruses, etc.—could easily take several hours. Preparing a Teletype message to be processed through an encipherment machine involved nothing more than typing the text.

Choosing the right encryption system wasn't a trivial problem, though. The use of a government encryption device was out of the question—its characteristics would have been quickly identified by Soviet and U.S. intelligence agencies and its use on a commercial ship would have been very suspicious. Our only option was to use a commercial system. The best commercial encryption device available in the early 1970s was the SABER encipherment device. Although the SABER system was the best available, we knew it would be little more than a privacy device if subjected to the code-breaking techniques available to the National Security Agency or the equivalent Soviet code-breaking facility. We hoped that wouldn't happen.

The weather van was absolutely vital to the successful completion of the mission. The operations of the recovery system were all dependent to some degree on sea state and weather conditions. Some of the operations, such as well gate opening/closing and docking/undocking, were critically dependent upon sea conditions. It was mandatory that we get the best two- and three-day weather forecasts that technology could deliver.

The best forecasting capability in the world was the Navy's Fleet Numerical Weather Central (FNWC) in Monterey, California. Their computer-generated weather models were the world's best. Even so, FNWC acknowledged that even the best weather models needed good observational data input and, unfortunately, there just weren't many weather observations coming in from the ocean areas around the target site.

FNWC's recommendation was to put one of their trained meteorologists onboard the ship with a full set of equipment for receiving and printing the FNWC worldwide forecasts and charts. The onboard meteorologist could also submit observations to the National Weather Service so that FNWC could continuously update their weather model for the central North Pacific area. The ship would have, in effect, a closed-loop prediction system with forecasts from FNWC continually corrected and updated with local conditions reported from the target site.

## Trouble Starts Early

The first sea trial was scheduled to begin on January 11, 1974. We were planning to operate the well gates and check out the performance of the docking legs, the gimbal system, and the heave compensator. We also planned to exercise the pipe-handling system, which had been giving us major problems. It had not been tested while the ship was on the East Coast (the lifting pipe was on the West Coast), and we'd been having trouble with the pipe-handling control systems ever since the ship arrived at Pier E. Engineers from several of the contractors had been drafted to work with Global Marine to get the control systems working reliably. Global Marine, MRI, Honeywell, and even CIA headquarters personnel were all working around the clock to debug the systems.

CIA engineer Geary Yost had been especially adept at interpreting the electrical drawings for the pipe-handling control systems and redesigning where necessary to get the various elements of the system to work together. One night in early January before the sea trials I climbed up to the rig floor to see how Yost was progressing—and perhaps to help. When I reached the rig floor, I couldn't even see the main deck. The wind was howling, a wet fog was blowing through constantly, and it was truly cold. Yost was all alone on the rig floor, soaking wet, trying to read the electrical diagrams for the transfer cart that was used to move pipe doubles between the main deck and the rig floor. I could see that I wasn't going to be much help—and I was already wet and miserable. With some embarrassment, I told Yost, "This is ridiculous!" and went back down below to get myself a cup of coffee. Some leadership, eh? Nevertheless, by the scheduled time for the first West Coast sea trials, we had the entire pipe-handling system working at least most of the time. Geary Yost got a major share of the credit for the job. He also got a cold that lasted for weeks.

———

The allowed time to complete sea trials and systems integration wasn't just a paper schedule that could be slipped. We *had* to meet that schedule if we were going to be at the target site during the couple of months out of the year that the sea conditions were quiet enough to permit recovery operations. We had done a lot of research on weather statistics for that part of the Pacific Ocean, and we knew that only the summer months, July and August, gave us a reasonable chance to complete the operation.

Global Marine would be in charge of the sea trials, but the designated mission personnel assigned by the CIA would be onboard to observe—and to learn something about operations at sea. According to our plans at that time, the shipboard organization and division of responsibilities for the mission had been tentatively decided:

- The Global Marine captain of the *HGE* would have ultimate responsibility for the safety of the ship. He and his Global Marine crew would be responsible for getting the ship to the target site. Once at the site, the captain would take instructions from the government's mission director, who had ultimate responsibility for success of the recovery mission. At all times, however, the ship's captain would have overriding authority to take any actions he felt necessary to ensure the safety of the ship.
- The mission director would be the senior government representative on the ship. He and his team would be responsible for carrying out the recovery and exploitation objectives of the AZORIAN mission. The mission director would have four deputy directors reporting to him: the deputy for recovery, the deputy for exploitation, the deputy for handling, and the deputy for operations.
- The deputy for recovery would be responsible for management and direction of those systems employed in the recovery operation, including the capture vehicle and the ship systems involved with

deploying the CV, lowering it to the sea bottom, capturing the target object, and raising the CV and target back into the ship.

- The deputy for exploitation would be responsible for managing the discovery, registration, preservation, and storage of items of intelligence interest from the recovered submarine.
- The deputy for handling would be responsible for ensuring personnel safety from any radiation hazards that might exist on the recovered wreckage, and for training exploitation workers on radiation safety.
- The deputy for operations would be responsible for managing the fourteen divers and the meteorologist. He would also be responsible for providing intelligence assessments to the mission director.

Although early operational planning assumed that most of the ship's crew would be contractor personnel, there were quite a few CIA men who were also eager to sign up. Responsibility for physical and psychological evaluation of the CIA crew candidates was assigned to Dr. Don Flickinger, who had provided me with the magic pills for seasickness when I was on the *Glomar II*. One day while I was back at headquarters, Flick approached me in the hall and asked if I intended to volunteer for the mission. He knew that I had participated in the *Glomar II* surveys and assumed that I'd also want to be part of the *Explorer* crew.

"I don't think so, Don. I'd rather not."

"Why not?" he asked. "I thought you did a good job on the *Glomar II*."

"Don, I think this is going to be an unpleasant mission. There are so many things that can go wrong with the recovery system, and none of the potential problems have a nice failure mode. You'll notice that it's not the design engineers who are volunteering. It's the ops people and the intelligence analysts who are eager. They don't know enough about the dangers to be afraid. Frankly, this system scares me. There's too much potential energy involved just waiting to be released catastrophically. All it would take is a little bad weather."

"You know that JP expects you to go, don't you?"

"Don, he'll be disappointed."

"Okay. I'll put a note in your file saying that you're off-limits as a crew member because of psychological problems."

"Thanks, Don—I think."

———

The first sea trial on the West Coast started in January 1974. As president of Global Marine, Curtis Crooke was in charge. (The agency hadn't formally accepted responsibility for *HGE* operation yet.) The mission director and deputy for recovery systems (both civilian contractors hired by the agency for this job) were aboard as observers. Some members of the CIA engineering staff, including me, were also onboard. This was the first chance for many of us to actually see what our engineering efforts had spawned.

When we reached the test site, the sea conditions were somewhat intimidating. Although no analyses had been performed to determine the maximum sea state for opening the well gates, and model testing technology wasn't sophisticated enough to get a good feel for the relative motions and loads, John Graham felt it probably would be unwise to attempt that operation with waves greater than eight feet. The significant wave height at the test site was probably about ten feet when we arrived. ("Significant wave height" is the term used to describe the apparent wave height as viewed by an observer. Statistically, the significant wave height—or $H_{1/3}$—approximates the average of the one-third largest waves.)

We sat around for several days patiently waiting for conditions to abate. After about a week, however, the weather wasn't getting any better—and the schedule for completion of sea trials was very tight. Crooke gave the order to prepare the well for flooding.

The well was allowed to fill with water, and the ballast tanks in the gates were partially flooded to make them neutrally buoyant. The conditions in the well while this was going on were disturbing. Due probably to the pitching motions of the ship, a large wall of water was moving back and forth from one end of the well to the other. This wall, about twenty to thirty feet high, was slamming into the fore and aft ends of the well with staggering force.

When the command to start opening the gates was given, all hell broke loose. The violent wave action just tossed the gates around in their guides as though they were little plywood doors instead of nine-foot-deep steel barges. Even though the clearance between the guides and the gates was only a couple of inches, the gates and the entrained water within them weighed thousands of tons. The forces of impact, as those gates moved up and down a couple of inches in the guides, made the whole ship shudder. We were too far along to stop at this point, so we just continued to drive the gates to the full-open position, where we could blow ballast out of the gates and lock them up solid against the hull.

Not to be. The pinion gears that drove the gates back and forth were completely stripped off by the dynamic forces. Now we had a situation where the gates were totally out of control, slamming back and forth into each other, as well as up and down in the guides. The noise of the gates slamming and the vibrations in the ship were dramatic, to say the least. Standing on the main deck, you could actually see physical deformation waves going up and down some of the ship structures, including the derrick, the docking legs, and the cart transfer boom extending from the main deck to the rig floor.

Tony A., one of the divers on the ship, volunteered to go into the well to inspect the damage and determine an appropriate course of action. He knew it would be dangerous, but his support team tried to set up safety lines that would keep him clear of the gates. Tony went into the water and swam over to the center of the well. Suddenly, he was sucked under the ship, straight down through the open well gates. Immediately after, the uncontrolled well gates slammed shut, with Tony either under them or between them—we couldn't tell which. We knew, though, that his air hose had been crushed. In the space of about thirty seconds, before anybody could react, the gates sprang open again and Tony popped up into the well from under the ship. He was pulled out of the water immediately, laid out on the deck, and his helmet was removed. His eyes looked like he'd seen a ghost, but he was fine. We were tremendously relieved for Tony, but we were beginning to have serious thoughts about how long the ship could sustain the dynamic stresses pounding away at it.

Fred Glassman, the CIA naval architect who had worked closely with John Graham during the design of the ship, was standing beside me on the main deck. He said, as seriously as I ever heard him speak, "Dave, if I ever get off this ship alive, I'm never, *ever*, going to set foot on it again!" (Glassman did, indeed, get off the ship alive and, indeed, he never set foot on it again.)

About this time, as (bad) luck would have it, a helicopter arrived with John Parangosky and the director of an influential government office that had provided key support to the AZORIAN program. This was the first visit either had made to the ship. What could be smarter from a security standpoint? Their visit to the ship would be unobserved, and at long last they'd be able to see, and stand on, the fruits of their collaboration.

The director was no dummy. He sensed trouble as soon as the chopper landed. Maybe the violent shaking of the helicopter pad gave him a clue. He asked Curtis Crooke (who had flown ashore so he could accompany the director and Parangosky in the helicopter), "Curtis, what the hell is going on?" Crooke filled him and Parangosky in on the problems and invited them into an office to get a full briefing on the sea trial events. The director, looking dubious, accepted the invitation but told the pilot before leaving the helipad, "Keep the rotors turning!" Fifteen minutes later, the distinguished guests were up, up, and away, heading back to the mainland. Those of us remaining behind thought seriously about donning life preservers.

The next half hour proved that all of our luck was not bad. The gates had been opening and slamming together for several hours by this time. But, because they were moving independently, just where they came together along the length of the hull was completely random. But then one coming-together occurred right in the center of the well and, automatically, the locking pawls that hold the gates in the closed position engaged. The gates were still banging up and down—but they were tied together. The crew quickly started blowing the ballast tanks, and before too long the gates were locked together *and* to the ship. The water was pumped out of the well and we were, relatively speaking, in good shape.

Actually, we weren't in all that great shape. The pinion gears for driving the gates open and shut were badly damaged, and the seals in the guides had been banged up. Some water seeped continuously into the well. This was a serious threat to our schedule. Here we had just started sea trials for the *Hughes Glomar Explorer* and we had already incurred damage that would have to be repaired before any further ship trials or integrated system testing could be started. And we were supposed to run the recovery mission in about six months.

Although the delay in testing and integration was a concern, the effect of the episode on the AZORIAN program management was even more traumatic. Our designated mission director withdrew himself from any further responsibility for the recovery mission. He believed that the ship was unsafe and that continued efforts to recover the Soviet submarine would almost certainly lead to a disaster with potential loss of lives. Some senior government officials agreed with him, forcing John Parangosky to emphasize that personal participation in the recovery mission would be entirely voluntary.

Some naval officers with key positions in the Pentagon—including our early supporter, Admiral Thomas Moorer—began to actively call for cancellation of the AZORIAN program, arguing that the CIA had wasted hundreds of millions of dollars on a technical "boondoggle." Before long, senior officials from other agencies joined the detractors.

On top of these problems, the security for the program was beginning to show signs of unraveling. Early in 1974, Seymour Hersh, the Pulitzer Prize–winning investigative reporter for the *New York Times*, approached CIA director William Colby with a story that he wanted to release. He told Colby that he had uncovered rumors of a CIA plan to recover a Soviet submarine (he referred to the program as "Project JENNIFER"), and that he was prepared to publish unless Colby could make a very convincing argument as to why he shouldn't.

Colby brought up the subject at a White House luncheon on January 22 with Dr. Kissinger, Secretary of Defense James Schlesinger, Joint Chief of Staff Chairman Admiral Thomas Moorer, and Major General Brent Scowcroft. Colby said, "Hersh has a story about the Soviet submarine. I would like to level with him and appeal to his patriotism."

Dr. Kissinger disagreed with the idea, but he asked for the views of everybody at the table. When the straw vote had been taken, the verdict was "No, let's not do it."[3] The luncheon group may have had a change of heart—or maybe Colby just went with his own gut instincts. In any event, he made a deal. He told Hersh that he would give him a complete briefing on the AZORIAN program if he'd hold off publication until the completion of the mission. Hersh agreed.

The CIA had dodged a bullet, but Colby knew that somebody—obviously briefed on many details of the program—had been talking. Whether this disclosure had been an inadvertent slip or an attempt to sabotage the program wasn't clear. Rightly or wrongly, Parangosky believed that the compromise had most likely come from a high-level naval officer who saw the CIA program as a threat to the growth of the Navy's own undersea warfare operations. Leaking AZORIAN to the media would have been a surefire way to kill the program. If the Soviets learned of the mission, program termination was a given.

———

Since I'd taken on the job of director of the WCPO, my relations with Global Marine's chief naval architect, John Graham, had continued to be rather strained. He and I butted heads frequently over numerous design and schedule issues. Graham knew what he was doing and didn't like the interference from a CIA engineer with no background in either naval architecture or marine engineering. I, on the other hand, had never let a lack of technical understanding restrain me from having a strong and vocal opinion. We were both too proud and stubborn to give in easily.

Curtis Crooke recognized that we were all going to have to accommodate each other's personalities and work together if we were ever going to be ready for a mission in June. He felt that a sail on his yacht, *Verve*, might work out some of the kinks in our relationship.

So, Crooke, Graham, Norm Nelson, and I set sail from Newport Beach to Catalina Island for an overnight stay and some relaxed conversation. On the way to Catalina, Crooke, Graham, and Nelson all lit up cigars—the better to enjoy the rolling motions of *Verve* in the Pacific swell. I passed on the cigar, but just smelling the smoke made me well aware of my susceptibility to *mal de mer*. Crooke and Nelson seemed to get a big kick out of watching me turn green, but Graham could see what was happening and tossed his cigar overboard. How could I not begin to like the man?

We moored the boat off Avalon, the largest town on Catalina Island, and took *Verve*'s dinghy ashore for a walk around the town. When we returned to the boat, we had a fine meal, some very good scotch, and a chance for Graham and me to get to know each other a little better before we turned in for the night. That cruise was a turning point in our relationship. Besides, the more I learned about the difficulties of designing and operating large shipboard systems, the more impressed I was with what Graham had achieved in such a short time.

## Clementine Meets the *Explorer*

In spite of the political problems with the program's future, we continued to focus on getting the *HGE* ready for the recovery mission. After the traumatic episode with the well gates during the January sea trials, Global Marine had managed to find an available graving dock in the Long Beach area and immediately moved the ship there to complete repairs to the drive gears and other well gate structural damage. These repairs were completed in several weeks, and we were ready to resume the sea trials by mid-February. The only reminder we had of the previous disaster was the seals for the well gates, which leaked forevermore. From that time on, we always had "stripping pumps" in the well to take care of the constant seepage.

Time was running out—we only had about four months to start the mission in the favorable summer weather window—and we still hadn't verified that we could use the heavy lift and pipe-handling systems to actually run pipe, or that the gimbal system and the heave compensator supporting the rig floor and derrick would do their jobs. All these systems had to be tested before we could even think about transferring the capture vehicle into the well of the ship.

One week before the start of our next sea trials, a personal tragedy occurred. Geary Yost—the CIA engineer who had been spearheading the effort to debug and redesign the pipe-handling control systems—received word that his young son back in Virginia had fallen through the ice and drowned in a pond near his home. The event was, of course, devastating to Yost, but it also strongly affected every one of our mission team. All of us had been sacrificing a lot of personal time for the last four years trying to prepare for the recovery mission. Many of the engineers had been spending more than half of their time away from their families. The sudden realization of how quickly one's life could be upended and shattered forced us all to think about those things that are most precious in our lives, and to reassess where our priorities should properly lie.

Steve Craig, chief of our West Coast security team, considered Yost—and all the other members of the program team—to be family. Craig made flight reservations for Yost to return to the East Coast that evening. He stayed with him all day, took him to dinner, and made sure that he ate something. Finally, he put Yost on the plane for that long, lonely trip back home to a family who was suffering as much as he was.

---

A week later, February 19, the *Explorer* left Pier E for a second attempt at completing our sea trials. We chose a test site fairly close to Los Angeles. We didn't need deep water—just a few thousand feet so we could lower and raise at least forty doubles (2,400 feet) of pipe and verify proper operation of the newly repaired well gates, the pipe-handling system, the gimbals, and the heave compensator. After successful completion of those tests, we planned to rendezvous with the *HMB-1* off Catalina Island so we could transfer Clementine, our 2,000-ton claw, into the well of the *HGE*. The transfer would take place at Isthmus Cove, a small recreation area on the opposite side of the island from Catalina Harbor and about twelve miles from Avalon, the island's largest community. The 160-foot water depth there was ideal for the transfer operation. The bottom was smooth, sandy, and level.

As soon as we arrived at the test site, with placid seas, we flooded the well and opened the well gates without a problem. Our next step was to start lowering the pipe string. The gimbals were to be locked in place until there was enough pipe deployed to counterbalance the derrick and prevent it from "tipping" or oscillating.

I was up on the rig floor with the lift system operators. We had run about 1,000 feet of pipe. This was over 600,000 pounds, so I thought it'd be okay to unlock the gimbals at that point. The gimbals were freed, and we continued lowering pipe. After fifteen minutes or so, one of the pipe handlers said to me, "I know that you guys [meaning the engineers] have explained to me how the rig floor stays horizontal while the ship is rolling and pitching—but if I didn't know better, I'd swear that this rig floor is moving." I chuckled and said something about optical illusions. Then, I took a hard look at the horizon. The pipe handler was absolutely right. The rig floor and derrick were, indeed, rocking back and forth while the ship was floating serenely on a perfectly smooth sea. There wasn't enough pipe weight hanging from the ship to prevent oscillations. Without wanting to cause any panic, I told one of the Global Marine engineers to lock up the gimbals until we had another thousand feet of pipe deployed. No harm was done, and we never ran into a problem like that again. I was truly embarrassed, though, and confessed to the rig floor crew that their intuitions had been absolutely right.

————

While the *HGE* continued checkout of the ship's systems, Lockheed was fighting heroically to deliver the capture vehicle to Catalina Island for the transfer operation. The *HMB-1*, with the CV aboard, had to be towed from Redwood City to Isthmus Cove—over 350 miles of open ocean. Under normal wind and sea conditions, the *HMB-1* could complete the trip in about forty hours. But the *HMB-1* wasn't encountering *normal* conditions.

Shortly after leaving Redwood City, the barge encountered steady-state winds of fifty-five knots for several hours with building seas. There had been some discussion about returning to Redwood City to await more benign conditions, but the critical urgency of getting the *HGE* and the capture vehicle mated so that integrated system testing could begin overruled such considerations. Lockheed decided to continue the tow.

Eventually, the winds built up to a steady sixty-seven knots with sea state 7 conditions—significant wave heights of up to thirty feet—way over the twenty-foot wave height limit specified for the towing operation. The tug and the barge were slowed by the fierce weather conditions, but they arrived safely at the sheltered waters of Isthmus Cove—only a day late. The *HGE* arrived at Isthmus Cove on February 27. The *HMB-1* was already positioning itself in the desired location with four anchors deployed by the support boats.

————

Here's how the transfer scenario was supposed to work: When positioned correctly and held in place by four large anchors—one at each corner—the *HMB-1* was submerged to the bottom by selectively flooding compartments in the hull and sides of the barge. When the barge was submerged up to the roofline, four large hinged pontoons provided the flotation and attitude stability. These pontoons, which rose into a vertical position as the barge descended, were selectively ballasted to keep the barge level until it was finally resting on the bottom.

Once the *HMB-1* was on the bottom, the *HGE* was moved directly over it. Tugs carried the *HGE* anchors out from each quadrant of the ship to establish a four-point moor. Then the mooring chains were adjusted until the ship was stable in the desired position directly over the submerged barge.

At this point, the telescoping roof of the *HMB-1* was opened. The *HGE*'s docking legs were tilted to the open position and lowered into the CV. When the docking leg keyholes were vertically aligned with the large support pins on either end of the strongback, the legs were tilted to the closed position and raised until the pins were firmly locked into the bottom of the keyholes. Then the legs were raised the rest of the way, lifting the claw out of the *HMB-1* and into the well of the *HGE*. The well gates of the ship were closed and the well pumped dry. The *HGE* was then ready to sail.

Although conceptually simple, the transfer operation was time-consuming (usually a two-day operation) and exacting. An error in the *HGE*'s anchor chain placement could (and did on one occasion) cause substantial damage to the sliding roof of the *HMB-1*.

Security was also an issue during the transfer operations. Although the roof of the *HMB-1* remained closed until the *Explorer* was moored in place above it, there was always some concern that a curious diver might attempt to take photos of the mining machine while it was being lifted into the *HGE*. To protect against this vulnerability, program security officers circled the ship continuously in small powerboats, warning off any private vessels that came too close. (That assignment, by the way, had no shortage of volunteers.)

Even though the risk of exposure was considered minimal, the cover story specialists in Washington arranged to have a small-scale model mining machine built that somewhat resembled the actual capture vehicle. This model had large finned propulsion wheels at each corner of the miner, and strange-looking nodule collectors mounted on the ends of clawlike tines that would ostensibly be dragged along the ocean bottom to collect manganese nodules. It was, indeed, an odd machine, and it might not have passed an engineering credibility test if exposed. Of course, the cover specialists never intended any pictures of this model to be shown publicly unless it was found absolutely necessary to respond to an inadvertent exposure of the CV. Fortunately, we never had a reason to take that step.

———

Our first transfer operation went quite smoothly. We arrived at Isthmus Cove on February 27 at 0700. By 1300 we had the mooring anchors set and soaking. We completed the transfer in the middle of the night. Floodlights were lined up all around the well to provide illumination for divers and the Lockheed technicians.

After the well gates were closed, we began to pump the well dry. Operations were normal for about fifteen minutes—then the pumps began to stop, one by one. After an inspection of the stalled pumps, the divers reported they were all jammed with calamari. As it turned out, the calamari were attracted into the well by the bright lights and ended up getting drawn into the well by the very strong suction forces. The divers cleaned out the pumps and we started them up again. Not to be. In about fifteen minutes, they were all jammed again.

The same operation was continued a couple of more times before somebody came up with the idea of reopening the well gates and hanging the lights over the outside of the ship to entice the squid to leave the well. That worked. After a couple of hours, the well gates were closed, the floodlights were brought back inside the well area, and the pumping was restarted without further problems. No harm was done to the pumps, but hundreds of pounds of calamari had to be shoveled out of the well once it was empty. The smell persisted for quite a while, but for the first time we had the entire recovery system together. The *HMB-1* was refloated and towed back to Redwood City. The *HGE* retrieved its anchors and departed for Pier E at Long Beach.

———

As you might suppose, the divers were very busy during the transfer operations. We had fourteen divers altogether. Most of them were former SEALs. The chief diver was an ex-SEAL named Bill Beaverton. Beaverton was an excellent manager—he had to be in order to keep fourteen divers with very diverse (and very strong) personalities content with their jobs. He looked out for his men and managed to negotiate some special perks to make their lives a little more interesting when they weren't actually working on the ship. Beaverton was able to convince our security people that the divers should be able to spend some time ashore during the transfer operations, drink at the local bar, and even sleep in the available tourist cabins at Isthmus Cove.[4]

The divers' time ashore was not completely uneventful. One of them, an ex-SEAL named Dan with a Silver Star, multiple Purple Hearts, and a chest full of scars from Vietnam, was a physical fitness addict. He stood about six and a half feet tall, with curly black hair, a walrus moustache, and (usually) a two-day growth of beard. Very imposing. Dan liked to run several miles every morning and found it entertaining to search out the indigenous buffalos on the island and run through the middle of the herd waving his arms and yelling, scattering them in all directions.

On one particular morning, a large male buffalo refused to be routed, standing his ground and looking menacingly at Dan. Since arm-waving and yelling didn't scare the buffalo, Dan slugged him in the nose. That didn't scare the buffalo either. In fact, the enraged bull started after Dan. The two of them, with Dan managing to stay slightly ahead, ran from the hills down toward the restaurant at Isthmus Cove. Diners sitting on the outdoor patio were surprised by sounds of yelling and snorting and, shortly after, the sight of Dan and the buffalo racing full-tilt toward the restaurant. Just as they reached the patio, Dan veered sharply from his course. The buffalo was not able to match the sharp turn and fell to the ground, sliding into the patio amidst the tables and diners. By the time the buffalo got up, Dan was long gone. The big bull looked around, shook himself off, gave one more bellow, and trotted back into the hills.

There were a couple of other minor incidents on Catalina Island, but nothing serious until one memorable night when the python got loose. (One of the divers had a pet snake, a giant python measuring about eight feet long.) When the ship was tied up at Pier E, this imposing pet was ritually fed a live chicken every morning. The snake was highly respected by all, seriously feared by most.

On this particular night at Isthmus Cove—after most of the divers had already gone to bed—the snake turned up missing. Its owner (only slightly less physically imposing than the python) was furious, believing that someone had stolen his pet. With more than a few beers under his belt, he proceeded from one tourist cabin to the next looking for his snake. His modus operandi was to approach the cabin, rip the door off the hinges, and look inside for the snake before moving on to the next cabin to repeat the search procedure. The authorities eventually arrived, and our security people had to talk fast and convincingly to get our diver off the hook. He wasn't fired. (He was a good diver—and cleared. We couldn't afford to lose a cleared diver.) Even so, the shore privileges of the divers were at an end. As for the python, it never turned up. It's possible that it lived many years on Catalina Island living on small wild goats.

———

The divers weren't the only ones who wanted to get off the ship. It was often hot during transfer operations and the ship wasn't moving—it was just sitting there under the hot sun. There was usually very little breeze. The sailboats were mostly motoring around the harbor with their sails furled.

The heat was made even worse by the required Global Marine shipboard uniform of long pants, work boots, and hard hats.

Adding to the frustration was the fact that lots of people all around the ship were having a great time in their own personal boats. These people, of course, were not wearing boots and hard hats. In fact, some of them weren't wearing anything at all. On one hot Sunday—while I was leaning on the rail of the ship watching the parade of curious boats—one of the sailboats came unusually close to the ship for a closer inspection. The captain of the boat was a bronzed young man wearing only a Speedo, and gold chains around his neck. Onboard with him were two young women, blondes, apparently twins, wearing absolutely nothing. I remember musing to my companion at the rail, "You know, one of these days I'm going to get myself a sailboat—and maybe some naked ladies, too!" Several years later, when the AZORIAN program was long over, I *did* get myself a sailboat. As for the naked ladies? Well, nothing's perfect.

———

On March 1, on the way back to Long Beach with the capture vehicle securely contained in the well of the ship, we tested the *HGE*'s roll stabilization system for the first and only time. This system had been added almost as an afterthought while the ship's design was being completed, and the need for it was hotly debated by the design engineers. We knew that the gimbal system would keep all bending loads off the pipe string so long as ship roll did not exceed ±8.5 degrees and pitch did not exceed ±5 degrees. As construction of the ship progressed, though, some of us couldn't help but wonder, "Would those angular limits be enough?" If ship roll *did* exceed 8.5 degrees, the gimbaled platform would go against the limit stops and large bending stresses would be put into the pipe string, quite likely leading to failure of the pipe and all of the predicted calamitous consequences.

Our worries about roll stability had started with the model testing being done for Global Marine at the David Taylor Model Basin (DTMB) in Carderock, Maryland. In the early 1970s, almost all ship model testing was done using sinusoidal waves of uniform period and identical height. From the testing we had done, ship roll was considered to be well within the gimbal limits for the relatively calm sea states that we expected to see at the target site during the summer months.

Then Jacques Hadler, program manager for the *HGE* model testing at DTMB, introduced some new uncertainties into the equation. He had been experimenting with a new, innovative model testing procedure that used random waves instead of sinusoidal waves. Hadler was able to produce waves that more closely duplicated realistic sea conditions, combining short-period broadband waves like those resulting from local wind conditions, and longer-period sinusoidal waves that resembled the swell resulting from distant storms. These are the kinds of sea state conditions that can produce the occasional rogue wave so feared by mariners.

What, we wondered, was the likelihood of encountering a rogue wave (and a resultant rogue roll) during the extended time that the ship would be raising or lowering pipe at the target site? How frequently did rogue waves occur? What was the likelihood that we would encounter anomalous weather conditions far worse than the statistical data suggested? We knew that if we spent a nominal two weeks for operations with the CV deployed, we would encounter up to 120,000 waves with periods between crests of ten seconds or more. How much faith, we pondered, should we place in statistical analysis and probability theory? Would it make more sense just to rely on the long experience and confidence of the ship's designer, John Graham?

Graham wasn't worried. He was confident that the ship would not exceed the roll limits imposed by the gimbals, but he couldn't counter the probability analyses of engineers, like me, who knew a lot more about the mathematics of random processes than we did about designing ships. Eventually, Graham gave in and agreed to put a roll stabilization system into the ship. Global Marine contracted with an experienced company, Muirhead-Brown in Scotland, to design the system for the *HGE*. It was the largest roll stabilization system ever designed by that company.

Since none of the Global Marine engineers felt the need for—or had any interest in—the roll stabilization system, I ended up in charge of the one and only test. I prevailed on the captain to give me an hour to test the system on the way back to Long Beach. The captain really hated to comply with my request because the test required the ship to be in the trough (taking the waves directly from the side of the ship), creating the maximum ship roll motion—and the greatest discomfort for the crew. Nevertheless, he agreed to give me an hour of uninterrupted time in the trough.

That test was the only time I experienced nausea on the *HGE*. As the experiment progressed, I had to run back and forth between the stabilization system's flapper valves to ensure they were opening and closing properly, returning periodically to a dedicated analog computer to adjust the phase relationship between the roll motions and the flapper valve actuations. The valves themselves were essentially steel gates about five feet square. Their function was to restrict on command the passage of air through the huge ducts connecting the stabilizing system's water tanks on either side of the ship. All of this plumbing was crammed into a space below the main deck that required me to scuttle around in a stooped position. The noise from the flapper valve operation was deafening (no sound insulation on that system!) and the air was stifling. I eventually managed to get one-half hour of data without the roll stabilizer, and one-half hour of data with the stabilizer. When the captain notified me that my time was up, I didn't argue. I couldn't wait to get back on deck and breathe some fresh air.

The system did actually work. When I completed analysis of the roll data, it turned out that the stabilization system had reduced the average roll motion of the ship by about 30–35 percent. I was satisfied. I was confident that we had a useful system that could be employed if conditions ever warranted—and I hoped we'd never encounter such conditions.

On March 2 at 1630, we docked the *HGE* at Pier E. We had twenty-six days before heading out for the first integrated systems test.

## Integrated System Testing

Shortly before beginning our first integrated systems test (IST), we reviewed our plans and schedule with the Lauderdale Panel, a high-level group of scientists, mariners, and engineers whom Carl Duckett had assembled to advise the program office. The panel was chaired by Duckett's deputy, Dr. Lloyd Lauderdale, an experienced ex-Navy officer who possessed an excellent understanding of marine engineering and operations. Other panel members included Dr. Duane Sewell, an associate director at Lawrence Livermore Laboratories; Dr. Alan Powell, director of the David Taylor Model Basin; William Perry, president of ESL Inc.; Clifford Cummings, former director of the Lunar Project at Jet Propulsion Laboratories; and Rear Admiral Nathan Sonenshein. The panel had about ten members, each of whom was a noted expert in one or more technical fields, including ship model testing, nuclear weapons, underwater optical and acoustic sensors, metallurgy, and hydrodynamics—all of which were critical to the success of our mission.

After approving, with some suggestions and recommendations, our test plan for the IST, the panel asked about our contingency plans for the mission itself. What were we going to do in the event of the ship breaking in two? What would we do if the Soviets showed excessive interest in our operations? What if a Soviet submarine surfaced and attempted to board the ship? We (the CIA team) just looked at each other blankly. Contingency plans? Who had had time to think about that? I guess each of us had some ideas on what an appropriate response for most contingencies would be, but we'd never really talked much about it and had certainly never formalized any of our thoughts by putting them down on paper.

The panel was dumbstruck. Lauderdale said, "Don't you guys know that you *always* have to have plans for contingencies?" He followed up by declaring that a full set of contingency plans would have to be produced and approved by the panel before the start of the mission.

Those of us in the room just looked at each other. We wondered who on earth was going to write those plans. All the engineers and crew members were working day and night trying to get the ship ready for the mission. There was precious little documentation of *anything* taking place, let alone contingency plans. Finally, Parangosky looked at Ott Schick, Lockheed's program manager, with raised eyebrows.

"Sure," Ott responded to the unspoken question, "I've got some systems engineering guys who have lots of experience writing contingency plans. They can turn out a plan in time for the mission."

So it was settled. Some of Lockheed's missile systems engineers were going to write the contingency plan for how Howard Hughes's ship—operated by Global Marine and managed by the CIA—was going to respond to everything from the ship breaking in two to an attempt by the Soviets to board and take over the ship. It sounded ridiculous, but we weren't concerned. At that time it seemed highly unlikely that we'd ever be able to start the mission, let alone worry about contingencies.

————

On March 28, at high tide, the *HGE* sailed away from Pier E for the first integrated systems test (we had to leave on the high tide because the ship was actually resting on the bottom at low tides). We knew this was going to be a long test period since practically every system on the capture vehicle had to be checked out for the first time. To simplify the logistics problems, the ship was operating fairly close to shore. That made it possible for a small support boat, the *Colleen,* to carry parts and personnel to and from the ship on a daily basis. For things that were really time-critical, we used a helicopter that commuted between the ship and the roof of the building that housed the Summa offices in El Segundo. Altogether, we spent about six weeks at sea trying to get the bugs worked out.

All the ship's systems (docking legs, pipe-handling system, heavy lift system, etc.) and all the capture vehicle systems (beam and davit actuators, sonars, cabling, CCTVs, lights, thrusters, etc.) had worked for at least part of the time, but we had experienced one failure after another throughout the entire test period. Although we had fixes planned for all the systems that were giving us problems, the outlook for getting the recovery system truly operational by mid-June did not look promising.

There was one operation in particular that we never got really comfortable with. That was the docking/undocking procedure. Undocking—deployment of the capture vehicle from the ship's well—was relatively straightforward. Once the well gates were open, the CV was lowered on the docking legs far enough to permit its lifting bridle to be erected. When the bridle had been rigged and attached to the pipe string, the CV was lowered until it was about 110 feet below the ship, with the docking legs still taking the full load. To initiate the actual undocking, the docking legs were gradually lowered until all of the load had been transferred to the lifting pipe. When the load transfer was completed and the docking legs were no longer supporting any weight via the CV support pins, the legs were quickly tilted back to move them longitudinally out of the way. When the legs were clear of the pins, they were raised at maximum speed while the pipe string was lowered as quickly as possible to get the legs away from the CV before significant relative motion between the two components could build up and result in collisions. The process of transferring the CV load from the docking legs to the pipe string sounds straightforward and simple—and it *was* simpler than the docking procedure—but there was never an opportunity to relax.

The docking procedure was simply the reverse of the undocking operation—with one huge difference. In the undocking maneuver, the docking legs simply let go of the capture vehicle and got out of the way as quickly as possible before significant dynamic motion of the claw, now swinging on the pipe string, could build up. In the docking operation, however, the relative motion between the ship and the CV was already in full swing. It was the job of the docking legs to somehow catch the CV's support pins in mid-fly and force the capture vehicle to move in sync with the ship's motions. Heavy physical contacts between the docking legs and the capture vehicle were expected—and planned for—by the ship's designers. Even with all the planning and expectation, however, the docking maneuver was nerve-wracking—and sometimes terrifying.

By far the greatest stress from the docking operation was experienced by the operators of the heavy lift system and the docking legs. Control of both of these systems, as well as the well gates, was managed from the heavy lift control room that was physically located belowdecks in the port wing wall. The wing walls on either side of the well, being the thinnest sections of the hull, suffered more flexing and vibration than the rest of the ship. Making matters worse, the control room was barely above the waterline, and the acoustic energy from the impacts was transmitted with little attenuation directly into the control room. The kinetic energy absorbed from a typical impact during the docking/undocking operations was equivalent to that of a Greyhound bus smashing into the docking leg at about forty miles per hour. The shaking and the noise experienced by the operators in the heavy lift control room were unnerving to even the most experienced Global Marine hands—most of whom were familiar with the violence of gales and even hurricanes on ships and oil rigs—but for the Western Gear engineers, the docking operations were really traumatic. Occasionally, one or more of the operators would have to come up to the main deck, visibly shaken, to smoke a cigarette and get a breath of fresh air before going back down into the control room to complete the operation.

In spite of the apparent violence of the docking operations, there was only minor—readily repairable—damage inflicted on the capture vehicle, the docking legs, and the ship during these docking maneuvers. John Graham's team and the designers of the claw had done their homework well.

———

On May 12 the ship tied up again at Pier E. We would have about two and a half weeks in port to repair broken systems and get ready for the next—and last—integrated systems test. Furthermore, because of the short weather window for attempting the recovery, we could only afford a couple of weeks for the final IST. By the middle of June, we'd have to start out for the target site.

Our situation wasn't encouraging. We had a recovery system with demonstrated capability but terrible reliability. We hadn't even had a chance to rehearse the critical bottom operations with the capture vehicle. Some senior officers felt we might be wiser to delay the mission a year until 1975. The crew hated the idea of delay—we looked at it as a kind of failure—but we couldn't make a good case for claiming full operational readiness by mid-June.

We brought the question up to the Lauderdale panel. When our technical team briefed them on our recent at-sea testing, they were unanimous in the opinion that we hadn't demonstrated readiness to attempt the mission. It would be technically prudent, they felt, to delay the mission until the summer of 1975.

However, the briefing from our security team took them completely by surprise and caused a reversal of opinion. The panel already knew about Seymour Hersh and his approach to CIA director Colby. Hersh had agreed to hold the story until after the mission, but he had not committed to stop probing for more information—or to stop talking to other reporters about the program. The security staff was concerned that perhaps Hersh wasn't the only reporter with the inside story on the program.

After a long discussion, the panel decided to approve a 1974 recovery attempt. They felt that the likelihood of technical success was limited, in view of our technical shortcomings. On the other hand, they felt that it was unrealistic to expect that the security required for a covert recovery operation would still be in place in the summer of 1975. They ended up recommending we take a stab at the recovery in 1974—and hope for the best.

———

Morale was at a low ebb. Both the government and contractor personnel were physically and emotionally exhausted. Most of the engineers had been pushing themselves hard for over four years to meet the ambitious program schedules. The excitement of AZORIAN had led all of us to extend ourselves well beyond reasonable healthy limits. The people on the West Coast seemed to be affected the most. Several of the WCPO engineers and analysts had suffered stress-related heart attacks during the preceding year. Many marriages were suffering because there just wasn't enough time or emotional energy to satisfy the demands of AZORIAN and still maintain a healthy married relationship. John Graham, who had tried to stop smoking because of diagnosed emphysema, had resumed his chain-smoking. About a year earlier, I had developed a stress-induced disease that allowed the fluid in both eyes to leak through holes in the retinas, leaving me with permanent partial blindness in one eye.

John Parangosky's plan to "kaleidoscope" time by handing the program off to the operations team never quite came to pass either. The sea trials and the systems integration tests had proven to be tremendously difficult challenges, requiring continued heavy involvement of the engineering team as the project continued. Some of the senior government and contractor managers slated for the mission had simply backed out.

We'd had several frightening and dangerous equipment failures during the testing, and there were growing concerns about whether the Soviets were on to our plans. The original choice for the position of director of recovery systems (D/R) had quit (along with the original mission director) after the first sea trials in January 1974. After the ship returned from the first integrated systems test in May, the replacement D/R opted out, too, having determined after almost six weeks at sea fighting continuous equipment problems that he preferred to support the program from the shore.

———

I had never planned to be part of the mission team. I had been enthusiastic about providing engineering support on the ship during the sea trials and integrated systems testing, but I didn't want to become part of the ship's management group. That would mean a firm commitment to participate in the mission, and I was definitely ambivalent about that. I'd had my fill of at-sea operations and seasickness several years earlier on one of the *Glomar II* missions. I had told Parangosky that I was not planning to volunteer for the mission. The potential danger from equipment failures and the threat of possible Soviet interference in the recovery mission were both strong negatives for me. I liked adventure, but I wasn't looking for *that* much adventure.

Ultimately, I had little choice in the matter. After the ISTs we had just completed, Parangosky found himself without anyone to manage the recovery systems on the ship. He flew to the West Coast and asked me if I'd take the job. I asked him whom else he was considering. He said, "Actually, nobody. It's too late to train a new D/R, and we need someone who knows the entire system inside and out. Will you do it?"

I couldn't let Parangosky down. And besides, I realized that deep down I really wanted to prove that the system design was sound and could do the job. So I became the director of recovery systems. I wasn't the first choice— or even the second choice—but I *was* the final choice. I would also continue as the director of the WCPO.

My decision to accept the D/R job came as a surprise to Dr. Don Flickinger, who was responsible for approval of all CIA crew selections. Flick knew that I had had reservations about going with the ship. My change of heart surprised us both.

When I told him that I'd decided to be part of the crew, he said, "But Dave, you said you were concerned about the danger of the mission, so I put you on the *psychologically unsuitable* list to make sure you wouldn't be pressured to go. Now you're saying you want to go. Do you have more confidence in the safety of the recovery system now?"

Of course I didn't. Sometimes the potential for disaster on the ship just scared the hell out of me. Furthermore, the likelihood of being confronted by a Soviet ship intent on boarding the *HGE* seemed very real in my mind.

"No, Don," I replied. "I don't feel good about it, but JP asked me to take the job and I'm going."

"Okay," Flick said. "I'll take you off the psychologically unsuitable list. Good luck!"

"Thanks, Don," I said, wondering how volunteering for this job could possibly be a measure of my psychological health.

## The Battle for Mission Approval

Somewhat to the surprise of everyone, the crew of the *Hughes Glomar Explorer* had demonstrated at least a marginal mission-readiness capability that very few had predicted. The CIA's oversight panel was satisfied that the mission team had a respectable chance of completing a successful recovery. The IST performance, together with the newly crafted contingency plans generated by the Lockheed aerospace systems engineers, justified in their minds their guidance to attempt the recovery mission in 1974.

It must be acknowledged that the oversight panel probably didn't read any of the contingency plans. The tome was almost three inches thick, with a table of contents that, by itself, would exhaust the amount of time that these talented and very busy scientists and managers could afford to spend in analytical study. That's probably a good thing. All in all, the contingency plans didn't make a whole lot of sense—having been written by spacecraft engineers unfamiliar with maritime law or the operation of a ship designed for ocean mining. But it was thick, and we had multiple copies with official cover sheets. In this case, style overruled substance.

Although the somewhat encouraging IST and the newly drafted contingency plan pleased the oversight panel, it caused a certain amount of desperation in the ranks of those government elements that had been opposing the mission on political and/or not-invented-here grounds. Concerns about program security, too, had continued to grow and there was increasing worry about a possibly strong Soviet reaction if the real mission of the *Hughes Glomar Explorer* was compromised.

With the security issues as a backdrop, we found that much of the U.S. government was looking for ways to kill the mission. Some Navy and State Department officials had openly indicated their strong reservations about continuing the recovery attempt. A full-blown inquisition was organized at CIA headquarters. Senior representatives from the State Department, the Justice Department, and the Navy were all present. John Parangosky had assembled his technical and security teams to provide the briefings, but it was pretty clear that the goal of many in the audience was to cancel the mission.

The people from the State and Justice Departments were especially troubled by the suspect legality of the proposed mission. Some legal authorities had already suggested that the recovery of a Soviet ship of state might, from the standpoint of international law, be considered piracy. The issue didn't especially alarm people back in 1971 when the security of the program was on really solid ground. Now, however, there was concern that the Soviets would eventually (if not sooner) find out about the attempt to recover their submarine. The fact that the Soviets had actually recovered—and used—a British submarine (the *L-55*) back in 1928 didn't alleviate their concern.[5] One of the State Department representatives pointed out that nuclear war was not a concern back in 1928.

The Navy representatives in that meeting seemed more concerned about our technical readiness to attempt the mission and our preparedness for dealing with contingencies. They pointed out that we had only tested the system in water less than half the depth of that in which the *K-129* rested. Furthermore, we had never attempted to actually drive the tines of the capture vehicle through sand or mud. They were right on both counts.

We would have liked to test the CV down to the same depths and water pressures that we would encounter at the target site. However, with the limited time we had, we couldn't afford to spend more than a couple of days transiting to and from the test sites. With that restriction, the deepest water we could test in was about 8,000 feet.

With regard to never testing the tines of the capture vehicle to ensure that they could, indeed, be hydraulically driven through sand and mud, that was a conscious decision that the AZORIAN program office made early in the project. We felt that there was a high likelihood that some minor damage (e.g., bending, twisting, cracking, etc.) would be incurred by the fingers of the claw when they were driven through mud and sand. We only wanted to encounter this problem once. Testing the actual ability of the tines to penetrate through the ocean bottom would have almost certainly resulted in several months of required refurbishment of the capture vehicle before it could be used for another test—or for the mission.

We did our best to convince our hostile audience that we were, indeed, technically prepared to complete the mission, but we weren't winning the arguments. I presented the briefing on our IST progress without impressing anyone. Norm Nelson took up the briefing chores where I left off, emphasizing the additional work that would be completed during a second IST before the mission. No sale. The questions were getting more and more heated when finally Parangosky had had too much.

He waved his arms and dramatically cried out, "Stop! Mea culpa! Mea culpa!"

This sounded rather generous to me and to Nelson—it looked like JP was willing to take some of the blame.

Then, Parangosky added, "It's my fault! I've hired incompetent people!"

I thought the room was going to erupt. The guys from the other agencies were all hooting with laughter, while Nelson and I stood red-faced and stunned.

Nelson reacted before I did, marching toward Parangosky shouting, "Just a damn minute now, John!" while shaking his five-foot briefing pointer threateningly.

JP realized he'd gone too far and backed up rapidly. It was an embarrassing and infuriating moment—but it broke the ice. From that point on, the audience wasn't quite so hostile. I began to think we might still have a chance.

I hadn't reckoned on the reactions of some of the Navy officers present, though—especially Captain Walter N. "Buck" Dietzen, who was on the staff of the new chief of naval operations, Admiral Elmo Zumwalt. Dietzen had read some of our contingency plans and he didn't like them one bit. Specifically, he didn't like our contingency plan for resisting a Soviet attempt to board the *HGE*. Our plan called for us to act and respond in a manner that would be consistent with our ocean mining cover story. For example, if a Soviet ship requested permission to come aboard, our captain would refuse permission on the grounds that our mining techniques had high proprietary value and the ship owner (Howard Hughes) was unwilling to show them to anybody.

If the Soviets made motions of trying to board in spite of our protests, our plan called for us to use fire hoses and spray the decks of the Soviet ship or submarine, making it difficult for the crew to rig any lines or launch small boats. If the Soviets responded with firearms, our plan called for us to essentially raise the white flag. Before boarding could be accomplished, we would have had ample time to jettison all the classified documents that we had in the control center. (They were stored onboard in steel mesh drawers that would sink rapidly when thrown overboard.) Visually sensitive systems, such as the claw, would hopefully be many thousands of feet under the water.

"Buck" Dietzen considered this plan cowardly and entirely unacceptable. He insisted that the *HGE* crew must be prepared to fight off any Soviet boarding attempt with firearms. To our protest that we didn't have any firearms, he yelled, "Get some!" I raised the question of where the nearest support from the U.S. Navy would be if we did, indeed, get into some sort of shooting situation. We were informed that there would be no U.S. Navy ship within 400 miles of the *HGE* at any time during the operation. Being closer than that, it was feared, might precipitate some kind of political incident with the Soviets. A State Department rep nodded his head approvingly. I couldn't believe my ears.

Someone from the CIA's office of legal counsel said, "Wait a minute! You're suggesting that the crew of CIA officers and contractors should get into a firefight with a Soviet submarine while the U.S. Navy stays well over the horizon to ensure that the Soviets aren't upset?"

Captain Dietzen grinned and said, "I'd never let any lily-livered communist pinko take over a ship of mine!"

I was furious. I said, "Who are you calling lily-livered when you're going to be more than 400 miles away? It seems to me—"

About that time I glanced over at Parangosky. He looked at me and, almost imperceptibly, shook his head. Perhaps he knew something that I didn't know. Or maybe he was just telling me to shut up. I did, but I wasn't happy.

When all the dust had settled, it turned out we had a deal. The CIA agreed to put up a "fight" (details to be resolved later) if Soviet boarding was attempted. The Navy confirmed that they'd be actively monitoring our situation at the target site from Pearl Harbor (about 1,800 miles away),[6] and the legal people seemed somewhat tolerant of the fact that the recovery operation was, arguably, piracy. (Perhaps their acceptance had something to do with their low confidence in our ability to successfully complete the mission.)

———

At the time, I could not understand the Navy's insistence that none of their ships would be permitted to come closer than 400 miles to the target site during the recovery operations. Now, over thirty-eight years later, several books have been written that offer some explanation for the Navy's position.

Two of those books, *Blind Man's Bluff* and *Scorpion Down*, describe in detail the aggressive tactics that both the U.S. and Soviet navies were using in trailing each other's submarines in the open oceans. Both books report that collisions (some resulting in damages) between the two governments' submarines occurred on more than one occasion. Details about such operations were, of course, tightly restricted. The crew of the *Hughes Glomar Explorer* did not have a need to know.

The Navy also would have known that Soviet submarine patrols regularly traversed the general area where the *Explorer* would be operating in the central North Pacific. It follows, then, that in some (almost all?) cases, those Soviet subs were being tracked closely—and hopefully covertly—by U.S. submarines. Quite possibly, then, whenever a Soviet submarine was in close proximity to the *HGE*, there was a good chance that a U.S. submarine would have been close by.

This situation would have caused a great deal of anxiety for the Navy. The last thing they wanted to do was to get involved in an altercation with a Soviet sub over a commercial ship, the *Hughes Glomar Explorer*. At least one alarmist in the State Department had expressed concern that the AZORIAN project could end up precipitating World War III.

———

After the mission approval meeting with the Navy, State Department, and others, John Parangosky briefed CIA director William Colby on the results and pointed out that the agency had agreed to put up a fight if any boarding attempt by a Soviet ship was made. "Hmm," Colby said. "How many platoons of marines will you be carrying on the ship?" Parangosky explained that there was no room on the ship to carry any marines. Colby just shook his head and said, "You'd better get some guns."

———

On May 31, just a few days after the headquarters meeting, the *Hughes Glomar Explorer* left Pier E for the second and final integrated systems test—and the last chance we'd have to show that there was some reason to be optimistic about the likelihood of mission success. About eight hours later, we arrived at the test site and began our mission rehearsal. For this IST, we actually lowered a special test target to the ocean bottom so that the CV sensors and positioning system could be realistically tested.

Amazingly, the rehearsal went like clockwork. After our long weeks at sea trying to complete the earlier system tests, we had left Long Beach with only cautious optimism and a nagging feeling that we might not get a final approval to proceed with the mission. The first IST had taken over forty days, and nearly every system had had repeated failures. This time was different. The second IST took us only eleven days, and we completed all of our objectives. Admittedly, we still had some reliability problems, but we had shown that we could complete the mission operations. After ten days at sea, the capture vehicle was back in the ship's well, the gates were closed, and the well was being pumped. We were heading back to Pier E. A mission-readiness meeting was already under way on the ship.

———

While all this testing and preparation for the mission were proceeding, events were taking place on both coasts that were critically important to the program. DCI Colby still hadn't received presidential approval to attempt the recovery mission. Ultimately, the responsibility for approval would fall to the 40 Committee. The 40 Committee reported directly to the president and was responsible for reviewing and advising the president on all major covert actions being considered for approval. Henry Kissinger, then the national security adviser to the president as well as the secretary of state, chaired the group. Committee approvals usually came down through Kissinger, with the approval cited as having come from highest authority. The term "highest authority" was conventionally recognized within the CIA as a euphemism for the president of the United States. By leaving his name off the official approval, the president retained the right of plausible denial if the covert operation was compromised with embarrassing ramifications.

DCI Colby delivered his briefing to Kissinger, ending with a request for permission to proceed with the mission. The president did not attend. In fact, none of the DCIs who took part in the AZORIAN program (Richard Helms, James Schlesinger, and William Colby) ever had much contact with President Nixon beyond formal occasions and social events. He preferred to have all intelligence matters pass through Kissinger.[7]

When Colby had completed his briefing, Kissinger showed little reaction. He inquired about the perceived intelligence value of the target and asked what the Soviet reaction would likely be if the mission were compromised. Then he thanked Mr. Colby and the other briefers and departed with no sign as to whether he was likely to recommend for or against mission approval.

On June 5, 1974, the 40 Committee met to consider the AZORIAN mission approval. Kissinger had prepared a memorandum for the president that explained the key technical, security, and political issues. On June 7, President Nixon approved the mission, stipulating that the recovery not be undertaken between June 27 and July 3. He would be in the Soviet Union during that time for SALT II negotiations with the Kremlin leadership. Kissinger commented that the president had been impressed with the co-operation and coordination among the various military and intelligence services involved in the program. *Highest authority* had weighed in. We had approval to go. The *HGE* would leave Long Beach on or about June 20.

———

President Nixon's decision to approve the AZORIAN mission was a bold and perhaps risky move. Since November 1969, the United States and the USSR had been actively negotiating ways to end the competition in proliferation of land-based and submarine-launched ballistic missiles. These Strategic Arms Limitation Talks (SALT I) had come to a successful conclusion on May 26, 1972, when President Nixon and Chairman Leonid Brezhnev both signed the Anti-Ballistic Missile Treaty and the Interim Agreement on the Limitation of Strategic Offensive Arms.

These negotiations and the resultant agreements were a high priority for the president, who was dedicated to the task of reducing the tensions between the two countries. Immediately after the conclusion of SALT I, the United States and the Soviet Union began the SALT II negotiations, aimed at replacing the interim agreement with a longer-term treaty providing for both qualitative and quantitative limits for strategic weapons systems.

The president had to be alert to the risk that compromise of the AZORIAN mission would certainly inflame Chairman Brezhnev and possibly upset the ongoing SALT II negotiations. His decision to approve the recovery mission anyway must be interpreted as a clear sign of his confidence that the ocean mining cover story would hold up.

———

Unfortunately, Nixon's confidence in the sustainability of the cover story might have been optimistic. At approximately 0045 on June 5—the same day that Kissinger briefed the 40 Committee—a Hughes business office on Romaine Street in Los Angeles was burglarized. Four men overcame the night watchman, who was blindfolded, gagged, and tied up. Over a time period of about three hours, the thieves cut through the door section of a Mosler walk-in vault and broke into several safes. They made off with $68,000 in fifty- and one-hundred-dollar bills, along with a number of antiques and collections, including two valuable Wedgwood vases. They also took an undetermined number of company files. It was front page news in that day's *Los Angeles Times.*

Early the next day, WCPO security chief Steve Craig received a phone message at his home from Bill Gay, one of Howard Hughes's principal representatives, requesting Craig to come to the Summa offices in Studio City as soon as possible. Gay believed something of critical interest to the agency might have been taken by the burglars.

At the meeting, this "something of critical interest" was described to Craig by Nadine Henley, Hughes's personal secretary, as a one-page handwritten document from a yellow legal pad. The notes were those of Raymond Holliday, perhaps Hughes's closest confidant, describing his briefing on the AZORIAN program by agency personnel. The notes also included the agreed-upon structure of the Hughes/agency cover arrangement. Henley said that these were the details that had been passed on to Howard Hughes in order to secure his approval of the arrangement. Neither Henley nor Gay was sure that the handwritten note had actually been in one of the burglarized safes. Henley acknowledged that she hadn't seen the document for some time and was uncertain who might have had it last.

The missing document set the AZORIAN security team back on their heels. They didn't know who the burglars were or what their objectives might be. One theory was that they were working for either government or business enemies of Howard Hughes, and that they were looking for evidence of criminal wrongdoings. Holliday's notes, if they actually *were* in one of the safes, may have just been a gratuitous find. But even if the burglars did find the note, would they realize its significance? And, if they did, what were they likely to do with the information? Some people even wondered if perhaps the Soviets were behind the operation.

Because of the sensitivity of the document, the CIA was forced to clear members of the Los Angeles Police Department (LAPD) who were conducting the investigation in coordination with the FBI.[8] We went from day to day waiting for the next shoe to drop, hoping without much confidence that the LAPD would honor our request to protect the security of the CIA operation.

———

It wasn't the best situation for the start of a mission that, if uncovered, would certainly inflame the Soviet Union to take action. But what kind of action? Would the Soviets simply demand that we leave the recovery site? Would they commandeer the ship and take it to a Soviet port? Would they simply *sink* the ship? And, with each consideration of what the Soviets might do, we wondered if any U.S. forces would be close enough to help us.

Most of the CIA personnel and contractors on the ship believed that we would essentially be "on our own" during the mission. If William Colby knew about probable U.S. Navy submarine presence during the AZORIAN mission, he never let on. In an interview given by Colby to the authors of *Blind Man's Bluff* many years after he had retired, he was asked what the *Glomar*'s crew would have done if the Soviets had tried to board the ship. He replied, "Probably dodge and weave." He then added, "We had some protection—we had a deal with the Navy. They were just down at Pearl Harbor," where, according to Sontag and Drew, naval intelligence was assiduously monitoring Soviet communications frequencies while the *Glomar* was at sea.[9]

Dodge and weave with up to three miles of pipe and 16 million pounds hanging below you? Probably not. And, having the Navy about 1,800 miles away at Pearl Harbor doesn't sound like much of a deal for ship safety. This whole discussion raises the embarrassing question of whether the CIA senior managers really appreciated the political risks they were taking or the personal danger they were expecting the crew to cope with on their own.

It was obvious (and understandable) that they didn't comprehend many of the technical details of the planned recovery operation, or the physical risks to the crew and the ship associated with some of the possible system failure modes.

When Secretary of the Navy John Warner was given his final premission briefing, I was told that he looked worried and said, "You know you guys are going to be on your own out there, don't you?"

The *HMB-1* submerging in about 160 feet of water in Isthmus Cove off Catalina Island. (Author's Private Collection.)

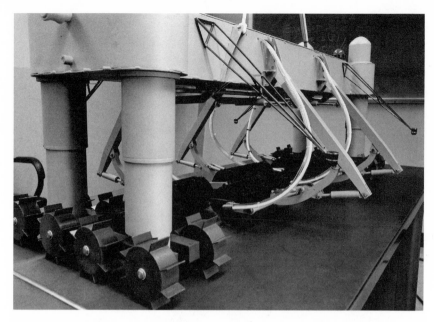

Model of a mining machine built to resemble the capture vehicle. The model was only intended as a possible publicity tool to support the ocean mining cover story in the event that a picture of the capture vehicle itself was exposed. (Author's Private Collection.)

Ott Schick, Lockheed's program manager for the construction of the *HMB-1* and the capture vehicle. (Courtesy of Oscar "Ott" Schick.)

Norm Nelson, one of John Parangosky's most trusted consultants. During the AZORIAN program, Nelson was employed by the Summa Corporation. (Courtesy of Curtis Crooke.)

Hank Van Calcar, senior Honeywell engineer and director of the capture vehicle operations during the recovery mission. (Courtesy of Henry Van Calcar.)

Participants in the formal signing ceremony for Summa
Corporation's acceptance of the *HGE* from Global Marine on
July 21, 1974. *Standing, left to right:* Chuck Goedecke (LMSC),
Chester Davis (Summa), Jim Lesage (Summa), Nadine Henley
(Summa), Bill Gay (Summa), Paul Reeve (Summa), Clint Morris
(Summa), Curtis Crooke (Global Marine). *Kneeling, left to right:*
Pat O'Connell (Honeywell) and Dick Abbey (Honeywell).
(Author's Private Collection.)

The offshore signing ceremony. *Left to right:* Chester Davis, Nadine
Henley, Paul Reeve, and Bill Gay, all from the Summa Corporation.
*Background:* Dave Sharp. (Author's Private Collection.)

The M/V *Bel Hudson* at the target site on July 13, 1974. (Author's Private Collection.)

The injured sailor from the *Bel Hudson* standing on the *Explorer* deck. (Author's Private Collection.)

The *Bel Hudson* lifeboat returning to its ship. (Author's Private Collection.)

Bow of the Soviet ship *Chazhma* in heavy fog. (Author's Private Collection.)

Helicopter taking off from the *Chazhma* helipad. (Author's Private Collection.)

Soviet helicopter during close-in reconnaissance of the *Glomar Explorer.* (Author's Private Collection.)

Aft view of the *SB-10*, a small Soviet trawler converted for use as an AGI intelligence ship. (Author's Private Collection.)

Front-quarter view of the *SB-10*. (Author's Private Collection.)

The *SB-10* crew relaxing on the afterdeck. The woman with the print dress appears to be having her picture taken with the *HGE* as background. (Author's Private Collection.)

A computer-generated image of the capture vehicle with the target in its grasp, right after liftoff. The four jettisoned breakout legs can be seen standing on the ocean bottom. (CGI Illustration Michael White ©2011.)

A computer-generated image showing the damaged capture vehicle with the bow portion of the target in the well of the ship. This image was specially created by Michael White for donation to the CIA's museum in Langley, Virginia. (CGI Illustration Michael White ©2011.)

Global Marine engineers on the ship. *Back row, left to right:* Jim McNary, Charlie Johnson, Sherm Wetmore, Don Borchardt (shore liaison), and John Parsons. *Front row, left to right:* Randy Michaelson, Bob Cooper, John Hicks, and John Owen. (Author's Private Collection.)

Some of the mission engineers from Lockheed, Honeywell, MRI, and Delco who supported the capture vehicle operations. (Author's Private Collection.)

Front page of the *Los Angeles Times*, February 7, 1975. The paper hit the streets just minutes before CIA security officers were able to talk to the editor and try to kill the story. (Courtesy of the *Los Angeles Times*.)

Bill Garner's political cartoon in the *Washington Star News* just days after the Jack Anderson exposé of the AZORIAN program on March 18, 1975. (Courtesy of William Garner.)

John Wayne's visit to the *Glomar Explorer* in 1976. *Far left*, Joe Gates (GMDI contracting officer); *fifth from left*, Bob Bauer (GMI president); *far right*, Don White (GMDI vice president); *second from right*, John Wayne. (Author's Private Collection.)

CIA director William Colby with Dave Sharp in April 1975. (Author's Private Collection.)

# 6

## The Recovery Mission

### En Route to the Target Site

For reporting the daily chronology of the mission, I use some of the comments and information from the deck logs of the *Hughes Glomar Explorer*. The logs are unclassified, written as though the *Explorer* were on a legitimate deep ocean mining mission. This information will be quoted directly.

I'll augment the entries from the ship's logs with notes from my personal journals, my own memory, and the recollections of other crew members about what was taking place each day of the recovery operation. This chronology begins with Day 1 of the mission.

*Day 1 (Thursday, June 20, 1974): A Mysterious Rendezvous*
Just after midnight on June 20, 1974, the *Hughes Glomar Explorer* and its crew of 176 steamed away from Pier E at Long Beach en route to the target site over 3,000 miles away. There are plenty of conspiracy theories about the departure of the *HGE* from Pier E in the middle of the night and a secret rendezvous with mysterious visitors. Some have suggested that the ship departed in darkness for reasons of security, and that helicopters were used to board additional personnel onto the ship after it was safely out of sight of land. The secret visitors were rumored to be special government operatives whose recognition factors were too high to risk their being seen at Pier E.

The rumored explanations for the midnight departure were way off. Security had nothing to do with it. It's just that we needed a high tide to ensure that the heavily loaded *HGE* wouldn't run aground getting out of Long Beach Harbor. As soon as the ship reached international waters, however, it stopped. There was still some unfinished business to attend to.

Shortly after dawn, a large helicopter arrived from the mainland and landed on the helipad. Nearly a dozen occupants got out of the helicopter and joined the ship's captain in the lounge. A helicopter of such size attracted a lot of attention from the crew, and rumors and speculation were rampant.

The real explanation for the activity was fascinating but not clandestine. The program's cover specialists were publicly staging this rendezvous to help bolster the DOMP cover story.

The helicopter was, in fact, bringing corporate officers of the Summa Corporation and their primary contractors—Honeywell, Global Marine, and Lockheed—to the ship for the official white-world acceptance of *HGE* ownership by the Summa Corporation.

The transfer of ownership was conducted in international waters to avoid the taxes that would apply if the transfer had been completed in Long Beach. Walt Logan, chief of the Commercial Operations Division, had taken great pains to ensure that the Los Angeles County tax assessor, Phillip Watson, was aware of the location of this transfer of ownership in order to preclude any dispute over taxation. (Watson accepted the legality of this transfer but didn't give up his quest for taxes.)

Bill Gay, Chester Davis, Jim LeSage, and Paul Reeve were all there to represent the *buyer*, the Summa Corporation. Nadine Henley, Howard Hughes's personal secretary, was also there to represent her boss. Curtis Crooke (Global Marine), Chuck Goedecke (Lockheed), Pat O'Connel and Dick Abbey (both from Honeywell) were there to represent the contractor team that had built the deep ocean mining system for Summa.

When the legal transaction had been completed, a celebratory cake was served and pictures were taken for DOMP publicity purposes. Finally, the visitors climbed back aboard the helicopter and returned to the mainland. The *Hughes Glomar Explorer*, now belonging publicly (if not actually) to the Summa Corporation, continued on its transit to the site of the *K-129*.

*Days 2–12 (June 21–July 2, 1974): En Route to Nodule Test Site*
As soon as the helicopter left, the captain turned the ship westward and we began the 3,000-mile voyage to the target site. The ship was literally a floating city. When filled to capacity, the *HGE* could carry 51,000 barrels of fuel, 400 tons of potable water, 1,028 tons of wash water, and 50,000 gallons of lube oil.

For this voyage, the *HGE* also carried armament. At the headquarters meeting with the Navy, State, and Justice Departments to decide whether the mission would be allowed to proceed, the CIA had acquiesced to the Navy's demand that the *HGE* crew put up a "real fight" if a boarding by a foreign ship was attempted.

But what was a real fight going to entail? Obviously, the *HGE* could not be fitted with deck guns or other weapons that, if observed or used, would clearly compromise the deep ocean mining cover story. *Any* armed resistance, in fact, would be inconsistent with our cover and could potentially endanger the lives of the crew members. The agency had continued to drag its feet with regard to actually putting weapons on the boat.

The foot dragging ended quite abruptly about one week before the ship was scheduled to depart. Colby personally called the AZORIAN program office and restated his opinion that a platoon of marines from nearby Camp Pendleton should be put onboard for the mission. He was told that not only was there no room on the ship for a platoon of marines, but the presence of forty-four soldiers with shaved heads and military bearing would almost surely compromise the commercial cover of the ship if it was observed by the Soviets at sea. Even so, Colby insisted, headquarters had agreed to have some firepower onboard—even if there was no intent to ever use it. He demanded that some action be taken to arm the ship. The program office, of course, acceded.

But where were the weapons going to come from? The WCPO couldn't just requisition government-issue weapons. They'd be really hard to explain on a supposedly *commercial* ship if they were ever discovered by a boarding party. So, with only a few days to go before the mission, our security team fanned out and bought a collection of guns from commercial sources. There wasn't time for compliance with all the usual paperwork for purchase of firearms in Los Angeles, but one of the security team in the WCPO, Brent Sparrow, was a retired LAPD officer. (Sparrow had also been the senior security officer onboard during the *HGE*'s voyage from Sun shipyard in Philadelphia to Pier E in Long Beach, California.) Brent knew the right strings to pull. He, Steve Craig, and Bob James quickly collected a total of eight assorted firearms—shotguns, sporting rifles, etc.—which (I discovered after boarding the ship) were stored along with ammunition and other sporting equipment in two large metal trunks under my bunk. So far as I know, Dale Neuwirth (the mission director), Jack Porter (the CIA security officer on the ship), and I were the only members of the crew who knew about the guns and their location.

James and Craig had also created cover stories to explain the presence of those firearms on a commercial ship—just in case the ship was boarded, the guns were found, and the boarding party wondered, "Why all the fire-power?" The shotguns were ostensibly for skeet shooting off the helicopter pad. James and Craig had also included several clay pigeon launchers and many gross of clay pigeons to lend credibility to this cover story. The sporting rifles were, so the cover story went, for shooting flying fish off the fantail of the ship. It all made sense, in a way. After all, some luxury cruise ships did have skeet-shooting facilities for use off the stern.

Of course, the *HGE* wasn't a cruise ship. And, to complicate matters further, the shotguns in the crate under my bunk were sawed-off shotguns—police riot guns with eighteen-inch barrels—and the only ammunition we had for them was equal quantities of double-ought buckshot and lead slugs. Just the thing for clay pigeons.

The sporting rifles were special, too. Steve and Bob had purchased a couple of high-powered hunting rifles with telescopic sights, and a couple of AR-15s, the sport version of the Army's M-16 automatic weapons. Just the thing for shooting flying fish off the fantail.

No one was complaining, though. The cover story for having the weapons onboard may have been a little weak, but for an emergency situation in which we might really have to repel a boarding attempt, those weapons were a professional's choice. Even Captain "Buck" Dietzen from the chief of naval operations staff—who had insisted that the *HGE* be prepared to fight off a boarding attempt—would have been pleased and impressed.

———

The *HGE* was under the command of Captain Tom Gresham, a no-nonsense, politically conservative, Global Marine veteran who spoke often and vehemently of his conviction that Henry Kissinger was a Soviet spy. Gresham had a deck department of twelve sailors. The first mate was James Drahos. Ron Howell was the chief steward in charge of three cooks, a baker, and all the other help necessary to feed and maintain the living quarters for a 176-man crew.

The Global Marine mining crew that included the crane operators, welders, pipe handlers, and roughnecks was headed up by my old friend from the *Glomar II*, Leon Blurton. Tech reps from Western Gear, Honeywell, Delco Electronics, MRI, and Lockheed had been hired by Summa and Global Marine for maintenance and repair of the major subsystems on the ship.

We had fourteen divers onboard, most of whom were former Navy SEALs. We also had a meteorologist, a retired Navy officer who had been trained at the Navy's Fleet Numerical Weather Central in Monterey.

The government management team included the following:

- Mission director Dale Neuwirth, a senior manager from one of the government's national laboratories who was signed up as a CIA contract employee for this mission;
- Deputy mission director Jack Sparkman, a career CIA employee;
- Deputy for recovery, myself, a career CIA employee;
- Deputy for exploitation Earnest Ruggles, and his assistant, Jack Nichols, both career CIA employees;
- Deputy for operations Fred Traner, a former Navy submarine captain;
- Deputy for handling, an expert on radiation safety from one of the government's national laboratories; and
- "Administrative officer" Jack Porter, a senior CIA security officer.

One man was missing from the deputy for recovery's engineering team. CIA engineer Geary Yost remained at headquarters after the loss of his son. Yost had been participating in the integrated systems testing, and he told Parangosky that he was prepared—and wanted—to go on the mission. But I had voted against it. I wasn't all that sanguine about the safety of the mission, and I felt that Yost's family had gone through enough pain already.

All government employees on the ship were using alias identities. This was a necessary by-product of the need to conceal all government involvement in the DOMP. In the event the boat was boarded and we were captured, we were hoping that our government and CIA affiliations would remain unknown.

The security people were very rigorous with regard to these identity changes. They maintained a safe-house apartment in Long Beach primarily for the purpose of changing identities. The apartment was a required stopping place for all government personnel going on the mission. When you walked in, all your personal belongings were taken from you and inspected. All name-bearing credit cards, driver's licenses, clothes with monograms, etc., were taken away and placed in storage. They were replaced with a new set of personal papers, credit cards (real ones), and other types of ID information with the alias name. An individual walked into the apartment with one identity. When he left, he was a different man.

We knew we'd have about two weeks to work on system checkout and training on the way to the test site. The *HGE* was no speed demon. It was capable of about 10 knots but usually sailed at an average speed of about 9.5

knots. We were glad to have the extra time, though. There were still many things to do in preparation for the recovery operation.

Morale on the ship was over the top. Everyone, from the mission director to the six young stewards responsible for cleaning the staterooms, was confident that we could pull it off. We'd come so far in such a short time, we could feel the momentum of the program. An anonymous contributor to the AZORIAN program history that the CIA released (in redacted form) in 2010 wrote:

> We could do anything. Let Headquarters give us a last-minute change of targets—with this crew and this beautiful ship, no task was too difficult. Mission impossible? Nonsense! "Impossible" was not in our vocabulary. Moments like this must contain the true meaning of team spirit, that extra ingredient that hardware will never possess. To experience it once is enough for a career.[1]

The next morning, Dale Neuwirth called all the CIA crew together for a meeting in the control center. When we got there, he asked how many of us had read and initialed the contingency plan for the operation. I've already remarked on what I thought of the plan, and I had to admit that I hadn't broken the seal on my copy. Neuwirth's first formal order to his staff was to read, understand, and initial the contingency plan. After that, he said, we could discuss it—and make possible modifications. I started reading. I can't remember all the details of the plan for attempted boarding. As best as I can recall, however, the guidance went something like this:

- Any request by a foreign ship to board people onto the HGE would be refused, citing the owner's (Howard Hughes's) concerns about company proprietary information and equipment.
- If boarding was attempted by small auxiliary boats, the HGE fire hoses would be used to discourage the effort.
- If boarding was attempted directly from a warship, the HGE fire hoses would be used to make crew movement on the adversary's deck very difficult.
- If the foreign ship continued boarding attempts, the firearms stowed under my bunk would be distributed to those divers with previous military training. They would use them to forcibly repel boarders.
- If the boarding of the ship appeared unavoidable and imminent, we would jettison—out of sight of our adversary—all classified documents in the control center. (Classified documents were stored in

steel mesh drawers with latching covers. Disposal was simply a matter of dropping the drawers down through a chute that led directly to the ocean.)

Resisting an attempt to board the ship from the air was pretty straightforward. We had placed some crates and boxes on the helipad, making it very difficult for a helicopter to land on the ship. The appearance was that the helipad was being used for temporary storage space. (After all, we weren't expecting any shipment of supplies by helicopter out in the central North Pacific Ocean.)

These instructions left a lot unsaid. For instance, what should we do if a foreign ship with boarding intentions began to fire back at our divers? Should the divers continue to test their wills against the firepower of a nuclear submarine? Surely a losing effort. On the other hand, if we laid down arms and permitted the boarding, how would we explain the fact that we had such weapons onboard in the first place? Would the boarding party buy our story that we just happened to have riot guns onboard for shooting skeet? And that the high-powered hunting rifles with telescopic sights were intended for target practice against flying fish? And what about the AR-15 automatic rifles? I kept wondering, "What were they thinking when they wrote this contingency plan?"

The next day, Neuwirth called his staff back to his office for another meeting. He asked if we had all finished reading the plan and signed off on it. We had. He said, "Fine. Now forget that plan. I'm going to tell you what the real contingency plan is going to be." He continued, explaining the real plan in detail. Here's the thrust of it:

If a boarding was attempted by a foreign ship, we would protest and use fire hoses—just as spelled out in the original contingency plan. However, if the adversary crew manned on-deck weapons and demanded they be allowed to board the ship, we would remind them that they were violating international law, that we would protest to an international court, and we would let them board. *We would not use the firearms stowed on our ship.* The boarding party would be treated civilly and escorted through the ship to verify that it was engaged in a legitimate mining operation. As in the original plan, all classified documents would be jettisoned prior to any actual boarding.

If, in fact, we were boarded, the new contingency plan became more improvisational. (Improvisation is a lot easier when you're at sea.) Neuwirth's plan went beyond just treating the boarding party with civility. The officers of the boarding ship would be invited to a suitable place for a meeting with the *HGE*'s principal officers, Captain Gresham and the mission director. Vodka and champagne would be available for refreshment, and we would try to establish a rapport with the boarding party (most likely Soviet, we assumed). A tour of the ship would be offered (including the control center only if necessary) and, hopefully, the Soviet officers would return to their ship—perhaps with a couple of cases of Russia's best vodka as a gift from their new American friends engaged in deep ocean mining experiments.

I liked the plan, but where were we going to get the vodka? Liquor wasn't allowed aboard Global Marine boats. As it turned out, I had underestimated (again) the resourcefulness and imagination of the WCPO security team. Steve Craig and Bob James had figured that a locker full of champagne and vodka would be a useful backup to the contingency plan. It couldn't be just any vodka, though. To impress the Soviets, they reasoned that the vodka must be good Russian vodka—and it must have Russian tax stamps to verify the country of origin. In 1974, in the middle of the Cold War, genuine imported vodka from Russia was not commonly available. Craig and James found a source, though, and spirited six cases onto the ship two days before departure. The vodka and champagne filled up an entire wall locker in my stateroom, only a few feet away from the crated firearms. Plan A and Plan B—right next to each other. So, that was the real contingency plan. We liked it. Understandably, it was never documented.

At the time, I believed that Neuwirth must have worked out this alternative contingency plan with Parangosky before we ever left port, and that it was never the CIA's intention that the crew go to war if the Soviets attempted to board the ship. Now, I find myself questioning whether Parangosky, Duckett, or Colby knew anything at all about the revised contingency plans. In conversations with some of the personnel who were in the headquarters program office during the mission, they all denied having had any knowledge of the locker full of vodka on the ship. The whole idea might have originated with the WCPO security team and been briefed to the mission director right before departure. Whether or not any high-level CIA officers at headquarters knew of the liquor locker as a backup to the riot guns is not an easy question to get an answer to. Dale Neuwirth, John Parangosky, Carl Duckett, and William Colby are all dead—and they're not talking.

———

Although we didn't expect it, we knew that there was always the chance that we would be boarded by a team intent on returning the *Glomar Explorer* to a Soviet port, or some other foreign port—the scenario that befell the USS *Pueblo* four years earlier. If that happened, we knew we'd be unable to communicate with headquarters by radio. We needed some way to signal that the ship was no longer under our control. The chosen method for signaling was green paint. We had bought about twelve quarts of a luminous green paint before leaving Pier E. These cans of paint were distributed, one can each, to certain members of the crew. If the ship was commandeered, each of those volunteers would attempt to spread the contents of his paint can on some part of the ship that would be clearly visible from the air—the helipad, the roof of the bridge, the forward main deck, etc. The paint could be detected easily by a reconnaissance aircraft or satellite. That would be the signal that we needed whatever help the U.S. government could provide. Just what that help might consist of, we didn't know—and we hoped we'd never have to find out.

———

Rumors about just what form that help might take had filtered through the crew prior to the mission. The story had spread that the CIA had made provisions to ensure that the ship would never be captured and returned to a Soviet port with hard evidence of intended espionage aboard. According to the rumors, explosive charges had been secretly planted into the bulkheads at each corner of the moon pool. If the Soviets captured the ship, the charges would be detonated by the CIA, sinking the boat within minutes.

The theory was preposterous, of course. Even if one assumed that the agency had such a plan of self-destruction, who would have done the actual implanting of the explosives in the bulkheads? Not Sun Shipbuilding—none of their employees were even cleared. Not Global Marine—those workers would never have installed such a self-destruct system without warning their friends on the "A" crew. The security for the implantation of explosives would not have held together.

Even so, many of the Global Marine crew took this rumor very seriously. Jack "Black Jack" Nichols—the principal instructor in the training classes for postrecovery exploitation of the submarine—was confronted by concerned crew members during one of his training sessions before the ship's departure for the mission. Nichols had been a Navy submariner for seventeen years when the CIA recruited him as an exploitation trainer for this mission. Nichols knew submarines inside and out—and he could read and write Russian, to boot.

These concerned crew members were not timid guys. They were all volunteers. They knew there'd be risks involved during the exploitation of the recovered submarine—especially if it turned out to be radioactive. They accepted those risks, but they didn't like the idea of being blown out of the water to prevent a foreign government from taking over the *Explorer*. They trusted Nichols, but they were looking for some honest answers.

Before the start of the training class, they demanded to know if there was any truth to the rumors they'd heard about CIA plans for disposing of the evidence if the ship were to be boarded, commandeered, and steered toward a foreign port. Nichols asked the rest of the training faculty to leave the area. Then he locked the doors to the facility and talked to the crew members at a highly classified level about the government's confidence in the cover story as well as the contingency plans that would apply in case the Soviets attempted to take over the ship. The crew had lots of doubts and many questions. They wanted to believe that the government would ensure their safety, but they were clearly shaken up by the stories they'd heard.

After a while, Nichols was able to calm down the crew. He reminded them that he himself had a wife and two young daughters—and there was no way that he'd be participating in the mission if he believed his own life would be put in jeopardy. The exploitation crew had an informal vote and decided that they'd stay with the program. Nichols unlocked the doors to the training center and exploitation classes resumed. The CIA had dodged a bullet, but very few government people ever learned about the incident.

———

During the trip to the target site, Honeywell's Hank Van Calcar—who, like many of the design engineers, had agreed to join the mission crew—continued training the capture vehicle operators using the simulator and target model that were still onboard the ship. For the operators inside the control center sitting at their mission consoles, the simulation was very realistic, and the stress level for the operators during the training sessions was high.

Van Calcar, the designer of the simulator, had incorporated the effects of all the ship's systems (heave compensator, heavy lift system, etc.) and ship dynamics (heave, roll, pitch, etc.) into the simulation. Sensors on the claw were modeled realistically. It was fitted with CCTVs that imaged the target model, allowing the operators to see realistic video presentations in the control center. Sonar returns were also displayed. The simulator's computer had target cross-section profile data from a scale model that had been built by the National Photographic Interpretation Center using the photographic imagery from the target surveys. A computer program calculated the profile each sonar would be scanning and displayed them on the sonar monitor in the control center.

The simulations ran in real time. Each second, the equations of motion of the ship, the pipe string, and the CV were updated and the integration gain was set to provide real-time response. To model realistic sea state motion, canned superposition of ship heave motion was used, enabling the operators to get used to looking at data with some low-frequency disturbance on it. The lift pipe model realistically simulated the pendulum motions of the pipe and CV, as well as the low-frequency vertical oscillations. All of the mechanical elements of the CV were simulated—breakout legs, tines, thrusters, etc. In addition, the soil dynamics were modeled in order to simulate the loads on the breakout legs and the dynamic forces of the breakout itself. All of the actuators, pressure sensors, and angle sensors were incorporated in the computer modeling. The simulator was actually a true closed-loop system test facility that could be used as a real-time trainer. The test manager had the ability to fail any combination of sensors, transducers, valves, etc., for the purpose of contingency training.

A side benefit of the simulator was that it gave us the opportunity to check out all the operational software. In the process of the training, it became very apparent that many of the documented procedures for bottom operations just wouldn't work. Some of those procedures were actually rewritten on the way to the target site.

By the time the capture vehicle operators had gone through several target recovery sequences with the simulator, they were fully trained and looking forward to the real thing. After the mission, some of the operators acknowledged that the actual mission operations had been less stressful than the simulations.

———

While Hank was training the CV operators, Dr. Earnest Ruggles and his deputy, Jack Nichols, used the time to continue training crew members in the techniques for recognizing, recovering, cleaning, and preserving objects of intelligence interest from the recovered submarine. Ruggles had his own dedicated personnel who were already skilled in these techniques. A few of them were trained to read Russian. Nevertheless, it was expected that once the recovery had been completed, the exploitation effort would be joined by all available crew members, including engineers and technicians from the recovery team.

We didn't know what the radiation problem might be during the exploitation. We knew that the *K-129* carried nuclear missiles—and possibly nuclear torpedoes—but we didn't know what the levels and nature of the residual radiation on the target might be. We were fully prepared for all cases. Radiation suits and masks were available for everybody working in the well of the ship. Educating personnel in the use of this protective clothing was of the highest priority. Training for radiation safety was conducted by the deputy for handling, who had many years of experience working with nuclear materials at one of the government's national laboratories.

In addition to the radiation levels, however, there were other significant uncertainties. The *K-129* had been underwater for over six years. The ambient temperature of the water was essentially a constant 32 degrees at that depth, so decay of perishable artifacts on the sub would have been minimal. However, the pressure at the target depth of 16,700 feet was over 7,400 psi—about 500 atmospheres. The effect of the pressure increase on electronic components, paper, and human bodies during the *K-129*'s descent was uncertain.

All items of intelligence value found on the recovered submarine would have to be cleaned, preserved, and stored as quickly as possible after their discovery. The *HGE* had seven large vans onboard that had been designed for exploitation functions such as crew dress-out, photography, cleaning, packaging, and refrigeration. Two other vans were available for office space and for storage. To aid the exploitation personnel in recognizing the nature and significance of recovered artifacts, courses in the Russian language were offered.

———

Bion Henderson and Tom Stockton of Delco Electronics were still working frantically trying to complete the software that would allow us to automatically adjust the spring rate of the heave compensator system to prevent the capture vehicle and the lifting pipe from going into a vertical resonance. Excessive vertical motions of the CV on the end of the pipe would raise the stress level in the lifting pipe itself and could make the final landing of the capture vehicle over the target impossible.

Here's how we wanted the computer program to work: At the target site, the *HGE* would deploy two (a primary and a spare) wave rider buoys. Continuous time histories of wave-induced accelerations at the buoys would be transmitted to the ship. These data would show how much wave energy, and at what frequencies, the ship was being exposed to. Plugging this information into an equation that included *HGE* model test data, deployed pipe length, and the load being carried at the end of the pipe string would allow us to calculate the optimum heave compensator air volume for minimizing vertical oscillations of the capture vehicle.

We hadn't been worried about vertical resonance during the integrated systems testing because we never had more than a few thousand feet of lifting pipe supporting the capture vehicle. The resonance period of the pipe and CV under those conditions was so short that almost all wave-induced vertical motion (heave) at those frequencies was essentially filtered out by the ship's huge mass. During the mission, however, the pipe length would be as long as 16,700 feet, and the load on the end of the pipe would include the target in addition to the claw. For these conditions, the resonant period of the pipe and payload would be much longer, and the *HGE* would not be filtering out all the vertical energy. Proper adjustment of the heave compensator to prevent resonance could become critically important.

The computer program we were trying to develop would seem trivial today. In 1974, though, the two Honeywell HC360 computers our engineers were using had less processing power than a modern cell phone. We were sweating to get the program completed before we got to the site.

———

During routine maintenance operations on the way to the site, we discovered problems from saltwater corrosion on the capture vehicle. The pan and tilt mounts for the cameras and sonars were deteriorating. The mounts for the high-resolution search sonars on the fore and aft ends of the capture vehicle seemed to be going especially fast. Over the period of a week, all of the moving mechanisms on the CV were inspected, refurbished, and tested by Lockheed and Honeywell engineers with help from the Global Marine riggers.

Assorted problems were also showing up during testing of some of the ship's systems. The heavy lift, heave compensator, and pipe-handling systems all required last-minute attention during the trip to the target site. We could only wonder how well these systems would hold up when actual recovery operations began. For all the hassle we were having, we knew that it would only get worse once we arrived at the site.

———

In spite of all the activity on the boat, there were still opportunities to marvel at the beauty of the sea and the sky thousands of miles away from any cities and the noise and commotion that go with them. One of the divers, a former SEAL, would spend about an hour in meditation on the foredeck every evening at sunset. I admired him for being able to break away from the routine—to preserve some time every day for contemplation of things more spiritually significant than recovering sunken submarines.

I tried to emulate him in my own way by writing poetry. My efforts were hampered by the fact that I wasn't much of a poet. Still, it made me feel better and provided a way to escape the routine of the ship. During one particularly beautiful sunset at sea, I wrote:

A deep blue color, but soft looking,
Not with the bright gemlike highlights of the sea when the wind spurs on the
    waves,
But a quiet steady blue, like an undulating, rather than rolling, carpet,
Beneath which we can imagine so many mysteries.
Not feeling quite safe on top of it,
But excited by the unfathomable secrets beneath.
On a day like this, the sea seems kind, and we take heart.
We gain a little confidence in our ability to work within—never master—the
    environment.

Looking at this poem today, I'm embarrassed. Even so, reading it also brings back the very clear and vivid memory of just how I felt on that ship on that evening.

*Day 14 (Wednesday, July 3, 1974): En Route to Nodule Test Site*
From the ship's log:

> Noon Position: Lat. 39°–29'N, Long. 174°–52.50'W
> 0400—Overcast, occasional light drizzle, slight SW'ly sea, moderate swell
> 0753—Reduced speed to 50 rpm/shaft, commenced test and calibration of uninterruptible power.
> 0820—Test and cal. of uninterruptible power completed, vessel returning to normal power levels, full power to port & stbd shafts, vessel returning to navigational speed.
> 2400—Vessel riding easily in low W'ly confused swell. Lookout posted on bow, running lights burning brightly. Vis. Good.

We were about two days from the target site, and we were beginning to think about schedule, sequence of operations, and—most important—the weather, which really controlled what we could do and when. At the 0700 weather briefing, our meteorologist, Dick Gilmartin, advised us that a front would be coming through tomorrow afternoon with six- to eight-foot waves. That was no big deal. But, he added, we could be seeing eleven to thirteen feet of swell by the morning of July 5 if an incipient low-pressure area at 35N, 171E increased its cyclogenesis. *That* would be trouble. From our January sea trial experience, we knew that we couldn't attempt to open the well gates with those sea states. It wouldn't stop us from deploying the beacons and transponders required for the automatic station-keeping system, though.

On arriving at the estimated location of the target, our procedures called for an acoustic beacon to be immediately deployed. That beacon would be used in conjunction with four hydrophone receivers on the four corners of the *HGE* hull to create a short baseline position reference system. The short baseline system was accurate to about 2 percent of water depth, or about 340 feet in a water depth of 17,000 feet. That was good enough to guide the ship's position during the deployment of transponders for the more accurate long baseline system. Six acoustic transponders would be deployed in a large circle (about four nautical miles in diameter) around the target perimeter. With pulse data from any three of the bottom transponders the position of the ship with respect to the transponder field could be calculated to within a ten-foot radius. We were estimating about forty-eight hours for completion of beacon and transponder deployment for the short and long baseline reference systems. We hoped that the predicted weather would be more favorable for well gate operations by then.

———

In the meantime, Chuck Canby, the Global Marine naval architect, had developed what we hoped would be very low-risk procedures for opening the well gates. Chuck had been on the frightening sea trial off Los Angeles in January when the gates had broken loose and put the ship in real danger of breaking. He shared the whole crew's concern about not wanting to repeat that experience—especially when hundreds of miles away from the nearest friendly port. Canby's ground rules stipulated:

- The gate-locking pawls would be cocked and ready to close before starting the gate ballasting.
- Four banks of the gate deballasting air would be precharged so that the gates could be quickly deballasted (made positively buoyant) if the action became too violent.
- People would be available to man all stations and air manifolds during the operation.
- Divers would be suited and on standby for whatever.

At the 1930 mission director's meeting, Gilmartin told us that the waves on July 5 might not exceed six feet. The low-pressure area off to the southeast had not developed as fully as feared in the morning briefing. This was good news. We crossed our fingers.

*Day 15 (Thursday, July 4, 1974): En Route to Nodule Test Site*
From the ship's log:

> Noon Position: Lat. 40°–02.0'N, Long. 179°–49.5'W
> 0400—Light overcast, light air, smooth sea. Low SW'ly swell.
> 0800—Overcast and cloudy. Distant showers.
> 1301—Commence backing down for approach to Site.
> 1306—Arrive nodule test site, beacon away
> 1310—Control assigned to aft bridge
> 1822—Completed Sat. Nav. location of the SBS beacon
> 2350—Change hdg. to 045° for weather.
> Positioning in auto-SBS. Vessel steady in slight sea. Vis. Good.

At 1301, with the ship still about a mile from the target site, the captain started backing down the main propellers. We had gotten a SATNAV fix (remember, no GPS in those days) a few minutes before, and the final approach was with dead reckoning. When we reached the estimated closest point of approach, an acoustic beacon was thrown overboard for use with the short baseline position reference system.

Five hours later, at 1822, we calculated the precise location of the beacon with another SATNAV fix. Now we knew where we were with respect to the target, and we could start deploying the six transponders around the perimeter of the site. By 1901 we had deployed the first transponder and were heading to the location for the second drop.

While deploying the transponders and confirming our position, the Western Gear engineers were bringing the heavy lift system up on line. All of the forty-eight high-pressure hydraulic pumps were readied and checked out to the 3,800 psi relief valve pressure. If all went well, we thought we'd be able to start the undocking operation the next day, July 5.

Not so fast. At the 1930 mission director's meeting, our meteorologist predicted eight to nine feet of combined sea and swell. That wave height was just over the edge of what we considered acceptable for well gate opening. With the prospect of improving weather on the sixth, we decided to hold off flooding the well for twenty-four hours.

## Recovery Operations

*Day 16 (Friday, July 5, 1974): At the Nodule Test Site*
From the ship's log:

0000—Holding in SBS auto, nodule test site

0107—Heading to wave rider buoy drop site

0145—Launch LBS transponder, under way to wave rider buoy site

0315—Wave rider hung up on bow.

0545—Workboat in water.

0715—Heave-to to retrieve workboat.

1122—5th transponder dead. Under way to 6th transponder site.

2000—Overcast and cloudy, continuous light drizzle, visibility fair.

2330—Under way to calibration point #7

Vessel riding easily in slight sea and SW'ly low / moderate swell.

Vis. Approx. ½ mi.


All day was spent deploying transponders and wave riders, and calibrating the LBS grid. The beacons and transponders operated on the bottom of the ocean. They were essentially a weighted battery pack connected to a slightly buoyant electronics package. The two were connected by a tether about thirty feet long. To deploy a beacon or transponder, the system was suspended by a crane from a pad eye on its electronics package, with the battery pack on the end of the thirty-foot tether hanging below. When the ship was in the correct position, the package was lowered until the battery was underwater and only the electronics package was visible. At that time, the crane operator would release the beacon (or transponder) so it could sink the three miles to the ocean bottom. The battery pack rested on the bottom, with the electronics package and acoustic transducer hovering about thirty feet above. These systems had been used for many years and were quite reliable—even when working under the high pressures at that depth.

The wave riders were a little more complicated. The electronics package, consisting of the accelerometers and a transmitter, was tethered with a polyester cable to a flotation buoy. The flotation buoy was connected to an anchor and anchor cable that extended from the surface to the bottom of the ocean. Each of the wave riders was essentially held in location with a three-mile-long cable anchored to the ocean bottom. Deployment of the wave riders was more complicated, as well. The crane operator had to hold the wave rider electronics package over the side of the ship while the surface flotation device deployed its anchor and cable. When the anchor reached bottom, the crane operator released the wave rider. The surface position of the flotation device was influenced by the effect of current on the anchor cable, but the wave rider instrumentation package, loosely tethered to the flotation device, was free to move in the orbital motions created by the passing waves.

The first wave rider deployment was a problem. The polyester tether connecting the wave rider to the anchor flotation drifted into the forward bow thruster of the ship. A workboat with divers onboard had to be deployed. In fifteen minutes, though, they had the problem resolved. The rest of the transponder and wave rider deployments went without incident except for one transponder that had a dead battery pack.

We had spent the entire day running the ship around the target site deploying and calibrating instrumentation devices. It was a dreary day, with the ship's whistle sounding fog signals most of the time.

*Day 17 (Saturday, July 6, 1974)*

The ship continued calibration procedures for the transponder grid on the ocean bottom. We knew the geographic coordinates of the target exactly from the *Glomar II* survey mission. But we only knew the precise coordinates of the *HGE* when we were able to get a reading from a passing navigation satellite. We had to calibrate the transponder grid so that we could continuously estimate the ship's position with respect to the target using the grid's acoustic signals.

These were slow and occasionally boring days. The fog was so thick that we never saw a horizon. Visibility was usually about one mile or less. There was nothing to look at over the rail of the ship except the ever-present albatrosses—or gooney birds—that flew around the ship looking for garbage.

After a meal, many of the crew members would line up on the ship's rail outside the mess hall for a cigarette and some small talk. Looking out at the sea, we'd occasionally see a couple of gooney birds fighting over an apple core. The only other thing to watch was the raw sewage being pumped out of the ship. You *know* that things were dull when the only thing to watch in the whole ocean was raw sewage being emptied into the ocean. Occasionally, the conversations were interrupted by comments like "Jeezus! Look at the size of *that* one! That guy must have been constipated for a week!" Such were the intellectual discussions of the crew while looking out at a gray ocean with no horizon.

*Day 18 (Sunday, July 7, 1974)*

The survey of the ocean bottom around the target area was completed today. The results were generally consistent with the earlier data taken from the *Glomar II* in 1970. We had a pretty good idea just where the target would be in our positioning grid. That was all good news, since the idea of dragging the capture vehicle around the ocean in a search pattern was really unattractive. Besides, the side-looking search sonars hadn't performed all that well during our integrated system testing. The side-lookers were so named because they radiated a vertical fan beam at a glancing angle to the bottom. What we'd be looking for was not a bright return from the target but an area of *no* return—a shadow—beyond the target. This shadow area would obviously be larger if the illuminating source (our sonar) was close to the bottom. So, there was a trade-off between getting the most effective search results from the sonar and running the risk of bouncing the capture vehicle off the bottom. Thinking about the challenge of a search operation was always guaranteed to make the CV operators in the control center nervous.

It looked like we might be able to start operations tomorrow. A weather meeting was scheduled for 1100. If the forecast was favorable, we'd start the CV wet testing in preparation for undocking.

### Day 19 (Monday, July 8, 1974)

The long-term weather prediction was encouraging, and it was time to start operations. At 0817, we started flooding the well. When the water level in the well was equal to the level outside the ship, the well gates were vented until they became neutrally buoyant. When they started banging around a little bit in the guides, the command to open the gates was given.

Each gate had to open 100 feet. Everything went well for the aft gate, but the forward gate stopped when the gauge indicated it was open only 85 feet. It looked like we'd have to put divers in the water to find out what the blockage was. Fortunately, prior to starting diver ops, a faulty gauge for the forward gate was discovered. In fact, the forward gate *had* opened the full 100 feet. Good news (especially for the divers).

Once gates were confirmed open, the docking legs gradually lowered the capture vehicle about 50 feet, putting the deck of the claw under water and permitting the wet check of the CV systems to be initiated.

### Day 20 (Tuesday, July 9, 1974)

By early morning we were progressing with the wet check of the capture vehicle, but things weren't going as smoothly as we'd hoped. The mounts for the aft docking leg cameras—used to show the underwater relative motions of the docking legs and the CV support pins during docking/undocking operations—had corroded badly again and were in no shape for an undocking attempt. They were replaced by the divers during the day.

One of the lights on the CV had also gone intermittent. It would go on for about ten minutes and then go off for a while before turning back on.

As an omen of problems to come, the pressure transducer on beam 8 of the CV failed. These pressure transducers were the only instrumentation we had to indicate what the total load on each beam was. Without those transducers, the process of trying to equalize the loads on all the beams and davits while we were preparing to lift the target would just be guesswork.

At 1300, Captain Gresham signaled for a fire drill. We had known that it was scheduled, but with all the problems we were having with the capture vehicle it was a frustrating distraction.

*Day 21 (Wednesday, July 10, 1974)*
At 0800, we started lowering the claw on the docking legs again, holding at fifty-six feet to configure the chain-link "net" that would be used to surround and support the top of the *K-129*'s number 3 missile tube. The photographs of the target suggested that the structure might be somewhat unstable, and we didn't want to take a chance of losing it. Everything, every little task, always took longer than we anticipated. This was no surprise for the Global Marine crew, but it was all new and unexpected for the CIA, Lockheed, and Honeywell guys onboard.

By early afternoon, we'd completed the wet check and had the docking legs down to 100 feet and holding. The next step was to complete the erection of the CV's tripod bridle and connect it to the end of the lifting pipe.

Before that could be completed, though, the forward well gate worked loose and started banging around in the guides. The gate was closed about six feet to allow access to the number 1 ballast tank. The tank was reballasted and the gate moved back into the full-open position. By 1750, the bridle was erected.

We were ready, finally, to think about undocking. As always, the long-range weather forecast would dictate the start of that sensitive operation. Our meteorologist started working on a thirty-six-hour and a seventy-two-hour forecast for wave and swell height. The decision to undock would be made after the weather briefing tomorrow morning.

———

During the day, one of the Lockheed engineers, Bob Mlady, suffered a mild heart attack. Mlady had volunteered to work in the pipe storage hold of the ship while he wasn't working on the capture vehicle. His condition was not considered to be serious, but we needed to find someone who could do his job. The call went out for a volunteer to work in the storage hold. We needed someone who could count and could stand on his feet for twelve hours at a time.

*Day 22 (Thursday, July 11, 1974)*

Ironically, just when we finally had the capture vehicle and all systems ready to begin descent, the weather turned bad on us. The 0900 forecast for thirty-six hours ahead called for seaways from seven to nine feet high, swell from four to seven feet, and fifteen to twenty-five knots of wind. The seventy-two-hour forecast called for heavy rain, fifteen to thirty knots of wind, and nine to twelve feet of combined sea height. The fog was thick and continuous. Visibility was down to one-quarter mile, and the ship's fog whistle was being sounded continuously.

Although the wave height on this day was within the limits for an undocking operation, the prospect of getting combined sea heights of up to twelve feet for the thirty-six- to seventy-two-hour period ahead of us was scary. Sea heights of that magnitude could produce ship roll angles of five degrees or more with *no* weight suspended from the derrick. The 2,000-ton capture vehicle and additional lift pipe that would be suspended from the lifting yokes—about 100 feet above the ship's center of buoyancy—after undocking would have an additional influence on roll by raising the center of gravity (CG) of the ship and reducing the roll stiffness. Since the derrick gimbals would only permit roll motions of up to ±8.5 degrees and pitch motions up to ±5.0 degrees (beyond which bending moments would be inserted directly into the lift pipe), we were very reluctant to see how close to the envelope we could push things. We decided to hold, with the docking legs lowered to 105 feet, until the anticipated storm had passed.

———

Bear in mind that in 1974 a seventy-two-hour forecast was little more than an educated guess. The Navy's Fleet Numerical Weather Central (FNWC) in Monterey, California, had the best weather prediction capability in the world, and they had already made some great strides in the direction of computer-based weather prediction models. Still, by their own estimation at the time, a three-day forecast had only about a 50/50 chance of being right.

On the ship, we were still leaning heavily on the recommendations of our own onboard meteorologist whom FNWC had helped us select. We had used several meteorologists during the sea trials and IST and found only one who was willing to go out on a limb and make a seventy-two-hour forecast that might differ from an FNWC computer-generated prediction. He was a retired Navy officer, Dick Gilmartin, who had been trained at FNWC. We decided that Gilmartin was the guy we wanted on the mission and we were lucky enough to get him. On several occasions, FNWC cabled the ship voicing strong disagreement with Gilmartin's prediction. Our man stuck to his guns. He had a great forecasting record for the entire mission, and the recovery crew considered him one of the most valuable members of the team.

On one occasion, I saw Gilmartin walking out of the weather room shaking his head, obviously disturbed. I asked him if he had a problem I should know about. He explained that he had just received a cable from FNWC. As it turned out, he had observed eight-foot waves at the target site and reported that information to FNWC via the National Weather Service. FNWC came back with a note stating that he must be mistaken about the measurement. Their computer model—in which they had full confidence— clearly predicted waves of three to four feet, and they were sticking by that estimate.

On another occasion, during our daily staff meeting in the mission director's office, I pressed Gilmartin for a four-day prediction on wave heights. We had been holding off the initiation of certain capture vehicle operations until we could get a high-confidence forecast of good weather for at least several days. The forecasts from FNWC had not been encouraging. Gilmartin, however, felt that the four-day outlook was pretty good. I asked him why he disagreed with FNWC's more pessimistic view. He said, "Well, the isobars and upper air currents on their charts don't look very convincing." He added, "They lack character." *Character?* What the hell did that have to do with weather prediction? I didn't understand his reasons, but I had a lot of confidence in Gilmartin. We decided to initiate the operations. As it turned out, Gilmartin had been right about the weather. As usual.

————

We also had some good news today. Bob Mlady, the Lockheed engineer who had suffered a heart attack the day before, was feeling much better.

*Day 23 (Friday, July 12, 1974)*
From the ship's log:

> 0000—Positioning in Auto-LBS. Continuing tests on mining system.
> 0400—Fog. Mist. Continuous sounding of fog signals.
> 0945—Intermittent ASK failures.
> 1000—ASK receiving no useful positioning data.
> 1150—Commence heading change to reduce roll & pitch and reduce noise in ASK system. Vessel pitching four degrees and rolling six degrees max. at times due to swells from two different directions.

Lookout posted on bridge, fog signals sounded on whistle—vis. ¼ to ½ mi.

1500—Long SW'ly swell to 12 ft. Considerable stress on docking legs.

2000—Large seas causing increasing pitching motion. Malestrom [*sic*] in docking well, docking legs moving actively. ASK acoustics overwhelmed by vessel noise. No mining activity. Continuous fog.

2400—Occasional rolling & pitching of 3° to 4°, with occ'l 12" to 15' swell. Fog signals sounded on whistle. Vis. Approx. ¼ mi.

ASK inoperative due to noise in water, holding position manually.

No mining activity.

We were really in an uncomfortable situation. The ASK became intermittent in the morning, due mainly to ship noise—a bad bearing in the aft docking leg was making so much noise that the acoustic return signals from the transponders on the bottom were drowned out—but also to the increasing noise of the growing seas. By noon, the ASK was completely inoperative. The mates were holding ship attitude and location as well as they could by manual operation of the ASK joystick.

As the seas picked up, they created havoc in the well of the ship. Huge twenty-foot waves were crashing back and forth in the well, putting extremely high stress on the docking legs that were absorbing all the dynamic loads from a 2,000-ton capture vehicle that was hanging 100 feet below the *HGE* while the ship was pitching up to four degrees and rolling as much as six degrees. One of the mates entered into the ship's log that the waves were creating a "Malestrom [*sic*]" in the docking well. That was about right. This was a phenomenon we'd only seen once before. The previous incident had been during the disastrous sea trials off the coast of Los Angeles when the well gates broke loose.

We were operating in an unexplored environment, hanging on and hoping for the best, but there wasn't much encouragement from our weatherman. The thirty-six-hour forecast called for seas of seven to ten feet and swells of eight to ten feet. The seventy-two-hour forecast hinted at only slightly better conditions. Beyond seventy-two hours? It was anybody's guess.

*Day 24 (Saturday, July 13, 1974)*
From the ship's log:

0400—Fog, Lt mist, sea & swell abating.

0800—Positioning in manual mode. No mining activity.

1145—Communication established with M/V Bel Hudson, home port

London, to effect medical aid emergency rendezvous for member of M/V Bel Hudson's crew who suffered apparent heart seizure.

1145—M/V Bel Hudson alongside stbd abeam @400 yds, maneuvering to launch stbd lifeboat.

1155—Bel Hudson's lifeboat alongside HGE. Crew standing by to assist lifeboat.

1342—Stretcher with patient and HGE Bosn lifted aboard by aft stbd crane. Patient removed to hospital for examination by ship's doctor.

1557—"Bel H" motor lifeboat underway to HGE. Dr. completed examination of patient.

1603—Lifeboat alongside to stbd. Patient ambulatory and in lifeboat.

2200—Various heading changes during watch to realize optimum heading/ roll & pitch minimum. Vessel riding easily w/occ'l heavy movements from occ'l hvy swells.

If we were beginning to weary of the monotony of high seas and apprehension, July 13 provided some needed relief. Just before noon, the ship got a radio call from a passing British ship, the M/V *Bel Hudson*. The *Bel Hudson* inquired if we had a doctor aboard, and getting positive confirmation, requested an emergency rendezvous for medical assistance.

The story they told was that one of the ship's crew had shown symptoms of a heart seizure and believed that he was dying. Since they had no doctor of their own, they wanted to bring the patient to the *HGE* on one of their lifeboats.

We had two concerns about this request. First, we didn't really want any uncleared people on the boat. The CV was well beneath the surface, of course, and the docking well would have been off limits to visitors anyway, but the possibility of having this patient onboard for the duration of the mission raised some real security worries. The second concern related to the difficulty, and danger, involved with trying to transfer personnel from one ship to another in a seaway with nine- to eleven-foot wave heights and deteriorating conditions.

In spite of the security problems, the mission director and Captain Gresham agreed that it would be unconscionable to refuse assistance to a sailor in apparently great medical distress. They offered to send our ship's doctor (Jim Borden), one of our paramedics (George Benko), and our "administrative officer" (actually our onboard CIA security officer, Jack Porter) to the *Bel Hudson* to examine the injured man. The *Bel Hudson* agreed to send over one of their lifeboats to pick up our medical team.

Easier said than done. Lowering a lifeboat in heavy seas can be very tricky. The harrowing phase of that operation is when the boat is beginning to make contact with the water, but isn't yet floating. The *Bel Hudson* was about 300 yards abeam of us, and we had a good view of the lifeboat launching activity. In the sea conditions we had, the lifeboat was alternately pulled up about ten feet from the surface of the water when the ship rolled away from it and then dropped suddenly down toward the water when the ship rolled back. At the instant the lifeboat impacted the water, the crews manning the lowering winches tried to release the lines quickly so the boat wouldn't be jerked up again. Unfortunately, the crews on the stern and bow lifting lines weren't coordinated. The stern of the lifeboat went down suddenly, but the bow lines were still taut and the bow was jerked upward. The lifeboat was now pointing up about forty-five degrees in the air, while the men in the boat tried to hold on for dear life. This carnival continued for about ten minutes before the lifeboat was finally floating on the surface and able to power its way to the *HGE*.

Having watched the launching difficulties, Dr. Borden and his team entered the lifeboat with some trepidation. Nevertheless, within about fifteen minutes—with only a few exciting moments—they were aboard the *Bel Hudson*.

The *Bel Hudson* seaman was examined, and didn't seem to be showing any signs of heart failure. Still, Borden felt that he really needed to bring him back to the *HGE* in order to give him a complete examination in the ship's hospital. Permission to transfer the patient was requested and granted.

Now the second part of the drama began to play out. The *Bel Hudson* crew put the injured sailor in the lifeboat along with our medical team and a crew of sailors and returned to the *HGE*. A rope ladder had been lowered over the side of the *Explorer*, but the patient claimed to be in too much pain to climb it. The only alternative was to strap him in a stretcher, and bring the stretcher aboard using one of the deck cranes.

Understand that the crane operators on the *HGE* were some of the best in the business. They had years of experience moving heavy objects to, from, and around rolling ships. This was a special problem, though, because the weight on the end of the crane's steel cable was so insignificant that it was difficult to get a *feel* for the natural rhythmic swinging motions that any object hanging from the end of a cable has. As a result, the crane operator wasn't able to compensate perfectly for the rolling motions of the ship. The patient in his stretcher was slammed into the hull of the ship several times as he was being lifted to the level of the main deck. Although he wasn't hurt by these collisions, he was understandably terrified by his experience. Jim Borden took him to the ship's hospital, where he was given a full battery of tests to determine the extent of his heart problem. As far as Borden could tell, his heart was in fine shape.

And then the true story came out. The patient admitted that he had gotten into a fight with his captain while they were drinking and enjoying the company of some women in the ship's lounge. Our patient had passed out after the fight, and when he woke up he felt a sudden sharp pain in his chest and assumed that he'd had a heart attack. Perhaps not remembering the probable cause for the pain, he panicked and convinced the ship's mate that he was going into shock, prompting the urgent radio call to the *HGE* for medical assistance.

With a few more tests and probes, our doctor was able to confirm that the wounded warrior from the *Bel Hudson* had suffered a couple of cracked ribs from his altercation with his captain.[2] Nothing more. Borden taped him up, and the *Bel Hudson* was notified that the patient was ready to be picked up.

When the lifeboat reached the lee side of the *Explorer*, Borden and the crew started to rig the stretcher in preparation for lowering the injured sailor back into the boat. When the patient saw the crane swinging around to pick him up, he jumped up off the stretcher and declared that there was no way he was ever going to make that trip down to the lifeboat via crane. He requested that we just lower the rope ladder, and he'd climb down on his own. And he did—without incident.

The *Bel Hudson* sailors had brought back a few bottles of fine scotch whiskey in acknowledgment of our assistance, and there were cheers from the crew of the *HGE* as we watched the final successful lifeboat recovery by the British freighter.

———

Jack Porter, the ship's gray-bearded security officer who accompanied Jim Borden on his visit to the *Bel Hudson*, shared a stateroom with me. He was perfect for his white-world role as the ship's administrative officer. Although he was an ex-marine who had fought in Korea before joining the agency, he was also a devout Catholic with great patience and understanding. With his strong New England accent that would have made President John Kennedy proud, Jack somehow came across as a father confessor to many of the crew. If he'd chosen to wear his collar backward, he'd have looked and sounded for all the world like the stereotypical priest from Boston. This was not a role that Porter sought; it was just unavoidable. Anyone on the crew with a personal problem ultimately ended up in "Gray Jack" Porter's office to confide.

That night before dinner, Porter carefully measured out one finger of the fine scotch whiskey from the *Bel Hudson* crew to each of our men as they entered the mess room. It might as well have been communion. Most of the crew found themselves involuntarily bowing their heads as they received their sip from Porter's "chalice." Some of them were caught involuntarily dipping their knees in genuflection as Gray Jack rumbled a kind word to each of them. It was a memorable scene. The whiskey was delicious.

---

With regard to our "mining" operations on that day, not much happened. The thirty-six- and seventy-two-hour forecasts were still calling for combined sea/swell wave heights of about ten to thirteen feet—way above what we could work in.

Meantime, the waves and ship motions were taking a toll on the recovery systems. The capture vehicle had been hanging on the docking legs about 100 feet beneath the ship for three days in heavy seas. The aft well gate had moved forward about one and a half feet, but it couldn't be repositioned because of the huge surge in the well of the ship. A couple of the tines on the capture vehicle had drifted down about five degrees, apparently due to leaking valves in the tine actuator mechanisms. The camera tripod on the forward docking leg had come loose, and we had only one additional spare unit onboard. Nothing could be done about that until sea conditions quieted down enough to permit the divers to work in the well. All we could do was wait—some more.

*Day 25 (Sunday, July 14, 1974)*
From the ship's log:

> 0000—Fog. Continuous sounding of fog signals.
> 0320—Both LBS A and LBS B ASKs malfunctioning and off line. Go to joy stick mode.
> 1415—Sherm Wetmore reports crack in fwd port docking leg.
> 2000—Positioning in auto-LBS. Overcast with patchy fog and hazy horizon.

The weather conditions began to lighten up in the morning. At noon the day before, the wave height had been ten to eleven feet. By noon on this day, it was down to seven to eight feet with six to seven feet anticipated for tomorrow. Looking ahead seventy-two hours, Gilmartin believed we might be seeing even milder sea conditions. Better yet, he predicted a cold front would pass through early in the period, getting rid of the continuous and oppressive fog we'd been seeing since we arrived at the site. If his forecast was right, we might be able to attempt undocking in a couple of days.

First, though, we had some repairs to make. Sherm Wetmore had found a crack in the forward docking leg, resulting from five days of turbulent wave activity in the well of the ship. One of the camera tripods on the docking legs had also come loose during the storm. The divers had already been engaged in so many rough water operations that their welding equipment had taken a hard hit. They'd started the mission with four welding machines. Only one of them was still repairable.

The CV had problems, too. We still didn't know the cause of the sagging tines that we'd noticed yesterday, but there was reason for worry. We weren't even sure if they could be repaired. That determination would have to wait until we were able to get the CV back into the well of the ship. If they weren't repairable, we could only hope that they didn't get worse. We'd have to bring the CV back into the well so we could close the gates, pump out the well, and make the necessary repairs. It felt like we were going backward.

――――――

During rough weather conditions like we'd been experiencing for the last few days, we couldn't make any progress toward preparations for undocking, and there were only so many maintenance items that could be handled onboard the ship while the seas were so rough. As a result, many of the crew members had more free time than usual to relax. The *HGE* had an extremely nice ship's lounge, with good chairs and lights for reading and a large TV for watching VCR tapes of the movies that had been brought onboard for the mission. The Global Marine personnel had picked out a good selection of first- and second-run movies, including comedies, dramas, and even some avant-garde films. One of my favorites—which I still enjoy although I've never found anyone else who liked the film—was *The Hired Hand*, with Peter Fonda and Warren Oates.

Someone (perhaps Global Marine, perhaps not) also brought on a copy of *Deep Throat*, starring Linda Lovelace. Now *that* was a crew favorite. It didn't seem to matter what time in the evening you came down to the lounge for some coffee and some conversation, *Deep Throat* would be playing. The soundtrack of that movie became the elevator music of the *HGE* lounge. I haven't heard that soundtrack for over thirty years, but I'm sure that if I did, I'd be spiritually transported back to the *Explorer's* lounge instantly. I think I'd enjoy that.

*Day 26 (Monday, July 15, 1974)*

Gilmartin was right again. As he predicted, the weather conditions improved significantly on Day 26, even though there was still too much noise in the water (either from waves, turbulence around the CV, or creaking docking legs) for the ASK to be used in auto mode. The helmsman on the bridge had to control the ship's position and attitude with the joystick.

Any thoughts we had with regard to planning another undocking attempt, however, were put on hold. We were already beginning to feel the effects of a distant storm, Harriet. Both wind and seas were building. We took advantage of this short lull in the weather and rushed to get the claw back into the well and the gates closed so we could work on it. With the seas building, we didn't have much time to spare.

Adding to our sense of urgency was the fact that the tilt cylinder relief valves on the docking legs were sticking. The shock absorbers built into the docking legs to absorb fore/aft surges of the CV when it was hanging beneath the ship couldn't do their job. The loads were being put into rigid docking legs, creating much larger stresses than the legs—or the decking they were attached to—were designed to take.

The divers started working in the well at dawn, the ship having been positioned in a direction to minimize the amount of water action in the moon pool. By the end of the day Clementine was secured in the well and we were preparing, once again, to close the well gates. We were essentially back to where we'd been a week earlier.

*Day 27 (Tuesday, July 16, 1974)*

The wind and seas had picked up a bit, thanks to Harriet. The storm was weakening, though, and the winds were expected to top out tomorrow. We used the time to repair all the parts that had broken during the last six days while the CV had been hanging in a churning sea 100 feet below the ship.

The camera tripods for the docking legs were repaired again (how many times had they broken already?) and Bill Beaverton, our chief diver, suggested an alternate location that would leave them less vulnerable. The divers were obviously getting pretty ragged with the near-continuous activity they'd seen on the mission so far.

All of the tilt cylinder relief valves on the docking legs were cleaned in order to free them up. The operation helped, but the port relief valve on the aft leg was still sticking. Not good. Each docking leg had two relief valves, one on starboard and one on port. When the fore/aft forces on the legs exceeded a design threshold, the relief valves were supposed to open in unison in order to limit the fore and aft loads on the legs. If one valve, say the port, did not open, the leg was subjected to twisting loads as well. The docking legs had already shown some weakness when subjected to high seas while extended. We had to get this problem corrected before we got into that situation again.

*Day 28 (Wednesday, July 17, 1974)*

Harriet dropped back to a depression and was dissipating. Although we were still seeing thirty-two-knot winds, they were expected to drop down to fifteen to twenty knots by noon tomorrow. The sea state was predicted to ease to about ten feet. The seventy-two-hour forecast called for sea and swell conditions that might permit us to attempt another undocking. Between now and then, we had to finish our repairs and get ready to go.

Tom Fry, the chief engineer of the Western Gear contingent, had been concerned for some days about oil leaking out of the heave compensator cylinders. They were still chasing the source of the leak(s), but there was concern that the problem was just a poor seal design—something we'd not be able to fix at sea. Some consideration was being given to adding grease to the heave compensator oil, but no one really liked that idea. Somehow it sounded like the old trick of adding oatmeal to a leaking automobile radiator. It would fix the leak, but it would also permanently clog up the radiator.

Meanwhile, work was continuing on the problems created during the worst of Harriet. The port relief valve (the sticking one) on the aft docking leg was being cleaned and reworked one more time; a new frame for the docking leg camera had been designed and was being built; and all electronic connection boxes on the capture vehicle were checked out and found to be in good condition.

Later in the day we got some good news on the heave compensator analysis. No leaks were found in the cylinder seals. The problem appeared to be simply a leaking fluid box. The Western Gear engineers added three to four gallons of hydraulic oil and called it "good."

If the weather forecast proved accurate—and if we didn't discover any new problems—we were hoping to start the undocking sequence sometime tomorrow.

*Day 29 (Thursday, July 18, 1974)*

From the ship's log:

> 0400—Positioning in Auto-LBS, no test activity. Vessel riding easily in moderate sea & swell. Fog. Vis. Approximately ½ mi.

0615—ASK exhibiting abnormal operational inconsistencies. Fog, blowing mist.

0906—Unidentified vessel continuously maintaining station 1½ to 2½ mi from HGE at various bearings.

1530—Fog lifts. Unidentified vessel close at hand to stbd.

1542—Observed helicopter taking off from vessel.

1545—Helicopter identified as *17, Russian.

1600–1745—Various signals made and received via blinkers/flags in responding to attempts by apparent Russian vessel to communicate with HGE. Helicopter flying extremely close and apparently taking photographs.

1900—Russian vessel identified by call sign as UMGT.

2200—Russian vessel leaves vicinity of HGE. Contact on radar last at 18 mi. Russian vessel hdg. 302° true @ 13.6 kts.

2341—Preparing to drop X-ponder. Vessel riding easily in low SW'ly swell & slight sea. Fog signals sounded on whistle.

Early in the morning, the bridge radar detected an unidentified ship circling around the *HGE* about two miles away. The fog was too heavy to permit visual observation. No attempts at communication were made by either the visitor or us. We continued our scheduled operational activity of dropping replacement acoustic transponders around the target site, but we kept looking through the fog—trying to see who was out there.

At mid-afternoon, the fog lifted very suddenly and we could make out a moderately large white ship, less than one-half mile away, with what appeared to be several large missile-tracking radar antennas. We weren't sure about the nationality of the ship, but we could see that there was a helipad with a helicopter on it. A quick check back to headquarters indicated that the ship was most likely a Soviet missile tracker, the *Chazhma,* out of Petropavlovsk.

Our immediate concern was that the Soviet ship might try to land its helicopter on the *HGE.* Landing a chopper on our helipad would not have been easy because we'd moved a number of crates and boxes onto the pad at the start of the mission in order to discourage any such attempts. Still, just to be sure, Jack Porter ordered some additional crates to be placed on the pad.

Sure enough, about fifteen minutes after the fog lifted, the *Chazhma's* helicopter took off and headed for the *HGE.* The nationality of the ship soon became very apparent as the chopper approached us. The side of the aircraft was marked with a large red star and the number seventeen.

I don't know if the Russians ever intended to land their bird on the *HGE,* but the helicopter crew soon realized when they saw all the junk piled on the pad that it would be impossible. Instead, they spent about fifteen minutes or so circling around our ship at very close range—taking photographs from all angles.

At first, we had some concerns that Clementine—now high and dry in the ship's well—might be visible. A quick look relaxed us on that count, however. There was so much structure around and above the well that photographs from outside the ship were unlikely to yield any useful intelligence about the shape or design of the mining vehicle within.

After the Soviet helicopter had been darting around the ship for about ten minutes, the Global crew began to get a little resentful and rowdy. There were lots of catcalls, some of the crew "mooned" the helicopter, and other crew members waved women's panties and other underthings (where did that stuff come from?) at the Russians. The mission director put a stop to those actions—we surely didn't want to challenge the Russians in any way, and after another five minutes or so the helicopter returned to its ship.

The *Chazhma* made several unsuccessful attempts to communicate with us using blinker signals and flags. Radio communications didn't work much better, but we were able to ascertain that the call sign for the Russian ship was UMGT.

About two hours later, the Soviet helicopter flew another reconnaissance sortie over the *Explorer*, this time flying very close and taking additional photos from a large camera mounted in an open doorway. That flight was followed by more attempts to communicate that eventually succeeded. The Soviets were interested in what we were doing and how long we expected to be there. We replied we were doing ocean mining experiments and expected to be finished in two to three weeks. Satisfied, the *Chazhma* signed off with "We wish you all the best."[3] By evening, the fog had drifted back in and the *Chazhma* left the area on a north-northwest course. By dark, we were all alone again in the fog.

———

Throughout the episode with the *Chazhma*, we kept working on the recovery systems to get them ready for another undocking attempt. We were still having trouble with the tilt-out capability on the aft docking leg, but by the end of the day it seemed to be working okay. Once again, we thought we were ready to attempt the undocking. (How many times have I said that already?)

*Day 30 (Friday, July 19, 1974)*
The day started and ended with frustration. The well gates were opened just after noon, but they only moved twenty feet. The air hose for the aft

gate had been misconnected to the forward gate and vice versa. The gates had to be shut again so the divers could correct the problem.

Eventually, we got the gates open and lowered the docking legs and the capture vehicle down twenty-three feet for bridle rigging. We ran into technical problems with the CV, though, and had to raise it back up to work on those problems. By late evening, we had it back down to twenty-three feet and bridle rigging had been started again.

On the positive side, while all the work in the well was going on we dropped the final replacement transponder and completed recalibration of the transponder grid. At least we knew exactly where we were with respect to the target. If only we could get the CV down there.

————

All of these delays and frustrations were having an effect on the crew. They were certainly affecting my attitude and outlook. We seemed to be going two steps forward, one step back, except sometimes we were going one step forward, two steps back. Operations, of course, continued on a twenty-four-hour basis. The Global Marine crew in charge of raising and lowering the pipe was prepared for this kind of activity. They had two teams of pipe operators, each working a twelve on, twelve off schedule. The engineers and technicians from Global Marine, Lockheed, Western Gear, and Honeywell didn't have that kind of redundancy, though. They were on call twenty-four hours a day. They had to fit in a little sleep or rest whenever they could.

The CIA people on the ship were on call twenty-four hours a day, too. Although Jack Porter and I shared a stateroom, we rarely saw one another in our quarters. We both found time to relax whenever we could, but those times seldom coincided.

Although Jack was tough enough to handle any situation, he was also a philosopher and he loved poetry. I was getting discouraged and beginning to give up hope that we'd ever be able to complete the mission. Jack mentioned a poem that he particularly liked, and which he thought applicable to our situation. He recited it to me and it struck just the right chord. He repeated it to me over and over until I had memorized it. I've never forgotten it. The poem, "Carrion Comfort," was written by Gerard Manley Hopkins. It went, in part:

Not, I'll not, carrion comfort, Despair, not feast on thee;
Not untwist—slack they may be—these last strands of man
In me or, most weary, cry *I can no more.* I can;
Can something, hope, wish day come, not choose not to be.

*Day 31 (Saturday, July 20, 1974)*

We made a lot of progress on Day 31, but things were still going much slower than expected. Rigging the bridle of the capture vehicle seemed to take forever. It was such a simple operation on paper—just drive some pins through some clevises to attach the CV bridle to the end of the lifting pipe. In practice, it was a daunting task. To begin with, the pins were about twelve inches in diameter and weighed about one-half to one ton each. Those pins had to be lifted and positioned precisely with respect to the clevises on the bridle and the end of the pipe so that they could be driven through. None of these components could be lifted by hand. All the loads had to be supported by cranes and other lifting devices. Further, the positioning operation was complicated by the motion of the ship and the capture vehicle. We weren't talking about a lot of relative motion during the bridle rigging operation— it amounted to maybe a few inches—but the clearance between the pins and the clevises was just a small fraction of an inch.

Nevertheless, the bridle rigging was completed by mid-afternoon. By late evening the CV was lowered on the docking legs down to 126 feet. By the end of the day, we were anxiously (and nervously) looking forward to undocking Clementine. The seas were calm, but the swell was running at about four to five feet. And it was expected to grow.

*Day 32 (Sunday, July 21, 1974)*

From the ship's log:

> 0000—Positioning in auto-LBS. Prepare to undock mining machine
>
> 0030—Commence undocking procedure. Heavy shocks and stress on derrick and heavy lift system. Undocking occurred at peak heave. Mining machine pins at bottom of key holes. Vessel in violent reaction to stress.
>
> 0040—Mining machine positioned back on docking legs. Shocks cease. Inspection made of entire vessel for possible damage. None found. Watertight doors secured.
>
> 0112—Commence lowering docking legs.
>
> 0125—Docking legs down full.
>
> 0127—Tilt docking legs to 7 degrees.
>
> 0134—Mining machine undocked. Commence raising legs.
>
> 0400—Clear, slight SE'ly sea and swell. Vessel riding easily.
>
> 1200–1500—Two joints of pipe down and brought back up. Faulty latch plate in upper yoke.
>
> 2020—Secure pipe handling for latch plate repair.
>
> 2145—Commence running pipe. Repairs accomplished.

2300—Vessel riding easily in moderate SE'ly swell. Fog signals on whistle. Vis ½ mi.

2400—Running pipe.

At 0000 hours, we were preparing for the undocking operation. The local sea was almost flat, but the swell was about four to five feet, causing the ship to roll and pitch slightly. Roll and pitch of the ship concerned us because of the fore-and-aft, lateral, and vertical motions induced on both the CV support pins and the docking leg keyholes. Relative motion between the pins and the keyholes resulted in impacts during the undocking. We wanted very much to keep those impacts at a low level. The ship was heading directly into the swell in order to minimize roll, so the fore-and-aft and vertical motions caused by the ship pitching would be the most significant.

Deciding just when to start the actual undocking of the capture vehicle was a tough call. We were actually experiencing swell from two storm sources at slightly different periods. The swell from these sources would "walk" through each other just about every five minutes. When the swells from the two different sources were in phase, we got maximum swell heights of about seven feet. When the two wave trains were out of phase, the swell heights would go down to about two feet. The average time between the peaks and the nulls of this process was about five minutes, but there was plenty of variation in this timing. We hoped that if we were able to sync the critical part of the undocking with a null in the wave train, we might be spared some of the brutal impacts that could accompany the docking and undocking maneuvers. Sea conditions were expected to get worse, not better, so we elected to start the undocking.

———

The undocking procedure consisted of lowering the docking legs while supporting the capture vehicle with the lifting pipe. As the legs were lowered, the forty-eight-inch-diameter CV support pins that rested in the vertical slots of the docking leg keyholes would move upward with respect to the docking leg until all of the CV weight was supported by the pipe. Once this load transfer had been made, the docking legs could be tilted back out of the way. The capture vehicle would then be totally supported by the heavy lift system. We'd be undocked—with Clementine hanging on the pipe.

———

Shortly after midnight, we started lowering the docking legs while taking up the CV load with the lifting pipe. We had tried to time the start of the operation with a null period of the interacting swell trains.

It didn't work out that way. We ended up with the separation of the docking legs and the capture vehicle support pins occurring in a period of maximum relative motion, with heavy impacts between the two bodies resulting. The energy in those impacts was incredible. The entire ship was shaking. It sounded like it was being torn apart. Physical shock waves from the collisions could be seen in the derrick structure and in the transfer boom used to transport pipe from the storage hold up to the rig floor. Fearing damage to the ship structure, the operators raised the docking legs so that the capture vehicle support pins were once again at the bottom of the keyholes and the weight of the CV was back on the docking legs. Undocking operations were stopped so a full inspection of the ship's structure could be made.

Western Gear's heavy lift operators and Global's docking leg crew came pouring up out of the control room located in the port wing wall. Being in the narrowest part of the ship, directly between the two docking legs and right under the derrick, this control room received more shock and acoustic barrages than any other place on the ship. The operators were justifiably alarmed. The only thing they wanted right then was some fresh air and a cigarette. It wasn't certain that all of those men would be willing to go back into that control room for another undocking try. Inspection of the ship's structure revealed no serious damage had been done, however. In spite of the violent shaking, the *HGE* had held up extremely well. We were ready to try it again.

About an hour after the first undocking attempt—and with restored operators—we started undocking again. This time we got our timing with the seas right. Within four minutes, the pins were in the wide part of the docking leg keyholes, and we started retracting the legs away from the capture vehicle support pins. Three minutes later, the CV was undocked—all of its 4 million pounds supported by the lifting pipe. Finally, after eighteen days on station, we were ready to start lowering Clementine to the target.

————

Our determination to attempt the second undocking maneuver in marginal sea state conditions—and immediately following a frighteningly physical first attempt—may seem odd. Especially considering how many times we had already aborted previous undocking operations. Up until now, we would have probably called off the attempt and waited another twenty-four hours or so to allow time to inspect the whole ship and its systems more thoroughly for damage. On this day, for some reason, the attitude was different. Perhaps it was the frustration that all of us were feeling after so many failed attempts to start the recovery operation. Or perhaps we were just getting more relaxed about the system failures that were occurring so often that they'd become a part of our daily routine. Sherm Wetmore, reflecting years later on our change of attitude that day, explained it this way: "We'd had so many technical problems. We were becoming comfortable with our own failures. We felt it was time to just *get it on!*"

———

The first two lowered pipe joints had to be brought back up again because of a faulty latch plate on the upper heavy lift yoke. This was readily fixed, though, and by the end of the day we were running pipe. Finally.

*Day 33 (Monday, July 22, 1974)*
From the ship's log:

> 0000–0400—Intermittent pipe handling operations. Vessel riding easily. Fog. Fog signals sounding, lookout posted fwd.
> 0700—Approaching vessel alters course towards HGE.
> 0725—Unidentified vessel hove to. Bearing 058°, dist. 2.0 mi.
> 0800—Positioning in Auto-LBS. Continue rigging divers' cage. Overcast, occasional passing fog with mist, light drizzle.
> 1142—Unidentified vessel hove to drifting on a 2 mi. perimeter from HGE.
> 1200—Prepared divers' platform. Commence intermittent pipe handling ops.
> 1805—Stop running pipe—transfer cart problems.
> 2215—Vessel riding easily in low SE'ly swell. Unidentified vessel lost on radar at 16 mi.
> 2315—Unidentified vessel reappears, visually reported by lookout. Apparently returning to close vicinity of HGE.
> 2400—Intermittent pipe handling activity.

Much of the morning was spent trying to lower pipe, but the divers were having a really tough time trying to trice the EM cable to the pipe as it was lowered. We had planned to have the cable tricing handled by an amazingly clever but fatally flawed automatic tricing machine. Unfortunately, we could never get that beast to work—either on the dock or on the ship. We finally just gave up on it and put the burden on the divers. It was manpower-intensive and much of the work had to be done at the sea-air interface.

Manually strapping the EM cable to each length of pipe was proving to be a lot harder than anticipated out in the North Pacific Ocean.

To ease this problem, the Global Marine engineers designed a cage for the divers that could move up and down with the lower yoke of the heavy lift system, giving them a chance to attach the tricing straps while moving in sync with the lift pipe. The machine was welded up and installed in about six hours. It was a great improvement. The divers still had a tiring job—they were forced to work in the sea-air interface with wave forces pushing them around constantly—but at least we could now start lowering pipe more or less continuously.

By late afternoon, we had to stop running pipe again because of a problem with the transfer cart. (The transfer cart carried the sixty-foot lengths of pipe from the main deck up to the rig floor on a special "railroad" track.) That, too, was fixed in a couple of hours.

Now that the capture vehicle was a couple of thousand feet below the ship, we added all 144 bottles of air to the heave compensator system, significantly increasing the isolation of the CV from the heave motion of the ship. The rig floor was now essentially fixed in elevation while the ship moved up and down beneath it.

Structural inspections of the ship continued on a routine basis—as they would from here on out. The ship was going to be undergoing higher stresses than it had ever experienced during the integrated system tests. We were in uncharted territory. Harry Jackson, a retired Navy engineer and a world-famous expert in submarine design, supported the inspection team. He reported a small crack that he'd found under the main deck, in the vicinity of the A-frame. Repairs were started immediately.

————

While we were struggling to establish a rhythm for our operation, a new unidentified ship was picked up by the ship's radar. It seemed to be hove to about two miles away. Visibility wasn't good enough to see it—but we knew it was out there.

After dark, the vessel appeared to be leaving the area. We lost it on radar at about sixteen miles, but about fifteen minutes later the vessel was spotted again by the bridge. This time the lookout visually detected its lights. The vessel returned and remained a couple of miles from the ship for the rest of the evening.

There was plenty of speculation as to the identity and nationality of the mystery ship, but we stayed on station and continued moving pipe. By the end of the day, the claw was about 3,000 feet below us. With over one-half mile of pipe string hanging below the ship, it didn't matter who or what the new visitor was. We weren't going anywhere fast. We just peered into the darkness, looking for the unidentified ship, and continued lowering pipe.

*Day 34 (Tuesday, July 23, 1974)*
From the ship's log:

> 0000–0400—Pos. in Auto-LBS. No pipe handling activity. Repairs being made to subspinner. 54 joints of pipe down. Good visibility, vessel riding easily.
>
> 0408—Unidentified vessel remains hove to at 5 mi. distant.
>
> 0800—Running in pipe
>
> 0850—Unidentified vessel observed close in to wave rider buoy, apparently observing it.
>
> 1000—Fire and boat drill. Sounded signals on gen. alarm and whistle.
>
> 1024—Dismissed from fire & boat drill. Drill was brief due to mining ops.
>
> 1055—Russian Tug SB-10 observed to be previously unidentified vessel. Approaches our stbd side & circles HGE at 200 to 300 ft.
>
> 1145—Tug SB-10 standing approx. ½ mi off HGE port side.
>
> 1200–1600—Positioned in Auto-LBS. Int. pipe handling activity. 85 joints down. Vessel riding easily.
>
> 2400—Vessel riding easily in low to moderate N'ly swell. Vis. Good. Vessel SB-10 keeping dist. of approx. 7 mi. from HGE.

We were running pipe, but it was slow going. Although the heavy lift system was designed to operate at a continuous speed of eighteen feet per minute, we were forced to go much slower because of failures. The sequence of raising a sixty-foot double from the hold, transporting it via the transfer cart railway to the rig floor, pulling it up into a vertical position in the derrick, lowering and screwing it into the box end of the pipe below it, and transferring the total lift pipe load back and forth between the upper and lower yokes was all supposed to work seamlessly with automatic control. In fact, we found ourselves having to operate much of the pipe-handling system in a semiautomatic mode, with manual control of some operations.

Early in the day, pipe-handling operations had to be shut down because of a problem with the subspinner—the device that rotated the pipe clockwise as it was being lowered into the box joint of the uppermost pipe joint. Later in the day, a cam roller on the lower yoke failed—apparently due to an undersized pipe joint that prevented the latching mechanism from working properly. (Two days ago, we had had the same issue on the upper yoke.) The basic problem was that, because of time constraints, we had never been able to completely debug the heavy lift control system. Instead, we were trying to do that during the mission.

Meanwhile, the unidentified vessel decided to come in for a closer inspection of the *HGE*. We had been watching the ship on radar since yesterday morning, but it never came close enough for visual identification. Early this morning, it had been observed on radar hove to in the close vicinity of our wave rider buoy, about four and one-quarter miles from the *HGE*. There was some question that mischief may have been intended, but that turned out to be an unnecessary concern. After about ten minutes, the still-unidentified ship moved and took up station about 200 feet from the wave rider.

A couple of hours later, the visitor decided to declare its presence formally. It sailed right up to the *HGE*'s starboard side and circled around it at a distance of 200 to 300 feet. It was identified as a Russian salvage tug, about 155 feet long with hull number *SB-10*. Although the ship was designed as an oceangoing tug, the Russians commonly used such ships as AGIs—intelligence-collecting ships. Clearly, the mission of the *SB-10* was purely intelligence collection. After the close-in inspection, the *SB-10* backed off to a distance of one-half mile, took up station there for a short time, and eventually left the immediate vicinity to hang out astern of the *HGE* at a distance of five to seven miles.

We soon realized why the *SB-10* had taken up that position astern. All the trash (garbage, mostly) from the *HGE* was being placed in plastic bags and dumped overboard. The plastic bags would eventually fill with water and disintegrate, leaving the garbage to be scavenged by seagulls and fish. The *SB-10*, however, was preempting nature's scavengers. The crew was picking up the bags of trash as they floated down-current from the *HGE* and examining the contents for any clues as to what we were doing.

This was a little surprising to us. We hadn't considered that a Soviet ship would be showing that much interest in our operations. The fix was obvious, though. All crew members were reminded that no classified information should be disposed of in the trash. Any documentation that might reveal information about the nature of our work or the problems we were having was placed in trash receptacles that were stored onboard.

———

Routine inspections of the hull and ship systems were also continuing. Harry Jackson found a new crack in the docking leg guide. The damage probably occurred during the traumatic first undocking attempt two days ago.

By the end of the day, we had about 5,600 feet of pipe out. That worked out to an average speed of less than 2 feet per minute since undocking. The learning process was painful. Unless we could improve our rate, it would take us four more days to reach the bottom. Motivating us to somehow improve that rate was the fact that tropical storm Kim, with wind gusts of up to forty-five knots, was about 1,200 miles southwest of us and heading our way.

*Day 35 (Wednesday, July 24, 1974)*
From the ship's log:

> 0000—Positioning in Auto-LBS, Hdg 310 deg. No pipe handling activity due to breakdown of EM cable winch.
> 0330—Pipe handling ops resume.
> 1000–1100—SB-10 passes down HGE's stbd side, at closest point approx. 200 ft, falling astern of HGE and taking station approx. 1.7 mi dist.
> 1045—Projected 3–4 hr hold on pipe running.
> 1500—Resume pipe handling. SB-10 passes close astern to stbd.
> 1825—Very heavy leak reported in Heave Comp. sync cylinder. Cautionary announcement made on P.A. system. All watertight doors secured. Attempting to isolate faulty cylinder.
> 1850–1925—SB-10 departs, moving away from HGE to vicinity of southern wave rider buoy.
> 1940—Heave Compensator problem resolved by isolating faulty cylinder. Resume normal HC operation.
> 2000—Running in pipe.
> 2055—Soviet Tug SB-10 makes pass close aboard to stbd at 100 yds. And then takes station approx. 1 to 2 mi dist.
> 2400—Running pipe.

In the middle of the night, the EM cable winch overheated and froze up, stopping all pipe-handling operations for several hours until it could be repaired. That kind of problem was frustrating but not frightening.

Later that afternoon, though, we had another problem—this one of the variety that was *very* frightening. A heavy leak was reported in the heave compensator, eventually traced to the port aft sync cylinder. This was serious. If the fore and aft heave compensator cylinders got too far out of sync, the misalignment could cause the gimbal system to bind up. Without the gimbals to isolate the normal roll and pitch motions of the ship, bending loads would be put directly into the pipe string. There was little reserve tensile strength in the pipe for off-axis loading. If the pipe was overstressed, it could break, possibly resulting in the failure mode that no one ever wanted to talk about—a ship broken into two main parts.

Recognizing the seriousness of the situation, a cautionary announcement was made on the public address system. Everybody (except the Global and Western Gear engineers trying to isolate and repair the problem) was ordered to leave the vicinity of the docking well. The watertight doors forward and aft of the well were closed and locked.

The problem was eventually resolved by lowering the heave compensator all the way down to the snubbers while the leaking cylinder was isolated from the system. Of course, with the heave compensator lowered to the snubbers, it was essentially "locked" in position. All the ship's heave motions were transmitted directly to the pipe string. This also raised the stress levels in the pipe, but the stresses were axial—not bending—and were of less concern. The problem was resolved in an hour or so and the heave compensator was once again performing its shock absorber functions. There was no damage done by the incident, but it was very disturbing. Under different conditions—during bottom operations, for example—a locked-up heave compensator could be disastrous.

The bridge also reported a problem with the ASK system. Of the six long baseline acoustic transponders on the bottom, two of them appeared to have failed completely. During the day, the *HGE* was maneuvered around the grid to the transponder positions and two new ones were dropped. We were back in business again with the ASK signals, but we only had three more of the deepwater transponder batteries remaining as spares.

All the while, the *SB-10* continued its reconnaissance of the *HGE* and our transponder deployment operations, alternately moving in close to within 100 yards of the ship and then retreating to greater distances to pick up the garbage.

––––––

By the end of the day, we had 9,600 feet of pipe down. With all the problems we were having with the ship and its systems, we still deployed 4,000 feet of pipe on our twenty-first day at the target site.

*Day 36 (Thursday, July 25, 1974)*
From the ship's log:

> 0000—Joy stick mode, proceeding to X-ponder drop site. Continuous pipe handling and operations.

0403—Pipe handling ops continuing. O'cast. Slight E'ly sea.

0730—"Rushin' Russian" begins morning run in from 9 mi. out.

1115—Under way to calib. pt. #4. Vessel riding easily in low SE'ly swell. Vis. good. SB-10 made one approach to within one-half mile of HGE, and then gradually drifted away. Present dist. 3.9 mi.

1200—Repairs to lower yoke. No pipe handling.

1355—SB-10 close at hand, to port.

2155—Commence transferring fuel oil to correct ½ deg list. SB-10 drifting away during watch.

2400—Running pipe. Positioning Auto-LBS.

———

In between minor breakdowns and delays, we were beginning to hone our pipe-handling skills. By the end of the day, we would have over 12,000 feet out. Anticipating a possible rendezvous with the target in a couple of days, the Lockheed and Honeywell teams started checking out the equipment on the capture vehicle. The TV optics looked especially good. With only one light on, we could see down the length of the claw about 100 feet.

Meanwhile, the *SB-10* (which the bridge officers had nicknamed the "Rushin' Russian") continued its reconnaissance operations. Several times a day, the *SB-10* would approach to within a couple of hundred yards of the *HGE*. The crew was clearly visible on the rail, many of them scanning our ship with binoculars or cameras. At least one (some of the crew swore they saw two) of the *SB-10* crew was a woman, usually wearing a simple print dress. The men were dressed very informally, most of them shirtless and hatless.

The close—and dangerous—maneuvering of the small Soviet tug was beginning to get on the nerves of our deputy director for operations, retired Navy captain Fred Traner. Traner was a former submariner, and he didn't take kindly to the harassment from the smaller ship—especially after dark.

The CIA had hoped that the Agreement on the Prevention of Incidents On and Over the High Seas, signed by the United States and the Soviet Union in 1972, would eliminate the kind of harassment that we had seen during the *Glomar II* survey missions in 1970. During those two missions, two Soviet ships—the *Gidrograf* and the *CC-23*—engaged in very aggressive behavior against the *Glomar II*. Although the 1972 agreement had been primarily intended to minimize the likelihood of dangerous incidents between Soviet and U.S. warships, the two countries had signed a protocol in 1973 that also pledged not to make simulated attacks against nonmilitary ships. Whether the close-in maneuvering of the *SB-10* qualified as a simulated attack was arguable. Still, it was certainly confrontational—and dangerous.

Well after sundown, Fred Traner was seething as he watched the *SB-10* maneuvers from the bridge. *HGE* captain Tom Gresham wasn't happy either, but he was used to this type of behavior from Soviet ships on the open ocean and he didn't want to start an altercation that might result in even more aggressive behavior. Fred Traner, though, had had enough. During one of the *SB-10*'s harassment runs, when it was approaching the *HGE* from dead ahead on a collision course, Traner took matters into his own hands. Without approval from the officer in command of the ship, he aimed the *HGE*'s bridge searchlight directly onto the bridge of the oncoming AGI—in clear violation of the U.S.-Soviet agreement to prevent incidents. The *SB-10* helmsman, blinded by the light, turned sharply away from the *HGE*, putting an end to the reconnaissance activities for that night.

If Traner considered turning the tables against the *SB-10* to be therapeutic, the feeling was not shared by Captain Tom Gresham. He was furious. He viewed the submariner's action to be extremely dangerous and irresponsible. Further, he considered it to be a challenge to his own authority as captain of the ship, responsible for the safety of the ship and all the crew aboard. Apologies and explanations had no effect on Gresham. He ordered Traner to leave the bridge immediately and forbade him to ever set foot on the bridge again. Gresham was the captain, and his word was law.

As it turned out, Tom Gresham's intuition might have been dead-on regarding the Soviet reaction to the searchlight episode. Thereafter, the *SB-10* was less active at night, but its behavior during daylight hours became increasingly aggressive and worrisome to the officers on the bridge. For the remainder of the time at the target site, the *SB-10* made frequent passes and circumnavigations of the *HGE* at separation distances of fifty yards or less.

*Day 37 (Friday, July 26, 1974)*
From the ship's log:

> 0000—Positioning in Auto-LBS. Continuing pipe ops.
>
> 0354—Cable to pipe cart counterweight parted, dropping counter weight. Pipe cart at top of transfer boom.
>
> 1010—SB-10 commences run along HGE's stbd side, dist. about 150 yds.
>
> 1100—Cautionary announcement made over ship P.A. system. Preparing to place pipe string on parking brake. Due to stress on upper double caused by broken counterweight, upper double must be removed.
>
> 1600—Positioning in Auto-LBS. O'cast moderate SE by S sea and swell. Vessel riding easily. Continue repairs to counterweight pennant.
>
> 2000—Positioning in Auto-LBS. Continue repairs. Overcast and cloudy.

2245—Repairs to pipe transfer boom completed.

2400—Lookout posted on fwd bridge. Vis. ½ mi. Vessel riding easily, moderate SSE'ly swell & sea. SB-10 not seen visually or on radar during this watch.

A couple of hours before dawn, we had another failure on the ship that really got our attention—audibly and physically. A 30-ton counterweight suspended from the rig floor dropped down on the main deck with a deafening crash when the steel support cable failed. Fortunately, no one was injured.

The counterweight was designed to compensate for the tilting moment applied to the gimbaled rig floor by the transfer boom. Recall that the sixty-foot pipe doubles were carried from the pipe storage hold to the rig floor via a transfer cart that traveled back and forth on a transfer boom, or railway. The upper end of the transfer boom rested on the aft edge of the rig floor. The weight of that boom, along with the cart and the pipe it was carrying, produced a large moment on the gimbaled rig floor that tended to make the derrick tilt aft. To compensate for this moment, a large cable-supported counterweight was hung from the forward section of the pitch gimbal box.

When the counterweight fell to the main deck, the entire moment of the transfer boom/cart/pipe resting on the aft edge of the rig floor was transferred to the lifting pipe. The pipe load was transferred from the lifting yokes to the parking brake while the counterweight assembly was repaired, but the uppermost pipe in the system had to be removed from the string because of the high bending stresses that had been imposed on it. How much stress was imposed on the pipe? According to the stress sensors on the lifting yoke, 135–145 kilopounds per square inch (ksi). The steel in the pipe would have failed at 170 ksi. Too close for comfort.

By late evening, the repairs were completed and we were back in operation. By the end of the day, we had 13,800 feet (over two and a half miles!) of pipe out, and the control center announced that we'd made the first sonar contact with the ocean bottom. Our progress was encouraging, but we were beginning to feel the effects of tropical storm Kim. Our thirty-six-hour forecast called for winds to peak at about fifteen to twenty-three knots, with seas of five to eight feet and swells of seven to ten feet. These conditions would be a serious challenge to the gimbal and heave compensator systems in our current situation with over 10 million pounds hanging from the heavy lift yokes.

———

As usual, the ever-present *SB-10* continued monitoring the *HGE* operations throughout the day. We were getting used to it. Then, surprisingly, the bridge reported it had lost track of the *SB-10*. The "Rushin' Russian" had not been seen visually, or on radar, during the last watch from 2000 to 2400. It looked like they'd gone home. We didn't bet on that.

*Day 38 (Saturday, July 27, 1974)*

In the morning we were getting the predicted heavy wind and swell from tropical storm Kim. Still, we continued running pipe without interruption. It was rough on the pipe-handling crew on the rig floor. They had no protection from the elements up there, and at times, when an especially heavy fog bank drifted through, they couldn't even see the main deck. They felt as though they were floating in space, and episodes of vertigo weren't uncommon.

The strain on the ship from the high loads being supported by the derrick was a major concern, too. The load—well over 10 million pounds now—was twice as high as we'd ever experienced during the integrated systems testing. The ship's operating crew was making hourly checks to affirm that the watertight integrity of the ship hadn't been compromised.

Of course, the heavy lift system was also being pushed to new limits every passing hour. The forty-eight hydraulic pumps, all operating in parallel, were delivering almost 1,200 gallons per minute of hydraulic oil at a pressure of over 1,800 psi. The straining pumps created heavy vibrations that shook the floor of the pump room. To those men overseeing the operation of the pumps, it seemed that something was going to have to give.

Shortly after breakfast, something did give. One of the forty-eight pumps on line simply exploded, showering the entire pump room with shrapnel and hot hydraulic oil. The pump technicians, fortunately, worked in a control room protected by heavy safety glass and were not injured. However, high-pressure hydraulic oil was spewing out of the broken lines, covering the floor of the control room in just a few seconds. The operators were able to isolate the disintegrated pump quickly, but the cleanup and pump replacement were going to take a few hours.

By late afternoon, we were running pipe again. Operations continued at a good pace until about 2000 hours, when a strong shock was felt throughout the whole ship. This time, it was the latch plate on the lower yoke that malfunctioned, allowing the lift pipe to actually drop a short distance. We'd had problems with the yoke latch plates before, but not with the kind of loads we were carrying now. In what had become a routine procedure, the watertight doors were checked to make sure they were secure, and the entire vessel was once more examined for any structural failures. Pipe-handling operations were stopped for the day. Continuing operation in these weather conditions just didn't make sense.

The control center crew didn't let the downtime go to waste, though. Earlier in the day some signals had begun to show up on the capture vehicle's continuous transmission frequence modulated (CTFM) search sonars. Was it the target object? Or the engineering section of the *K-129*? We couldn't be sure. We were still about 1,000 feet from the bottom—too high for effective searching by the side-looking sonars—but we thought we might be able to find out more by looking at the object from different directions. The positioning maneuvers were done with the ship and the capture vehicle working together in what was called auto-LBS track mode. In that mode, the *HGE*'s ASK system was programmed to follow exactly the position of the capture vehicle on the ocean bottom. Position control of both the CV and the ship was in the hands of a single CV operator in the Lockheed control center.

———

Repairs on the heavy lift system continued through the last watch. The worldwide weather forecast from the Navy's FNWC in Monterey suggested we had already seen the worst of tropical storm Kim. The winds were expected to drop to eighteen to twenty-three knots after midnight, diminishing thereafter. Tomorrow we could start moving pipe again. At the end of the last watch, we had deployed 15,673 feet of pipe and had been seriously scared twice in one day. The prospect of better weather was welcome.

*Day 39 (Sunday, July 28, 1974)*
From the ship's log:

> 0000—No pipe handling ops. Repairs being made to lower yoke latch plate.
>
> 0255—Heave Compensator system out of sync due to malfunction of electronic component. Precautionary announcement made. Capt. and engine room notified.
>
> 0345—All gimbal bearings free & working.
>
> 0800—Vessel riding easily in confused moderate S'ly swell. Vis. approx. ½ mi.
>
> 1145—Commence pumping from stbd to port fuel oil transfer to correct ½ deg stbd roll.
>
> 1200—Undergoing heave comp. & lower yoke repairs.
>
> 1600—Continue in track mode. No pipe handling activity.
>
> 1705—Unidentified vessel previously circling HGE at 1.5 mi. or more seen momentarily through poor visibility. Appears to be similar to Russian tug formerly in vicinity.

2010—Unidentified vessel appears to be on collision course to HGE. Turn on aircraft warning light as a precaution due to poor visibility. Call unknown vessel on channel 16 VHF to warn him we cannot maneuver.

2020—No contact could be made on channel 16.

2023—Closing vessel's bearing changes, appears to be changing hdg. while 6 mi. from HGE.

2040—Closing vessel one mi. from HGE.

2200–2400—Unidentified vessel drifting from 2 to 4 mi from HGE. Vessel riding easily in moderate sw'ly swell. Vis. ½ mi. Repairs in progress.

Just before 0300, I was awakened suddenly by thunderous noises and heavy shocks running through the ship. Racing out on deck, I could see that the source of the problem appeared to be up near the gimbal platforms at the base of the rig floor. I couldn't make out what had happened—the power for the derrick lights had failed—but about once every minute or so the ship would shudder, accompanied by a sheet of flame shooting out of the gimbal area and an explosive crash. There was no option to wait until daylight to analyze the situation. The Global Marine engineers had to go after the problem and inspect for damage *now*, with their hearts in their mouths and only flashlights for illumination. Everybody who wasn't involved in problem analysis was ordered to stay in the aft or forward sections of the ship.

After climbing up to the rig floor, we could see that the outer gimbal ring that was supported by the two heave compensator cylinders had been tilted forward so far that the aft side was three to four feet higher than the front. One of the Global Marine electrical engineers, John Owen, crawled down from the rig floor onto the catwalk that surrounded the gimbals to get a better sense of what was going on. While he was inspecting for damage, the ship lurched again, accompanied by another burst of blinding light and thunder. In the short time that the flash persisted, I could see the gimbal catwalk bending and twisting with Owen trying to hang on—and this was about eighty feet above the main deck. Amazingly, Owen kept his cool and, with only his flashlight for illumination, completed the survey.

It was determined that the forward and aft heave compensator cylinders had gotten wildly out of sync, the aft cylinder pushing the outer gimbal ring so high that both gimbals had become locked up, unable to move freely. Whenever an especially large roll of the ship would occur, the torques on the two interfering gimbal rings got high enough to force some relative movement between the two. The stress concentrations at the gimbal interference points were so great, though, that any relative movement of steel against steel created a brilliant flash of light accompanied by a thunderous explosion.

Unfortunately, since the gimbals were no longer able to adjust for ship roll and pitch, the bending loads were being absorbed by the lifting pipe, creating a real risk of pipe breakage. A check of the stress sensors on the lifting yokes showed that the pipe was experiencing stress levels of 140,000 to 145,000 pounds per square inch. To put that in perspective, the yield strength of the 4330V Mod lifting pipe steel was only 150 ksi, the breaking strength 170 ksi. The pipe string and the ship were in serious trouble.

Once the problem was diagnosed, the Global Marine engineers figured out a way to operate the heave compensator cylinders in a manual mode. First, they drained oil from the aft cylinder until it was about level with the forward cylinder. Then they stationed a man with a long calibrated rod at the base of each cylinder. These men read off the heights of the cylinder they were monitoring, and the engineers controlled the pumps manually to keep the cylinders at approximately the same height.

Several Lockheed technicians and engineers had volunteered for this job of reading off the heave compensator cylinder heights. Their duties onboard had previously been limited to the relatively comfortable confines of the control center, and this exposure to the wet, oily, and risky nature of the heavy lift operations was quite a shock. Wayne Ellingson, a highly skilled electronic engineer from Lockheed, was standing on the main deck with hydraulic oil from the heave compensator running over his boots, holding a long calibrated rod and reading off the heave compensator height every thirty seconds—knowing that if the ship *did* break apart, he was right in the middle of the section that would break. These Lockheed engineers never flinched or complained, but I'm sure they were second-guessing their reasons for leaving the comfort and safety of northern California.

———

Years later, I talked to John Owen about that episode and his experience on the gimbal catwalk. He recalled that the scariest part of the situation for him wasn't the deforming catwalk, but the bolt heads that were flying all over the place as they were being sheared off because of the stresses. The catwalk was surrounded by lots of ship structure—the gimbal rings, the heavy lift cylinders, the heave compensator rams, etc.—and when one of the bolts sheared off, the bolt head would fly around in that partially enclosed area at very high speed, bouncing between the structural elements like a bullet. Owen said, "I kept thinking it was like a gun battle in an old Hopalong Cassidy Western, with every bullet ricocheting off at least one boulder. I was glad I had my hard hat on, but I didn't know which way to duck!"

After some more analysis, we discovered the actual *cause* of the heave compensator unsync problem. Each of the compensator's two pistons had a fine piano wire pennant attached to it. This piano wire, with a weight attached to its end, went up and around a pulley that was directly attached to a potentiometer. As the piston went up and down, the potentiometer resistance would also rise and fall. The heave compensator sync system used the outputs from these potentiometers as inputs to the control system for keeping the pistons level. The piano wire used to measure the position of the aft heave compensator piston failed, causing the sync system to believe that the aft piston was too low. To correct the apparent problem, the sync system kept pumping oil into the aft cylinder, tilting the outer gimbal forward until the gimbal rings were "two-blocked."

It wasn't hard to fix the piano wire/potentiometer system, but why did it fail? A quick analysis revealed that a length of steel wire of the thickness we were using—when turned around a pulley of the diameter we were using—would suffer a fatigue failure after about 50,000 cycles of operation. Some elementary arithmetic disclosed the not-too-surprising fact that the piano wires had gone through just about 50,000 cycles of operation. It was a design failure we just hadn't anticipated. Fortunately, it wasn't fatal.

———

Practically everything on the ship was run by hydraulic power, and it seemed that every one of our hydraulic systems sprung at least one leak during the mission. Each failure resulted in gallons (sometimes hundreds of gallons) of hydraulic oil being spilled overboard. We speculated on the always visible oil slick that disappeared over the horizon. "How many miles did the slick extend before it was dissipated by wave and wind action?" "Will we run out of hydraulic fluid before the mission is over?"

———

We continued to work on the heave compensator and yoke latch plate repairs through the day, but by late afternoon some of our attention was refocused on yet another unidentified ship approaching the *HGE*. This ship, observed momentarily during a break in the fog, looked a lot like the recently departed Soviet tug *SB-10*. Attempts were made to contact the vessel on VHF channel 16 but without success. At the end of the day, the new mystery ship was hove to about four to six miles from the *HGE*.

The attempt begun the day before to verify the identity of the object detected on the ocean bottom by the capture vehicle's search sonar was aborted. We were still too far away. The control center moved the ship and the CV back into a position directly over the object and held there. When pipe-lowering ops could resume, we'd be able to get a better look at whatever it was.

———

For the twenty-four-hour day, we had lowered about 300 feet of pipe and were beginning to truly wonder if the ship was going to survive the ordeals of this mission. But we were getting closer to our target every day.

*Day 40 (Monday, July 29, 1974)*
From the ship's log:

> 0000–0400—Work in progress on lower yoke, gimbals, and heavy lift system. Fog signals sounded. Lookout maint. Smooth seas, moderate swell, vessel riding easily.
>
> 0455—Heave compensator bottles on line.
>
> 0655—Commence running pipe.
>
> 0800—Positioning in Auto-LBS/Track. Running in pipe. Engaged in bottom survey operations.
>
> 0814—Traveling block of draw works is lowered and falls on pipe in draw works. Shut down pipe handling ops to inspect for damage.
>
> 1020—Repairs completed, commence running pipe.
>
> 1200—Continuing bottom survey.
>
> 1300—Sounded signals for fire drill.
>
> 1316—Sounded signals for abandon ship drill.
>
> 1325—Recently unidentified vessel approached to .25 mi off port side and was identified as the "SB-10", the Russian tug previously watching HGE.
>
> 1600—LBS auto-track mode. Continue bottom survey. Vessel riding easily.
>
> 1600–2000—Watertight doors checked hourly. "SB-10" hove to 2–3 mi off port quarter. Overcast with low ragged clouds. Passing squalls.
>
> 2004—Frequent rain squalls with occ'l heavy rain.
>
> 2350—Preparing to remove one double on the lower yoke for inspection of a leaking joint. Positioning in Auto-LBS "Track" mode. Various repairs and preparation being made prior to operation of mining machine.
>
> 2355—Cautionary announcement made. Pipe on pipe transfer boom is loose and held precariously at the box by the pipe subspinner.

The Global and Western Gear engineers continued working all night trying to repair the lower yoke, gimbals, and the heavy lift system. A couple of hours before dawn, the heave compensator was ready to go. We started running pipe again, and a couple of hours later we were close enough to the bottom to start seriously searching for the target. At about 650 feet, the profiling sonars were close enough to the bottom to produce returns, providing strong evidence that the object we were holding over was, indeed, the target. By late afternoon, the capture vehicle was only a couple hundred feet above the bottom and we were beginning to get video returns from the CCTVs—final and indisputable confirmation that we'd found the target object that we'd been chasing for so long (this was our twenty-sixth day at the recovery site). It was in the exact location pinpointed by Jack Sparkman and his team during the target site survey with the *Glomar II* over three years earlier.

———

With so much pipe deployed, the ship was straining heavily under the load of about 12 million pounds hanging from the lifting yokes. This focused weight in the center of the ship put a giant bending load into the wing walls on either side of the well. The *Explorer*'s naval architect, Chuck Canby, understood the stresses the ship was undergoing better than anyone, and he ordered hourly checks of the entire ship to ensure watertight integrity and to look for any signs of cracks in the hull. All watertight doors at either end of the well were kept closed and locked. For the man in charge of maintaining the structural integrity and stability of the ship, these were tense times.

———

In order to maneuver the capture vehicle, we had to stop pipe-running operations and attach a hydraulic subassembly to the top of the lifting pipe. High-pressure (2,000 psi) seawater with a lubricity additive was then pumped down the six-inch center of the lift pipe in order to operate the hydraulic thrusters controlling the CV's fore and aft motions. We couldn't add or remove doubles from the string while we were pumping water down the pipe.

Connecting the hydraulic subassembly to the top of the pipe was an awkward operation, and we hadn't had much chance to practice it during the ISTs. Today's attempt to get hydraulic power to the CV didn't go well at all. First off, the traveling block that pulls the box end of the pipe up into a vertical position in the derrick fell, crashing into a piece of standing pipe and shutting down operations until a damage assessment could be made. Once the hydraulic hose was finally connected, it was observed that the pipe joint resting on the lower yoke was leaking. Apparently, it hadn't been torqued up before being lowered into position. When we tried to remove pipe from the string so we could torque up the leaking joint, one of the pipe sections failed to set on the transfer cart properly, leaving us with a sixty-foot double weighing 20 tons hanging precariously at the top of the transfer boom. The crew could appreciate the implications of that sixty-foot pipe section sliding down the transfer boom directly into the mess room. People grabbed their coffee cups and ran, not walked, quickly to the port or starboard side of the ship.

————

While all this was going on, the "mystery" ship came within a quarter mile of us and was easily identified as the same Russian salvage tug that had been so diligently monitoring our progress previously. We wondered, of course, why the *SB-10* had left the area and then returned. Possibly it had rendezvoused with a Soviet submarine to provide some sort of operational support. We knew that our position was close to the normal routes used by the Soviet subs on their typical patrols. Our coordinates were just a convenient crossroads. So far as we knew, however, none of the Soviet submarines that might have passed through our area had spent any time to stop and observe us.

*Day 41 (Tuesday, July 30, 1974)*
From the ship's log:

> 0000—Positioning in Auto-LBS Track Mode. Operations continue to secure pipe in transfer boom.
> 0300—Pipe secured to boom cart.
> 0315—Pipe down and off cart.
> 0425—Run in one double.
> 0645—Run in one double.
> 0800—Rigging S.W. hydraulic sub (again!). Broken overcast with low clouds.
> 1200—Preparing for mining machine bottom ops.
> 1500—SB-10 125 yds to port beam and holding position.
> 1600–1700—SB-10 made several passes, some dangerously close, apparently in disregard of common sense and good judgment!
> 2000—Positioning in Auto-LBS. Continue NCV[4] checkout/calibration. SB-10 hove-to 1.5 mi. off stbd. quarter.

2322—Enter 600' SE off-set in 100' increments at 0.1 kt from c.c. to put vessel in deeper water to add one more double to pipe string.

2325—Commence de-rigging hyd. subassembly. Vessel riding easily in low to moderate SW'ly swell. Vis. 6–8 mi, occ'l passing mist.

2400—Continue offsets in "track" mode, continue to de-rig hydr. subassembly.

The mining crew got the wayward double under control early in the morning and began running in additional pipe sections to get the capture vehicle within about 100 feet of the bottom. When the CV was at the right altitude, we started rigging the seawater hydraulic system for powering the CV thrusters and the tines. We were more careful this time, and we didn't have any pipe doubles flying around out of control.

By mid-morning, we had started the alignment of the capture vehicle with the target—the final step before we actually lowered the claw to the ocean bottom. The control center operators were amazed at the quality of the CV images we were getting from the closed-circuit TVs. The water was incredibly clear—we could see the whole length of the target object with the pan/tilt cameras. And, reassuringly, the target looked almost exactly as we expected. Hank Van Calcar was stunned to note that the real submarine was almost indistinguishable from the target model he had used in the simulator to train the CV operators.

There was one artifact that looked odd to Van Calcar and Earnest Ruggles, though. They noticed a large hammer lying on the hull of the *K-129*. They'd never noticed a hammer on the sub's deck during the many hours they'd both spent examining the hundreds of target photos before the mission. The mystery was finally solved by one of the Global Marine pipe handlers. He recognized the hammer as one of the standard tools on the ship and further remembered dropping one overboard while he was working up on the rig floor during the descent. By an amazing coincidence, the hammer had fallen more than three miles through the water and ended up precisely on the deck of the submarine we were hunting.

There were also many types of ocean life, perhaps attracted by the lights on the CV, that could be seen clearly by the cameras. Dozens of crawling, crablike crustaceans were visible, as well as a large, apparently white (we didn't have color TV on the CV), sharklike fish measuring perhaps eight to twelve feet long.

While we were getting our first look at the target, the *SB-10* suddenly became much more aggressive. Perhaps its crew could tell from our operations that we had reached the ocean bottom. It made several passes that were well within fifty yards, causing a great deal of anxiety for the seamen controlling the ship. It was absolutely critical that the *HGE* maintain its position (or its course, if moving to an offset location) very closely during operations around the target object. Maneuvering to avoid the Soviet tug was out of the question.

---

Throughout the day, the CV was undergoing final checkout for bottom operations. All systems were looking good—so far.

*Day 42 (Wednesday, July 31, 1974)*
From the ship's log:

0000—Continuing running offsets in track mode.

0050—Run one joint of pipe, commence rigging S.W. hydraulics.

0316—Enter offset to nodule site @ .15 kts. Various offsets entered by C.C. to return to site. Complete rigging of SW hydraulics.

0627—Completed setpoint to final nodule test site.

0800—Positioning in Auto-LBS. Continued NCV check-out. Overcast, cloudy, w/distant squalls.

0800—Auto-LBS in "hold set point" mode.

0854—SB-10 approaches HGE from dead ahead & makes a slow run alongside HGE's port side at about 50 yds dist. Q & Delta flags hoisted on HGE.

0900—Commence final lowering of mining machine to bottom. Final checkout completed.

0916—Mining machine on bottom.

1200—Continue mining machine bottom ops.

1240—SB-10 closes to approx. 100 yds to port.

1650—Commence lowering docking legs to 85 ft.

1913—Heave comp. sys. develops problems with make-up pump. Secure operations.

1930—SB-10 approaches close aboard and circles vessel several times.

1935—Commence raising docking legs to 45 ft.

2000—Positioning in Auto-LBS. Heave compensator repairs in progress.

2302—SB-10 dangerously close amidships to port—our windward side. Estimated less than 50 yds dist. Signal SB-10 on flashing light DDD (Keep clear of me. I am maneuvering with difficulty). Also signal AAA (calling signal) but received no response.

2305—Commence lowering docking legs in preparation to putting pipe on parking brake for heave comp. repairs.

2315—SB-10 moves away & along port side, crosses bow & stops .8 mi off stbd bow.

2325—Docking legs at 80' for G.M. compensation. SB-10 drifting along stbd side of HGE, 100–200 yds, moving from stbd bow to stbd quarter. Occ'l blowing mist. Positioning Auto-LBS. Water tight doors checked hourly. Vessel riding easily in low confused swell.

2400—Bottom ops secured due to heave comp. repairs in progress.

Having located the target and rigged the seawater hydraulic system, we realized that Clementine was still too far off the bottom to permit us to lower it onto the sea floor without adding pipe. And, we couldn't add pipe with the seawater hydraulics connected. Much to the disgust of the crew working on the rig floor, it was determined that we'd have to derig the seawater hydraulics and add another section of pipe.

When the hydraulic subassembly was eventually reconnected, the control center operators moved Clementine directly over the target, an operation they'd been practicing on the simulator for months. The capture vehicle's positioning control system, powered by the eight hydraulic thrusters located at the corners of the strongback, was able to hold the CV's position to within about ±1 foot. The electric thrusters used for azimuth control kept the heading of the CV within about ±.5 degree.

As the capture vehicle moved very slowly over the target—preparing for the final descent to the bottom—the operators were gratified to see that the visibility remained excellent, even with the hydraulic thrusters stirring the water with hundreds of horsepower. This was an unexpected bonus. Many of the oceanographers whom we had consulted during the mission planning phase had assured us that any disturbance near the bottom would raise a huge cloud of mud that would hang in the water for many minutes— even hours—effectively precluding the use of TV cameras for positioning. We were prepared for this eventuality. We had profiling sonars all along the backbone of the CV that could be used to precisely position our claw over the target regardless of water clarity. Still, the extra assurance that came from actually seeing the details during the descent over the sunken submarine was a great confidence builder.

About 0900, after a final check of Clementine's systems, we started the final lowering to the ocean bottom. The breakout legs had been adjusted to match the topology of the area around the target. All four legs were adjusted so that on touchdown the capture vehicle would align properly with the submarine hull. The aft breakout legs touched down first. Then, while controlling the azimuth of the CV with the hydraulic thrusters, the bridle was lowered until the forward part of the CV had pitched over far enough (about ten degrees) to enable the forward legs to impact the bottom. At that point, the claw was lined up with the axis of the *K-129*'s hull and ready for final adjustment to put it in the capture position.

All those hours of simulator training really paid off. Fifteen minutes after beginning the final descent, the capture vehicle was resting on the ocean bottom with the cookie cutters completely engaged into the sand. An additional 1 million pounds was offloaded from the heavy lift system to anchor the CV solidly to the bottom. It was almost a perfect touchdown, although there was a slight list of the claw to port—perhaps because of an observed leak in the aft port breakout leg (number 3).

Before touchdown, the tines had all been extended out as far as possible. The tips of the davits were barely touching the soil. The next step was to offload tension from the pipe string, effectively driving the tines down through the muddy bottom until they could be closed under the target—capturing it for the eventual ascent to the surface.

The lowering operation didn't go smoothly, though. The soil surrounding the target was harder than expected, resisting penetration by the tines. We weren't overly surprised that our estimates on soil density had been off. When the "Dork" had broken during the *Glomar II* survey mission—precluding us from getting core samples of the soil around the target—we knew that our assumptions about soil hardness would be no more than intelligent guesses. We'd hoped that those assumptions would be on the conservative side. Not so.

We started out by removing a million pounds of tension on the bridle while allowing the breakout legs to vent freely so they wouldn't be supporting much weight. Penetration was minimal. Then we offloaded another million pounds. Still, not much progress. Finally, we offloaded a total of 2.5 to 3 million pounds, still trying to get the tines—with water jets on full force—to penetrate to the depth required for capture. The CV operators were getting anxious. The capture vehicle itself only weighed about 4 million pounds. Taking any more tension from the bridle might cause the claw to list further to port, or even to start sliding downhill.

The control center operators had one more trick up their sleeve. They commanded the heavy lift to increase tension by a million pounds. This provided some righting moment from the bridle apex to correct the port list of the claw, and it also disturbed the soil around the tips of the tines, allowing the water jets to work more effectively. When the extra tension was taken back off the bridle, the result was an additional two feet of grabber penetration. That was just enough. One by one, the tines were driven down through the muddy bottom and under the target.

Once the davits were under the submarine, they were raised carefully until they made contact with the sub. Further positioning adjustments were made to distribute the weight of the target properly on each of the davits. When the target capture process was finally initiated, the work went fast. It took about eight to ten hours to drive the tines under the submarine and adjust the davit loads. The process was somewhat iterative since increasing the load on one davit would affect the loads on the other davits.

It was during this iterative adjustment period that we first began to notice some problems. Some of the seals on the actuators controlling the position of the beams and davits had developed small leaks, making it difficult to maintain the tines in a fixed position. We also noticed that a couple of the gauges that measured the position of the tines and the pressure being applied to each tine had failed.

We thought that the leaking seals on the actuators might have been due to mud being forced past the seals as the tines were driven through the ocean bottom. We hoped that this problem would be self-correcting once the actuators were clear of the bottom. The problems with the gauges, however, were an enigma. All of the electrical contacts for these gauges were housed in individual welded pressure vessels that had been leak-tested using helium gas at the time of manufacture. The gauges had all worked well during integrated systems testing. We had no good ideas about what might be going on to cause them to fail.

Fortunately, the TV cameras were still working properly. We hoped that by visually monitoring the position of the beams and davits during the ascent, we'd be able to pause, if required, to connect the seawater hydraulics and drive the claws back into the correct position. Not an ideal situation, but with all the problems we'd been able to overcome so far, we felt confident that we could overcome this one, too.

As we prepared for the breakout, the control center and the heavy lift operators reviewed the procedures thoroughly. Most of the force necessary to break the submarine loose out of the mud would come from the four breakout legs on each corner of the capture vehicle. Low-pressure seawater would be driven down the pipe into these legs, pushing the pistons in the cylinders downward against the ocean bottom, and forcing the CV and the target up and clear of the mud. But the breakout legs couldn't do it all. The heavy lift system also had to maintain a large lifting force to ensure that the capture vehicle remained stable and level as the submarine actually broke loose from the mud.

After breakout and liftoff, the heavy lift system would be operating at its maximum load, supporting the weight of 16,700 feet of lifting pipe, the claw, and the target. With all of that weight hanging from the heavy lift system, the effective center of gravity of the ship would move higher and the ship would become more top-heavy. Chuck Canby, our naval architect, was understandably nervous about this situation. The higher center of gravity would make the ship less stable and could possibly result in roll angles outside the 8.5-degree limit of the gimbal system. Just to be safe, he directed that we lower the docking legs 85 feet before breakout. The extended docking legs would lower the center of gravity of the ship and also act as a deep keel to help damp the roll motions of the ship. It seemed like good insurance. With the docking legs lowered, we were ready to initiate the breakout.

The breakout went smoothly, just as it had in the simulator training. Pressure was applied to the forward legs first. This tended to *pry* the target up out of the bottom, and it also put the CV back into a more level position for the final liftoff by the heavy lift system. Once the scanning sonars showed that target breakout had actually occurred, we prepared for liftoff—and the long ascent back to the surface. The recovery operation was proceeding by the book. How long would our luck hold out?

Not for long. Just prior to actually beginning liftoff we encountered another problem—the heave compensator system again. One of the makeup pumps. It couldn't have come at a worse time. All liftoff operations were suspended while the Western Gear engineers analyzed the situation. It wasn't going to be a quick and simple fix.

The seawater hydraulic system providing pressure to the breakout legs was shut down and the heave compensator was lowered all the way to the snubbers so the engineers could work on the failed makeup pump. The capture vehicle, with no water pressure available, slowly settled back into the soil with the target as the breakout legs leaked down.

The Lockheed engineers were shaken. The breakout legs were expected to leak water. They weren't designed for a situation in which they'd have to support the capture vehicle and the target in the same position for an extended time. And the tines? They'd been designed to lift, not push.

The situation with the tines was analogous to how your own fingers work. In a curled position your fingers are capable of lifting very heavy loads, like lifting a set of barbells. On the other hand, you'd never use your curled fingers to try to support your weight while doing push-ups. Your fingers just aren't designed to take compressive loads. Neither were the tines of the capture vehicle.

On top of everything else, the heave compensator would no longer be able to isolate the pipe string from ship motion. Every foot of ship heave or tidal change was going to change the pipe string tension by about 220,000 pounds. Fortunately, both the wave and swell heights were moderate—combined sea/swell height of about six feet. Even so, we'd be experiencing a fluctuating pipe string tension of about ±400,000 pounds due to tides and ship heave motion. What should we expect from the capture vehicle under conditions like these? We didn't have any actual or simulated test results to guide us. We could only cross our fingers and hope for the best.

Several hours after the heave compensator failure, we had to raise the pipe three to five feet so the load could be shared equally by the upper and lower yokes, reducing the strain on the heavy lift pumps. The seawater hydraulics were reconnected at that time, and while the pipe handlers raised the top of the pipe string, the control center operators extended the break-out legs downward, lifting the target from the ocean bottom once again. This operation was almost complete when there was a strong shock transmitted up the pipe and into the ship. Either the target object had shifted its position in the claw or part of the claw's structure had failed—perhaps both. Inspection with the CCTVs and sonars showed that the sail section of the *K-129* had rotated downward, but we couldn't determine if a structural failure of the CV had also occurred. We wouldn't know the full extent of any damage to the claw until it was back in the well of the ship.

———

While we continued to wrestle with the heave compensator, the *SB-10* was causing more anxious moments for the seamen on the bridge of the *HGE*. The Soviet ship would come in very close—within fifty yards—and circle the ship, sometimes several times in succession. Because of the bottom operations, the helmsmen knew they had to hold position precisely. The concentration required to perform this job was hard to maintain when they had to keep constant watch simultaneously on a smaller vessel maneuvering dangerously close to our ship. Several attempts were made with flags and lights to warn the Russian ship that we were "maneuvering with difficulty." The bridge also tried to establish some communications with the *SB-10* so we could explain the precarious position we were in. Nothing worked. The Russians ignored our call for more maneuvering room and appeared to have no interest in conversing with the *HGE*. These harassment tactics were not unusual in the Cold War years—we had no reason to believe that the Soviets knew what we were up to—but they made a tough situation a whole lot worse for us.

By 2400, our bottom operations had been shut down for over five hours. We suspected we might have had a structural failure of the claw. And the heave compensator repairs were still continuing.

*Day 43 (Thursday, August 1, 1974)*
From the ship's log:

> 0000—Positioning in Auto-LBS. Continue with repairs to Heave Comp. Watertight doors checked hourly.
>
> 0400—Overcast, occasional light rain squall. Vessel riding easily.
>
> 0435—SB-10 makes run up stbd side, heaves-to ¾ mi stbd bow.
>
> 0500—SB-10 drifting down stbd side, less than 50 yds off at stern, ends up hove-to 1–2 mi. distant.
>
> 0800—Positioning in Auto-LBS. Continue heave comp. repairs. SB-10 approx. 100 yds off port side. Vessel riding easily in low W'ly swell & slight NW'ly sea.
>
> 1200—Continue heave comp. repairs.
>
> 1435—Repairs to Heave Comp. completed. Resume mining machine bottom ops.
>
> 1700—Control Center reports the Collector control systems alarmed. Exact status unknown, but both manual and auto terrain guidance controls malfunctioning. CC investigating.
>
> 1929—Commence unrigging S.W. hydraulic sub.
>
> 1930—Off track mode.
>
> 1940—Hydraulic sub off; commence pulling pipe; NCV off bottom.
>
> 2008—First double pulled.
>
> 2310–2400—Commence correcting ½ deg port list, fuel oil transfer by engine room. W.T. doors checked hourly. Vessel riding easily in low WNW'ly swell. Intermittent pulling of pipe. SB-10 continues circling (5 times so far) at dist. of 75 to 125 yds.
>
> 2400—Holding for repairs.

In the early afternoon, after almost twenty hours, the repairs were complete and the heave compensator was moved back up to its mid-position. The seawater hydraulic system was rigged so that low-pressure seawater could be pumped down the pipe into the breakout legs. We prepared—again—for liftoff.

Once again, the breakout legs would be slowly extended while the heavy lift system applied the maximum safe load on the lifting pipe. Once the target was eased clear of the ocean bottom, the heavy lift system would take the full load of the capture vehicle and the target. The breakout legs would be jettisoned and left standing on the bottom.

Before the actual liftoff procedure could be started, an alarm sounded in the control center. Both the manual and automatic terrain guidance control systems for the capture vehicle were showing a problem. An inspection of the CV status using the CCTVs was initiated, but results were inconclusive. (Only two of the CCTVs onboard had pan/tilt capability, limiting our diagnostic capabilities.) Given the situation we were in, we decided to continue with the liftoff sequence. There was no way to repair the CV—if anything *was* broken— and it was getting increasingly difficult to make any additional adjustments to the tines because of the leaking seals and failing pressure gauges.

The docking legs were extended down eighty feet in order to lower the center of gravity of the ship, and we started pumping seawater down the pipe into the breakout legs. Water was directed to the forward legs first, in order to level the CV. Then, water was pumped into all four legs—maintaining near-maximum lift forces with the heavy lift system—until the target was completely free of the bottom. The liftoff itself went smoothly except for one small glitch. One of the four breakout legs wouldn't jettison. Larry Musselman, one of the Lockheed engineers, quickly diagnosed the problem and rerouted the hydraulic control through redundant hoses. The recalcitrant breakout leg, along with the three others, was successfully released. Within a couple of hours, the capture vehicle and target were clear of the bottom, leaving the breakout legs, clearly visible, standing on the seafloor. The seawater hydraulic subassembly was removed from the top of the pipe, and the target started the long trip back to the surface and the well of the *Hughes Glomar Explorer.*

*Day 44 (Friday, August 2, 1974)*
From the ship's log:

> 0000—Positioning in Auto-LBS. Continue with repairs.
>
> 0215—Complete repairs. Commence pipe handling ops.
>
> 0400—Cont. pipe handling ops. Watertight doors checked hourly.
>
> 0420—SB-10 approaches from astern; heaves-to ahead; drifts to 2.0 mi. off stbd beam.
>
> 0810—SB-10 approaches from stern, commences slow circling of HGE 75–150 yds dist.
>
> 1330—Raise docking legs to 45 ft.
>
> 1500–1600—Watertight doors checked hourly. Continue pipe handling ops. Light o'cast, slight SW'ly sea. Vessel riding easily.

1700—Stop pulling pipe. Repairs to hydraulics on stbd tripod.

2000—Positioning in Auto-LBS. Repairs in progress. Broken overcast.

2100—Commence pipe ops.

2125—Secure pipe ops due to critical sensor reading.

2128—Cautionary announcement made to crew due to possible stress on pipe.

2150–2225—Communication exchanged w/ the tanker, "Bangkok", call letters HSKB. Communication on channel 16 originated with "Bangkok." He was curious as to the nature of our vessel. "Bangkok" was bound for San Francisco, passing HGE at 4 mi.

2240—Announcement made danger of pipe stress is over.

2400—Continue repairs. Vessel riding easily in low WNW'ly swell & slight SW'ly sea. Lookout posted on forward bridge, special purpose lights burning brightly. Vis. 6–8 mi.

The heavy lift system was really straining now. Including the weight of the lifting pipe, the capture vehicle, and the target, we were trying to raise over 14 million pounds from the ocean bottom. The sea states were reasonable and the ship was stable, but the heavy lift system was stressed to its limit. Failures were frequent. It seemed as though we were spending most of our time fixing problems rather than pulling pipe.

At 2125 the notes from the ship's log indicated that we had another problem with the heavy lift hydraulic system that pushed the stress on the pipe past the acceptable limit. A warning announcement was made to the crew. Once again, everyone not involved in the actual repair process was expected to stay out of the midsection of the ship. The crew was growing weary of these high pipe stress announcements—they seemed to be occurring with more and more regularity.

————

Our progress during the last few weeks had been excruciatingly slow. When we arrived at the site on the Fourth of July, the optimists among us expected to complete the operation in about six days—one day to deploy the wave rider buoys and bottom transponders, two days of pipe lowering at six feet a minute, one day of bottom operations, and two days to raise the pipe. As of this day, August 2, we'd been working for thirty days and had encountered more problems than even the hardest-core pessimists had predicted.

Still, however slowly, we were making progress. By the end of the day, the target was back up to 13,800 feet. We had pulled almost 3,000 feet of pipe.

*Day 45 (Saturday, August 3, 1974)*
From the ship's log:

> 0400—Broken clouds, slight SW'ly sea. Confused low swell. Repairs continue to pipe handling system.
>
> 0800—Positioning in Auto-LBS. Continue repairs on hydraulic system. High and medium broken overcast.
>
> 1154—Commence pipe handling ops.
>
> 1200–1600—Positioning in Auto-LBS. Pipe handling ops cont. thru watch.
>
> 1815—SB-10 approaches to port from 9.0 mi. astern and heaves-to on port bow; commences drifting aft.
>
> 1910—Resume pulling pipe, albeit slowly! Docking legs to 40 ft.
>
> 2000—Pulling pipe. Scattered low clouds—thin, high overcast.
>
> 2400—Continue pulling pipe. Watertight doors checked hourly.

Yesterday's high pipe stress incident was a real wakeup call for the pipe-handling crew. They realized we were operating right on that thin line between normal operations and total disaster. By midday, repairs to the heavy lift hydraulic system were completed and we were ready to start pulling pipe again. Because of yesterday's scare, however, the pipe-handling operations were resumed at a *very* slow rate, with each transfer of load from one lifting yoke to the other being watched carefully by the operators.

We continued the lifting ops for over twelve hours, and the speed kept increasing. We were making good progress, and every double of pipe recovered reduced the total load on the heavy lift system by about 40,000 pounds. It felt as though the removal of each pipe double from the string allowed the lift system to work a little easier and faster. We were all getting cautiously optimistic. It was becoming easier to believe "We just might be able to pull this operation off after all!"

*Day 46 (Sunday, August 4, 1974)*
From the ship's log:

> 0000–0400—Pipe handling ops in progress. Passing rain squalls, moderate SW'ly sea, W'ly swell.
>
> 0555—SB-10 approaches from port quarter; crosses bow at approx 75 yds; heaves-to on port bow and begins drifting aft.
>
> 0625—Stop pulling pipe.
>
> 0659—Heave comp at top of stroke.

0800—Positioning in Auto-LBS. Repairs in progress to hydraulics. Mainly overcast and cloudy. Occasional passing light rain.

0830—SB-10 makes run from astern to along port side, dist. 200 yds.

1144—Commence fog signals on whistle due to heavy rain squall. Vessel riding easily in moderate SW'ly sea and WNW'ly swell.

1200—Continuing repairs.

1315—Resume pipe ops.

1433—Commence raising docking legs.

1535—Docking legs in full up.

1612—Stop pulling pipe. ARN problems.

1750—Resume pulling pipe.

1850—SB-10 begins approach from 3.0 mi. on port quarter. This sea-going kamikaze passes close under stern, goes up stbd side, passes close under bow, and goes down port side.

2000—Pulling pipe. Overcast and cloudy. Passing rain occas., distant and near-by squalls.

2400—SB-10 ¼ mi. off stbd. bow. W-T doors checked 2200 & 2400. Continuing pulling pipe.

Just after breakfast, I was walking along the main deck speculating on how much longer it would take us to bring the target to the surface. Sherm Wetmore was sitting in the mess room having a second cup of coffee. Hank Van Calcar had just sat down at his desk in the control center to make a routine check on the status of the capture vehicle. Chuck Canby, our naval architect, was just beginning his daily calculations on weights and ship stability.

Canby had raised the docking legs from 85 feet to 45 feet. We had already pulled almost 8,000 feet of pipe, and he was less concerned now about the ship's center of gravity. I figured that if the heavy lift system could continue at the pace we had been maintaining, we might be ready to dock Clementine and its cargo in a couple of days. We were all feeling a little more comfortable with our recovery status. I was actually beginning to relax a little.

Suddenly, there was a slight jolt in the ship. Instinctively, I looked up to the rig floor to see if something had happened. Sherm Wetmore left his coffee and went out on the deck to investigate. Van Calcar looked around at his instruments, monitors, and gauges. Everything looked okay, he thought—so what caused the bump?

Something looked strange to me as I looked up at the rig floor, but I couldn't identify what it might be. Then I realized the heave compensator had moved to its highest position and was locked in place there against the snubbers. Why? My first thought was that the control system for the heave compensator had malfunctioned again, causing it to drive itself all the way up to the snubbers. This wouldn't have been too serious, since we were in a moderate sea state and the loads on the lifting pipe had been coming down steadily.

Then it suddenly occurred to me that it might not be a heave compensator malfunction at all. Perhaps the load on the pipe string had been suddenly reduced. Perhaps we had a problem a lot worse than a heave compensator control system. I finally put two and two together and connected the slight bump I had felt with the behavior of the rig floor. Perhaps we had lost part of the target—and maybe the capture vehicle.

I rushed up to the control center and found the watch operators intently looking at the images from all the CCTVs. It was obvious that some kind of calamity had occurred, but they couldn't identify the exact nature of the problem. They'd turned on the television and sonar displays immediately when they felt the bump as the heave compensator topped up against the snubbers, and they expected the worst. Surprisingly, everything looked okay. The CCTVs showed the target in position and in one piece, just as it had been when it was lifted off the ocean bottom. The sonars, though, were indicating that all was not well. Some of the profiling sonars attached to the strongback weren't seeing any target at all.

It didn't take long to resolve this contradiction. When the CCTVs had been turned on, they were showing the most recent images they had scanned. When the CCTVs were commanded to refresh, the pictures changed, confirming that we had, indeed, lost part of the target—and maybe part of the capture vehicle as well. We tried to interpret the tine position sensors and the actuator pressure gauges to get more information about the extent of the problem, but we had so many failed sensors that it was impossible to make any kind of accurate assessment.

Eventually, we were able to put most of the story together. When the truth had sunk in, the control center operators sat at their consoles staring blankly into space. They couldn't believe that after all the obstacles that had been overcome, we'd have a problem like this. I spoke to Van Calcar, but he didn't hear me. His mind was miles away, trying to assess the cause of the failure and asking himself what we could have done differently to prevent the failure. Success had seemed so close. And we still didn't know how much of the target had been lost—or how much was remaining.

Obviously, there was nothing we could do other than accept the fact that part of our target was now back on the ocean bottom, and take what steps we could to ensure that we could retrieve what still remained in the claw up to the surface and into the well of the *Explorer*.

Our first task was to get the heave compensator lowered to its vertical midpoint so it could resume its function of isolating ship heave motions from the pipe string and capture vehicle. With most of the target now on the bottom, the air pressure in the heave compensator chambers was way too high. When the valves were opened to bleed the system, the shriek of the escaping air actually caused physical pain to the ears of those working in the vicinity. This eerie scream continued for many minutes until the excess air was bled off and the heave compensator adjusted itself to its proper vertical position.

While the heave compensator adjustments were continuing, the control center personnel checked and recorded the readings of each of the still-working gauges and sensors on the tines. We didn't know how the loads were distributed on the tines, but it seemed prudent to try to maintain the positions of those that still had working sensors. Whatever part of the target we still had we wanted to hold on to.

———

Mission director Dale Neuwirth notified CIA headquarters immediately. Using secure communications, he reported that a large part of the target had fallen back to the ocean bottom when it was about 9,000 feet from the surface, and that we were preparing to continue lifting the remainder of the target to the surface.

Within an hour, we got a reply from headquarters: "We do not agree with the plan to continue raising the capture vehicle to the surface. We prefer you return to ocean bottom and recover that portion of target that broke away."

When we received the headquarters cable, Neuwirth handed it to me and said, "I guess you'd better answer this one."

I wrote a cable explaining our situation in more detail. I pointed out that at least two of the tines that had been supporting the lost part of the target had already been broken off or rendered unusable. Further, few of the sensors for the tines still worked. We'd have no way of knowing what their position was or how much load they were being subjected to. Also, we had no breakout legs to support the weight of the CV on the ocean bottom. (The breakout legs had been jettisoned right after liftoff.) Finally, we had no way of knowing what configuration the broken target might be in as it lay on the seafloor—or how many pieces it might be in. We thought we might be able to find it, but whether it would be resting in a configuration that would allow us to capture and lift it was highly doubtful. In short, there was virtually no way that we could return to the bottom and recover the remainder of the K-129.

This time the answer came back almost immediately: "Return to ocean bottom and recover remainder of target. This is not a request. This is an order." The identity of the sender was Carl Duckett, the CIA's director of science and technology.

Obviously, my cable hadn't been convincing. I went back to my desk and started thinking about how I could persuade Duckett that we really didn't have any option except to continue the ascent. Although Carl was a strong advocate and supporter of the AZORIAN mission, his knowledge of the technical details of the recovery system was limited. I knew I'd have only one more chance to make my case. If I failed, we'd have no choice but to descend once more to the ocean bottom and attempt the location and capture of the lost portion of the target—a mission that we all believed to be impossible.

I was ready to submit a second response when I was preempted by another cable from headquarters. This one said, simply: "Proceed with plan to continue ascent. Disregard previous order." The mission director and his deputies breathed a collective sigh of relief. We resumed our plans to try to recover at least *something* into the well of the ship before this operation was all over.

———

How could we best ensure that we'd be able to get the remainder of the target into the well of the ship? We considered readjusting the tine loadings to distribute the remaining load more evenly, but that idea was overruled. At least for now, we thought we had a *stable* situation. If it became apparent during the ascent that the tine positions were shifting, we could stop the ascent, reconnect the seawater hydraulic subassembly, and try to bring the tine positions and pressures back to where they were. For now, though, we decided to just continue raising the damaged claw and the remaining portion of the target as quickly as we could, without tempting another failure of the heavy lift system. We were in a race against time.

———

After the mission was over, I had a chance to get some headquarters perspective about the exchange of messages following the target breakaway incident. There were few hard facts available. Parangosky wasn't talking. In fact, no one really wanted to talk about it. Eventually, though, I was able to put the following story together:

Our first message to headquarters arrived late afternoon. Parangosky immediately called Carl Duckett and requested that he come to the AZORIAN Situation Room. When Duckett arrived and heard the news about part of the target breaking away, he was so upset that he was figuratively bouncing off the walls. He insisted that a cable be sent to the ship ordering us to descend and recover the rest of the target. Shortly after that direction was sent to the ship, headquarters received my response explaining that we didn't have the capability to fulfill that request—that we were not able to return to the bottom and collect the rest of the target. I must have used the wrong tone in my message, because it infuriated Duckett. He immediately sent a response indicating that his direction to go back down was not a "request," but an "order!"

By this time, it was early in the morning on the East Coast. Duckett was insisting that Parangosky patch him through to the ship with an open (unenciphered) telephone so he could verbally command us to return for the rest of the submarine. Realizing that such an open-line conversation between Duckett and the ship would assuredly compromise the mission and endanger the ship and crew, Parangosky—very calmly—explained to Duckett, "We can't do that, Carl." Finally, at about 0200, Parangosky called Geary Yost, our mission crew member who had been left behind, and requested him to come to the Situation Room.

Yost was unable to say anything for a couple of hours. Duckett was doing all the talking and getting more frustrated and angrier by the minute. He was still insisting that he be allowed to talk to the ship by radiotelephone. John never raised his voice. He just kept repeating, "We can't do that, Carl."

Finally, Duckett calmed down enough so that Yost could start explaining the situation. All the drawings of the recovery system and its parts were in the Situation Room, and Yost explained, clearly and convincingly, why the *Explorer* crew had no real choice at this time except to continue the ascent. Around 0500, Duckett conceded. But he hated it. We had come so close to recovering the entire target. He was devastated.

Yost was probably the only engineer at headquarters who could have convinced Duckett that the mission director and his deputies were doing the right thing. He was the only engineer remaining in the program office who truly understood the technical details of the entire recovery system. Many times during the mission, I'd wished that Geary had been on the ship to help work through the system failures we were having. But I'm grateful that he was in Washington on the day we had our worst failure.

*Day 47 (Monday, August 5, 1974)*
From the ship's log:

> 0448–0625—Stop pulling pipe for upper yoke tele. tube repair.
> 0620–0710—SB-10 from port quarter to stbd bow; commence drifting down stbd side.

0650–0730—Stop pulling pipe for ARN repair.

1015—Commence pipe handling ops.

1035–1055—SB-10 approaches from port quarter, runs along port side at 150 yds, crosses bow at 50 yds & drifts down stbd side within 50 yds before heeding "D" flag and backing down to approx. 150 yds from stbd side to commence drifting.

1645—Docking legs lowered to 90 ft.

The rate of pipe recovery was picking up, probably due to several factors. First, the load on the heavy lift system was decreasing constantly as the pipe doubles were removed from the string and placed in the storage hold. Second, the operators were becoming more skilled in the operation of the heavy lift and pipe-handling systems with all their idiosyncrasies. Third, there was a sense of urgency to get the remaining part of the target into the well of the ship before we had another breakaway experience. With the gauges and sensors for the tines working less and less reliably, we couldn't afford to lose any time. We were now pulling pipe at a rate of about 4,000 to 5,000 feet per day. If we kept that up, we'd be ready for docking tomorrow.

In anticipation of the docking, the legs were lowered to ninety feet. In that position we could check out the docking leg subsystems (i.e., tilt controls for both fore and aft legs, the sliding cylinders that controlled lateral motion of the keyholes, and the underwater cameras). Perhaps our lowering of the legs was what motivated the SB-10 to come in for another very close reconnaissance. Perhaps—if they'd been counting the doubles removed from the pipe string—they also knew that we were nearing the surface and getting close to the end of the operation. And this brought up some new worries.

What if the Russians' curiosity prompted them to put divers in the water to inspect the underwater operations during docking? If they had any notion that we were recovering their submarine instead of a mining machine, they might use a diver to confirm their suspicion. Even if they had bought our deep ocean mining cover story, they might still be curious enough to want to get intelligence on Howard Hughes's ocean mining techniques. It would certainly be easy enough for them to deploy a diver without our knowing it. The SB-10 had been spending time each day within fifty yards or so of our ship. A diver entering the water from the side of the boat away from the HGE would never be noticed. Even easier, they might choose to deploy a diver at night when the entire moon pool of the HGE was brightly illuminated. They'd have no problem observing the operations.

Since detection of the divers wasn't a viable option—and, what would we do if we did detect them?—there was some speculation about possible ways to discourage diver operations. What if we were to set off underwater charges at random intervals? This would certainly discourage the use of divers, but it would likely make the Russians very suspicious about why we were doing it—and what were we trying to hide? And then there was the risk of actually harming, or even killing, a Russian diver. Any injured diver would probably have to be brought aboard the *HGE* for humanitarian reasons. We had a doctor and sophisticated medical equipment. The *SB-10* likely had a medical technician onboard, but they were almost certainly unprepared to deal properly with a life-threatening injury.

Ultimately, the mission director made the only decision he felt he could conscionably defend. He would not risk losing more lives over the *K-129*. Ninety-eight Soviet sailors had already perished. If there was going to be an international incident over the CIA attempting to raise a Soviet submarine, the situation wasn't going to be exacerbated by the death of yet another Soviet sailor. There were going to be no underwater explosives.

Everyone felt comfortable with Neuwirth's decision. We all breathed a collective sigh of relief, and hoped that the Russians had no clue as to what it was that we were planning to recover into the well of the ship the next day.

*Day 48 (Tuesday, August 6, 1974)*
From the ship's log:

> 0400–0405—SB-10 hazarding HGE with unreasonably close approach. Warned off with flashing light; heaves-to 1–2 mi on stbd qtr.
>
> 0822—SB-10 approaches stbd side from astern, dist. 200 yds, reverses direction, runs around stern & up port side & down stbd side dist. 150 yds.
>
> 1335—Lower docking legs to 133 ft, then raise to 100 ft at 7 deg tilt. Discontinue pipe handling ops.
>
> 1645—NCV blocking ASK acoustics; shift to joystick—manual inputs to thrusters/mains.
>
> 1714—Last double off rig floor.
>
> 1809—On parking brake. Commence well diving ops.
>
> 2000—Manual inputs to thrusters/mains, joystick mode. Continue diving ops in preparation for docking. High thin o'cast.
>
> 2045—Commence lowering docking legs. SB-10 approaches stbd abeam, 50 yds. Flashed ("delta") "D" on blinker to SB-10, and SB-10 commences backing away from vessel.
>
> 2100—Crew members of SB-10 wave good-bye & three long blasts are blown on the whistle by SB-10 as he crosses our stern at 50 yds.

2117—Mining machine hitched to docking legs.

2118—Commence raising docking legs.

2145—Heave comp. off line, derrick gimbals locked.

2148—Commence raising docking legs.

2315—Commence diving ops in moon pool. Vessel riding easily in low moderate swell.

The heavy lift and pipe-handling systems were still chugging along. We were taking doubles out of the string and putting them in the storage hold with a regularity that was foreign to us. It really did look like we'd be docking that day. The docking legs were lowered all the way down, tilted seven degrees (maximum "open"), and raised back to 100 feet in anticipation. We only had a few hundred feet to go.

Then we got a new surprise to blast us out of our euphoria. As the remaining portion of the K-129 was getting closer to the ship, it was beginning to feel the effects of subsurface wave action. The swirling water was beginning to loosen some of the detritus that the target had been carrying with it. Some of this debris—fuel containers, clothing, etc.—had surfaced in the well of the ship. We didn't know if any of those artifacts had floated up on the outside of the ship or—if they had—whether they'd been noticed by the crew of the SB-10. Certainly, the SB-10 had been showing a great deal of interest in everything that floated free of the HGE for the last couple of weeks. Did they still have that same intense curiosity?

There was nothing we could do about it, so we just continued with our docking plans. When the capture vehicle was about 150 feet from the ocean surface, pipe-handling operations were discontinued and the lift pipe was placed on the parking brake. All the air bottles were shut off from the heave compensator, locking it in place to minimize relative vertical motion between the docking legs and the CV. The divers were sent down to begin preparations.

At this critical time, the SB-10 came in for another close reconnaissance. The HGE bridge, alarmed at the aggressive action, sent a "D" signal with the blinker lights to warn the Soviets that we could not maneuver to avoid contact. We wondered if the SB-10's crew was going to find floating objects from their submarine, confirming suspicions they might have about the true nature of our activities. Paranoia was running rampant as we got ready to dock.

Maybe it was because the sea state was relatively calm—and maybe it was because we were finally getting the "hang" of the docking/undocking maneuvers—but we managed to capture Clementine without a hitch. We had her and the abbreviated target on the docking legs about 110 feet below us. We were ready to bring the payload into the well.

But the *SB-10* was only fifty yards away. We knew that even as we continued the docking operations, the Russians could easily deploy a diver to inspect the payload. We thought about just holding in our present position until the *SB-10* backed off. On the other hand, Clementine and its prize were now being subjected to the same dynamic motion and wave action that the ship was seeing—and we were concerned that the claw's grip on the target might be precarious. We didn't want to lose any more of the *K-129*. With one eye on the *SB-10*, we started raising the docking legs to bring the capture vehicle up high enough to permit bridle derigging. If the Russians had deployed a diver at this point to inspect the mining machine, he would have gotten an eyeful.

But luck was with us. The Russian ship, which had been at close quarters for much of the day and had only responded sluggishly to repeated "D" signals from the *HGE* bridge, casually crossed our stern at under fifty yards. At that point, the whole crew of the *SB-10* lined up on the rail and mooned the *Explorer*. Hank Van Calcar and some of the other crew members stared in disbelief as they witnessed the spectacle from the *HGE* fantail. Quickly coming to their senses, though, they immediately dropped their pants, turned around, and mooned the crew of the *SB-10*. The Soviets cheered, waved goodbye, and with three long blasts of their horn headed off over the horizon. We never saw them again.

*Day 49 (Wednesday, August 7, 1974)*

While the bridle was being derigged, the divers went down to inspect the capture vehicle and the remaining portion of the *K-129*. They confirmed that a couple of the tines had broken away, allowing most of the submarine to fall back to the ocean bottom. The remaining portion of the target, however, seemed to be contained securely within the forward tines. It also appeared that the total envelope of the CV and the remaining part of the target were well within the limits defined by the well size and geometry. There was no need to do any cutting or trimming before raising Clementine into the well.

When we got the divers' reports, our worst fears about what part of the target had been lost were confirmed. We had part of the submarine, but we had lost that portion that was of most interest to us. As William Colby poignantly wrote in the French edition of his memoir, "only the forepart, about one-third of the ship was eventually brought back to the surface, while the aft fell to the bottom of the sea with its nuclear missiles, its guiding apparatus, its transmission equipment, its codes, in other words with all the things the CIA had hoped to recover."[5]

By early evening the capture vehicle had been fully raised. By 1800, the well gates had been closed and the water was being pumped out of the well. The entire crew was charged up with the anticipation of finally seeing at least part of the *K-129* submarine that we'd come so far—and worked so hard—to recover.

*Day 50 (Thursday, August 8, 1974)*
From the ship's log:

> 0705—Depart site. Maneuvering to retrieve northern wave rider buoy.
> 0822—North wave rider and anchor buoy aboard.
> 0830—Change heading to retrieve south wave rider.
> 1025—South wave rider aboard.
> 1040—Transfer control to forward bridge. ASK secured. Full ahead, 3 motors on each shaft.
> 1042—Departure nodule test site. Hdg. 151 deg. true course.
> 1200—Underway to 126-1 site.

While the moon pool was still being pumped, the ship was steered to the north and south wave rider buoy locations and the buoys retrieved. We wouldn't be needing the continuous power spectral density information on sea and swell anymore.

With completion of this minor housekeeping, control of the ship was transferred to the forward bridge and we departed the target site. Our destination was referred to simply as Site 126-1, in the general direction of Midway Island.[6] In accordance with the cover plan, a message had gone out in the open commercial channel on August 3. The *HGE* had reported that the "nodule collector vehicle might have collided with a hard silt-covered outcrop." This fictional casualty, reported in the clear, could be used as an excuse for the *HGE* to request permission from U.S. naval authorities to enter Midway for repairs to the vehicle before proceeding to Lahaina for replenishment of supplies and a crew change.[7]

By noon, we were well on our way. As soon as the well was pumped, we'd begin the exploitation phase of the mission.

*Day 51 (Friday, August 9, 1974): En Route to Site 126-1*
When the well was almost completely pumped out, we could finally see the portion of the target object that we had recovered. It wasn't a pretty sight.

It was so mangled that it was difficult to identify the features. To me it was just a gray mass of metal that bore very little resemblance to a submarine. It was impossible for me to say, "Oh, there's a torpedo tube," or "Over there's the mount for the deck guns." It was massive, and gray, and looked very formidable.

The exploitation team was eager to get started. Fortunately, the submarine looked cleaner than we'd expected. There seemed to be very little mud and silt raised with the target, and that would simplify the exploitation process.

First, however, the onboard radiation experts did a thorough inspection of the wreckage to determine how much and what kind of radiation there was down in the well of the ship. This survey would determine what kind of protective clothing the exploitation crew would have to wear, and what kind of precautions would have to be taken to prevent inhalation of radioactive smoke from the cutting operations. We were prepared for all conditions, but we were hoping for a relatively safe environment.

I'll confess, I wasn't eager to take part in the exploitation. I knew that all of my recovery team would be needed to help with the salvaging, but the thought of the Soviet sailors, some presumably still in that twisted wreckage, was very sobering.

The radiation checks were reassuring, though. The contamination levels were lower than anticipated. Evidence of plutonium was found—probably from the detonation of one or both of the high-explosive fuses in the submarine's two nuclear torpedoes. Fortunately the contamination was in a hydroxide form, so there was little chance of airborne particulates.[8] Paper jumpsuits, good for one wearing, would be adequate to protect the exploitation crew.[9] On Day 51 of the mission, exploitation of the K-129 submarine was finally started.

*Day 52 (Saturday, August 10, 1974): En Route to Site 126-1*
From the ship's log:

> 0000—Advance clocks 1 hour to Z+11. Underway to Site 126-1. Heading 153°.
> 0935—Changed course to 152°. Vessel riding easily in low to moderate NNE'ly swell. Visibility excellent.
> 1820—Changed course 126°—Alter course toward Lahaina, island of Maui, Hawaii, per instructions Mining Director.
> 2155—Changed course 128°. Vessel riding easily in low NE'ly swell. Occ'l rain squalls. Lookout posted on bow—vis. approx. 15 mi. Running lights burning brightly.

When we started exploitation yesterday, the target was sort of grayish, and it had a distinctive smell—vaguely metallic, with an acrid odor somewhat like a pickle brine. Now the warm temperatures and oxygen-rich environment were already beginning to work on the target hull. The gray was turning rapidly to rust. And the metallic pickle brine odor was also changing. It was getting stronger—a smell that was completely foreign to me. I didn't believe it was the smell of decaying bodies—I had grown up in rural Virginia and I was very familiar with the smell of decaying wildlife. The smell rising up from the well was not like that. The divers knew what it was, though. Most of them had experienced the smell of human death before. They assured me that what we were smelling was, indeed, distinctly human, and that the odor would be getting a lot worse in the next few days.

The exploitation was progressing rapidly, though. The bow section that we had recovered was yielding its secrets much more quickly than the sail section of the submarine—our primary objective—would have done. It was obvious that we'd be able to finish the exploitation in much less time than originally envisioned. This consideration, along with the low level of radiation found on the target, convinced the mission director that it probably wouldn't be necessary for us to stop at Site 126-1 for a prolonged exploitation period. It looked like we could probably finish much of the job en route to—or in the near vicinity of—Lahaina.

Neuwirth instructed the captain to change course. He followed up with an unencrypted message to Summa headquarters indicating that the problem with the nodule collection vehicle was not as serious as first believed, and that the planned voyage to Site 126-1 would be cancelled.[10] We would be going directly to the port of Lahaina Roads on the island of Maui.

That was a very popular decision. The crew had been at sea for fifty two days so far. That's not a long time for the Global Marine crew or Navy personnel—especially submariners—but it seemed like a long voyage, indeed, to the civilian government personnel and the contractor engineers who had tired of the novelty of shipboard living weeks ago.

*Day 53 (Sunday, August 11, 1974): En Route to Lahaina*

As we sailed farther south, the weather got warmer and accelerated the decomposition of both the metallic and human wreckage in the well of the *Explorer*. The odor from the well now permeated the entire ship. Even though we were underway, the smell hung in the air, refusing to be blown away by the almost ten-knot breeze that the *HGE* was creating as it steamed toward Lahaina.

I was reminded of the lines from Shakespeare's *King Henry V* spoken by

King Henry before the battle of Agincourt. On the night before the battle, the king of France sends a messenger to King Henry demanding surrender. In answer, Henry acknowledges that many Englishmen will die on the battlefield, but tells the messenger that the sun will "draw their honors reeking up to Heaven, leaving their earthly parts to choke your clime, the smell whereof shall breed a plague in France!"

Indeed, the honors of those Russian sailors who died in the defense of their country were now being drawn reeking up to heaven. Recalling those lines increased my admiration for those brave Russian sailors who had died as patriots serving their country. In my mind, their reeking honors no longer represented the embarrassment of their death but rather the celebration of their heroism.

*Day 54 (Monday, August 12, 1974): En Route to Lahaina*
From the ship's log:

> 0000—Under way to Lahaina, isle of Maui. Course 129°.
>
> 0049—Radar plot of unknown vessel indicates CPA of approx. 7 mi on port to port meeting. Vessel approaching from port bow with no indication of course change on near collision course. Order given to helmsman for a 040 deg change to stbd to effect approx CPA of 2 miles. Helmsman unable to check vessel swing to stbd with full left rudder order. Rudder will not go past midship position. Switched to port steering pump. Rudder locked at midship. Switched to N.F.V. steering and rudder responds. Vessel swing stopped at 220 deg and heading returned to 169 deg. Notified engine room. Unidentified vessel did not appear to make any alteration of speed or heading. CPA approx 1.79 mi.
>
> 0110—Returned to course 129 deg.

The "A" crew's exploitation team was finally getting the opportunity to put their extensive training and high technology to good use. We knew that the submarine and its contents had been well preserved for over six years while lying on the bottom of the ocean. The temperature at that depth was just about a constant thirty-two degrees. We were less confident about damage that might have been done by living organisms at that depth, however. In fact, we didn't have a very good idea about what kind of living animals even existed down there until we landed over the target and used the CCTVs to explore the ocean bottom.

The challenge was that, although the target had probably suffered very little from decay and oxidation while submerged, those processes were greatly accelerated when we got the bow portion into the well of the ship. We were running a race with time to recover and preserve documents, electronics, and mechanical systems before they were degraded beyond any useful intelligence value.

*Days 55–57 (August 13–15, 1974): En Route to Lahaina*

Even though we were working with a much smaller part of the *K-129* than planned, the exploitation operations were not without problems. The interior of the forward section of the submarine had been compressed very tightly into the bow, and only a limited number of exploitation team members could simultaneously access that section of the boat. Removal of the artifacts had to be done very carefully to ensure that they didn't break apart, tear, or crumble as they were being separated from the surrounding wreckage. As work progressed, it became clear that the trained exploitation specialists could best be used in the forward areas of the bow, while the untrained laborers (like me) picked through the rubble remaining in the rest of the recovered target section.

As the experts worked their way through the submarine uncovering objects and documents of intelligence value, they also uncovered the bodies of the Soviet sailors. Somewhat surprisingly, the bodies were mostly intact, with their features very well preserved. The explanation was that when the hull imploded (or whatever caused the massive destruction of the submarine interior), the wall of water coming forward into the bow forced everything—equipment, mattresses, and sailors—into the forward section containing most of the sleeping quarters. The mattresses compressed around the sailors, protecting them from the fish and crabs that were all over the ocean bottom and which would have otherwise stripped their bones bare. The bodies were removed with great care and stored in a refrigerated van. They would remain there until such time as they could be interred with dignity and an appropriate ceremony.

Throughout the exploitation, the *HGE* welders and crane operators had been systematically cutting up and disposing of the *K-129* hull. Of course, samples of the pressure hull and other parts of the submarine that revealed construction techniques and materials were saved for follow-on analysis, but the massive radioactive outer hull wasn't needed and would be hard to get rid of once the *HGE* was in port.

As the exploitation crew stripped the intelligence from portions of the submarine, the welders cut the outer hull into small pieces that could be handled by the ship's cranes. The crane operators picked the hull sections out of the well and dropped them overboard into the ocean. To prevent any inhalation of radioactive smoke from the cutting operations, a positive pressure differential was maintained in the well at all times. Air was continuously being forced into the lower part of the well, forcing a steady flow of the residual air and smoke upward and out of the ship. Within a couple of days, most of the "scrap" sections of the submarine hull had been disposed of.

*Day 58 (Friday, August 16, 1974): En Route to Lahaina*

From the ship's log:

> 0000—Under way to Lahaina isle of Maui. Course 140 deg. Speed 9.8 kts.
> 0314—Kaena Point Oahu abeam. 11.3 mi off to port.
> 0529—Barbers Point Light abeam to port, bearing 015 deg T @ 5.0 mi.
> 0704—Diamond Head Light abeam to port, bearing 018 deg @ 7.56 mi.
> 0817—Chopper N-1459W aboard and away w/passengers.
> 1019—Laau Point port abeam @ 5.6 mi.
> 1200—Proceed into Lanai Molakai channel.
> 1408—Commence slowing down.
> 1424—Arrival at Lahaina.
> 2000—Anchors checked, anchor lights burning brightly, gangway rigged & lighted, awaiting crew change.
> 2200—Crew change. Capt E. A. Thompson relieved Capt T. Gresham.

After all the time at sea, many of us got up early just to see the lighthouses of Hawaii as we swept by them, leaving them to port. It was really exciting just to see land again. Captain Gresham anchored the ship in twenty fathoms of water, about one mile from Lahaina.

The Global Marine "B" crew had been flown over to Hawaii, and were now in Lahaina ready to be taxied out to the ship. Global Marine's Captain E. A. "Tommy" Thompson would relieve Captain Tom Gresham. The "B" crew had been thoroughly trained in exploitation techniques, and they'd been waiting for months to get on the ship and do what they'd been trained to do. The "A" crew would be going home immediately.

For the most part, the mission crew felt pretty damned good about what we'd accomplished. We'd overcome a lot of adversity, been scared badly on several occasions, and been emotionally crushed when we lost a portion of the target, but we still managed to come back with at least part of the K-129 and many recovered items thought to be of high intelligence value.[11] Sure, we'd have liked to have recovered the entire target, but given the short time available to prepare for the mission, and the number of serious technical problems we'd encountered during the mission, we felt like we'd done well.[12]

———

That good feeling was, of course, short-lived. As soon as the gangway was lowered at our anchorage off Lahaina, a "Tiger Team" of engineers and scientists rushed aboard, proudly announcing their chartered responsibility for determining where the blame for failure should be placed. I knew that a thorough analysis of the technical and procedural problems we'd had was vital if we were going to have any chance of successfully rebuilding the system to complete the recovery objectives in 1975, but I didn't expect the second-guessing to start so early. Clearly, DCI William Colby and S&T Director Carl Duckett were already planning on another mission and taking the first steps to implement it.[13]

Standing on the boat deck of the HGE, I watched the Tiger Team members disperse around the ship, questioning anybody who had the time—and the patience—to talk. It didn't take them long to convince themselves they had all the answers. One of the Tigers approached me after he'd been onboard for about fifteen minutes. He stared me straight in the eye and said, "If I'd been onboard this ship, none of these problems would have happened!" I thought he was joking at first, but he didn't crack a smile. I didn't know whether to be amused or dismayed. I felt the best thing I could do at this time was simply to get out of the way—let the Tiger Team burn themselves out.

A little later, another visitor came onboard, one whom I was really pleased to see—Curtis Crooke, the president of Global Marine Development. Crooke and I had some brief words about the nature of the technical problems, and then he handed me a package—a small box measuring about 12 × 12 × 6 inches. It was addressed to "David Schoals [the alias name I used while on the ship], Mining Superintendent, Hughes Glomar Explorer." Crooke and I took the box up to an office, where I opened it. It contained a clear plastic bag filled with what looked like shards of white bone. On the plastic bag was a tag that read "John R. Graham."

Graham had died shortly after we departed on the recovery mission. I knew he'd been in bad health, but this was an unexpected shock. He believed that the Glomar Explorer was his greatest technical achievement. He had requested his family to send his ashes to the ship, to be scattered off the fantail with a simple ceremony.

I thought about the last time I had seen Graham. Although he hadn't been feeling well, he had come aboard for a day during one of the at-sea tests of the *Explorer*. He wanted to see the ship in full operational trim before it departed on its mission. We toured the ship together with Graham rattling off some of the design criteria he had used for the major subsystems. I was surprised by his knowledge of so many small details of the design, but I'd been amazed for quite some time by the design of the ship itself. The more time I spent on the *HGE*, the more awed I had become over that incredible engineering achievement. That ship was John Graham's masterpiece.

We didn't do much climbing between decks during our tour. The stress from leading the design and construction had been hard on him—and the years of heavy chain-smoking hadn't helped either. When we finished the walk-around, we stood on the main deck leaning on the ship's rail, Graham catching his breath.

"John, this ship is an amazing engineering achievement," I told him. "You should be very proud."

"Thank you," he replied, "I *am* very proud of it. I wish I could be going with you."

"The ship will be fine, John," I told him. "The ship's going to work just fine."

He didn't reply. He just looked out at the ocean. When I turned to look at him, tears were streaming down his face. I didn't realize just how much emotional strain he had been going through. I should have, but I didn't.

———

The arriving "B" crew and the departing "A" crew were both in high good humor. The "B" crew was eager to continue the exploitation that had already been started. The "A" crew was looking forward to getting their feet on solid ground and going home.

Bob Mlady, the Lockheed engineer who had suffered a minor heart attack on July 10, was one of the "A" crew members returning home. At the Oahu airport, he and the others had to run to catch a waiting flight. Tragically, after boarding the aircraft, he collapsed in his seat with a massive heart attack and died.

## Exploitation and Burial at Sea

*Days 59–71 (August 17–29, 1974): At the Exploitation Site*

Early on the morning of the seventeenth, Captain Thompson moved the *HGE* to a new location, about four to five miles from Lahaina, to continue the exploitation process. We would remain at that location for thirteen days while the real "dog work" of exploiting the recovered submarine took place.

The "B" crew included an entire cadre of engineers and technicians who had been trained in techniques required for the exploitation process. One of those men was Manfred Krutein, the German immigrant who had previously served on World War II U-boats, and whom Global Marine had hired as a consultant in ocean mining technology. In his book *Amerika? America!* Krutein described the "suiting-up" process for those working in the well.

Even though only paperlike radiation suits were required for outer covering, the crew working in the well had to don two layers of underwear under their regular work clothes. They wore surgical gloves over their hands and elastic booties over their steel-toed work boots. Both the gloves and the booties were taped to be airtight. Finally, they had to don a hood over their hard hats.[14]

The standard procedure for removing articles from the target consisted of photographing the part before removal to show its location in the submarine; attaching tags with a number and a brief description; placing the article in a plastic bag that was sealed and put into a second plastic bag; registering the part; and, finally, storing everything in drums. The drums would later be placed into crates for transporting. A number of food cans were discovered, some containing potatoes in good condition. Reportedly, an apple was discovered that actually looked fresh enough to be edible.

Preserving the paper documents recovered from the target required some high-tech procedures. The documents were placed in a liquid bath that penetrated the pages. Ultrasound was used to aid the penetration of the liquid between the pages and facilitate their separation. A camera, operated by a foot pedal, was placed at every workstation so each page could be photographed as it was carefully pulled away from the document. After separation and photographing, each page was individually placed in a plastic bag with the appropriate information regarding the source and nature of the page and the parent document.[15]

While Krutein was going through one particular document, the fading ink became unreadable. A recording expert was called in who added a different liquid. Under ultraviolet light, the writing became legible. These specialists in exploitation techniques were truly impressive. Their training had been thorough, and the hard work was paying off.

———

On Monday evening, August 19, Captain Thompson, Curtis Crooke, Global Marine foreman Jim Rogers, I, and perhaps some others that I can't recall gathered on the fantail of the *Hughes Glomar Explorer* to fulfill John Graham's last request. The captain said the formal words appropriate for a burial at sea. Crooke and I said a few words about what Graham had meant to us. Then his bleached bones were scattered into the ocean. Some mild air turbulence caused some of the fine ash to drift back around our feet, creating a fine white covering on the deck. Looking downward with my head bowed, I noticed a couple of little dark spots in the ashy covering where a few tears had dropped from our cheeks.

The ship's log for that day read, "At 1906 hours the cremated remains of John Robey Graham were dispersed at sea in Latitude 20°–46.5' N, Longitude 156°–38' W (Burial Permit 8642)."

———

It's now been thirty-four years since we scattered John Graham's ashes, and I still feel a terrible sadness that his achievements are known to so few people. The AZORIAN recovery system was arguably the most impressive feat of marine engineering of the twentieth century. Certainly, nothing of that scale has ever been attempted before or after AZORIAN. Graham's contribution to that effort was immense. Many of the ideas and concepts for the design came from smaller-scale technology precedents, but these technologies were extrapolated out to a scale never previously imagined. As Global Marine's chief engineer, Graham was responsible for completing the final design, managing the acquisition of the thousands of detail drawings needed for construction, and overseeing all the work at Sun Ship to ensure that the design was correctly implemented. And, he did it all in about three and a half years!

Graham has never received the recognition he deserved from the CIA because the design and details of the AZORIAN program have never been made public. Although DCI Robert Gates officially acknowledged the mission of the *Hughes Glomar Explorer* in a meeting with Russia's Boris Yeltsin in 1992, the CIA has been loath to say anything more.

In contrast, the great Clarence "Kelly" Johnson of the Lockheed Skunk Works was acclaimed by the CIA during his lifetime. The CIA was proud to describe the U-2, OXCART, and SR-71 reconnaissance aircraft that the agency and Kelly had teamed to produce. That generosity of spirit and pride in accomplishment have never been shown for the AZORIAN program.

———

After a little less than two weeks, the removal, registration, cataloging, and storage of those parts of the target that had intelligence value were largely completed. The only remaining materials in the well of the ship were large sections of the pressure hull.

There were only two things left to be done. The hull sections would have to be cut up and dropped overboard into the ocean, and the bodies of the Soviet sailors would have to be given a formal and respectful burial at sea. But not at the exploitation site. The water was only about 180 feet deep. The final resting place of the Soviet sailors had to be in water deep enough to ensure that they would never again be disturbed. The remaining pieces of their ship would be buried in the same location. At 1300 hours on August 29, the *Hughes Glomar Explorer* left the exploitation site and steamed to a location about 170 miles southwest of Lahaina.

I left the ship before its departure to the burial site. There were lots of questions to be answered back at Langley, and we had to begin the necessary analysis to determine if a second mission to recover the lost portion of the target would be possible in 1975.

*Days 72–77 (August 30–September 4, 1974): At the Burial Site*
The ship arrived at the burial site on August 30. The water at the site was too deep for anchoring, so the ship just drifted into the area, steaming back to the designated site every hour or so.

The first few days at the site were devoted to cutting up the massive pressure hull. The pieces were lifted out of the well by cranes, lowered until underwater, and then released to sink to the bottom. When this task was completed, only one job remained.

The burial was held on September 4, 1974. Participating members of the crew were all dressed in white. Large flags of both the Soviet Union and the United States were hung side by side behind the large steel container that would be the coffin of the Soviet sailors. After the bodies had been placed in the coffin, the national anthems of the United States and the Soviet Union were played over the ship's public address system. Then Dale Neuwirth, the mission director, spoke:

> This service is being conducted to honor Viktor Lokhov, Vladimir Kostyushko, Valentin Nosachev, and three other unidentified submariners who perished in March 1968 in the North Pacific Ocean when their ship suffered a casualty of unknown origin.
>
> In a very real way, this ceremony has resulted from the continuing contentions between our two nations. Their casualty happened at a time when they were engaged in activities which they deemed to be in their national interests and protection. Their bodies have come into our possession some six years

later through activities on the part of our country which we feel fit the same criteria. The fact that our nations have had disagreements does not lessen in any way our respect for them and the service they have rendered.

And so, as we return their mortal remains to the deep, we do so in a way that we hope would have had meaning to them, enclosed with a representative portion of the ship on which they served and perished. As long as men and nations are suspicious of each other, instruments of war will be constructed, and brave men will die as these men have died in the service of their country. Today, we honor these six men, their shipmates, and all men who give their lives in patriotic service.

May the day quickly come when men will beat their swords into plowshares and spears into pruning hooks, and nation shall not rise up against nation, neither shall there be war, anymore.

Appropriate prayers were said both in the English and Russian languages, and "Eternal Father, Strong to Save"—more often referred to as the "Navy Hymn"—was played as the steel coffin with the sailors' bodies and part of their ship was lowered beneath the waves. When the casket was fully submerged, it was released by the crane, allowing the Soviet sailors to reach their final resting place. (During Robert Gates's meeting with Boris Yeltsin in 1992, he identified the burial site as being "located approximately 90 miles southwest of the Island of Hawaii at Latitude 18° 29.0 N, Longitude 157° 34.0 W.")

After the burial ceremony, the *HGE* returned to Lahaina. Remaining CIA members of the "A" crew disembarked and flew back to Washington. The "B" crew and the ship left soon after to return to Pier E in Long Beach, California.

## What Went Right? And Wrong?

When I returned to Washington, the gears were already turning for another mission in 1975. Bill Colby and Carl Duckett were determined to complete the job they'd signed up for and wasted no time in lobbying the Ford administration and Congress for their support.

Before that support would be forthcoming, however, we had to establish the fact that the portion of the *K-129* that had broken away during recovery was, in fact, recoverable. Obvious questions were: Is the remainder of the target still in one piece? Or did it shatter into a number of smaller pieces on impact with the bottom?[16] Even if the remaining portion of the *K-129* was essentially in one piece, was it lying in a configuration/position that would be amenable to recovery by a modified capture vehicle?

Another issue was the feasibility of using the same equipment for a second attempt. We'd had major reliability problems with the entire recovery system during the 1974 ISTs and during the mission. Arguably, with the reliability problems during the mission we'd been lucky to recover *any* portion of the *K-129*. Clearly, some changes in the system were required to give us improved reliability. But were these changes feasible? And could they be implemented and tested in time for the June–August weather window in 1975? The Tiger Team was working furiously to provide convincing answers to these questions.

———

As soon as the ship returned from Lahaina, the large crates containing the documents and other artifacts of intelligence value from the target were off-loaded onto the Pier E dock for shipment to various locations for detailed analysis.[17] Shortly after, the *HGE* and the *HMB-1* rendezvoused at Isthmus Cove, Catalina Island, to transfer the capture vehicle out of the ship's well and back into the *HMB-1*. *Clementine* would be going to Redwood City along with the control center vans for modifications and refurbishment. When the ship returned to Pier E, the well was thoroughly scrubbed and cleaned, removing the last traces of residual radioactivity from the *K-129*.

Lockheed, Global Marine, Western Gear, and Honeywell immediately started tearing down their systems and analyzing all available data to determine the causes of known failures or problems during the mission, and to identify any incipient failures that might have been ready to occur.

## No Good Deed Goes Unpunished

The primary tasking for the Tiger Team was to determine the cause (or causes) of the structural failure(s) that resulted in the target breakaway. This group of highly skilled engineers, metallurgists, and analysts reviewed all the instrumentation and video that had been fed into the control center during the mission. They also interviewed many members of the recovery crew to get their firsthand recollections of the breakaway incident and the events leading up to that fatal failure.

The Tiger Team concluded that at least one of the beams (number 4) had actually broken off during the breakout procedure. (That conclusion was later proved correct when postmission images of the recovery site showed the broken beam standing upright in the ocean bottom—along with the four breakout legs.) Careful examination of the video recordings revealed that cracks in some of the other beams and davits had also occurred prior to the start of the liftoff sequence. The team theorized that cracks in the remaining beams and davits had propagated during the ascent, ultimately resulting in the failure of one or more additional tines, quickly followed by the loss of others as the loads were suddenly shifted and increased. The tines holding the bow section of the target retained their structural integrity and continued to support that portion of the submarine, while the rest of it fell back to the ocean bottom.

The Tiger Team's finding that cracked beams and davits were the direct cause of the breakaway only confirmed what many had suspected. The more important issue, though, was identification of all the technical factors that might have contributed to the tine failures. There was no single, identified cause for the fracturing. Rather, there appeared to be a number of problems experienced during the mission that led to the eventual failures. The contractors and the Tiger Team came up with the following list of technical issues that might have contributed to the breakage.

*Material Selection for the Beams and Davits*

The selection of Maraging 200 steel for the beams and davits had never been universally popular. At the time of the capture vehicle design, there was not a very large database on the performance of that steel in extreme environments (such as freezing temperatures and very high pressures). Lockheed, however, had felt strongly that it was important to take advantage of the high-tensile-strength material in order to keep the weight of the capture vehicle within reasonable limits. The metallurgy team doing the postmission analysis was divided on the extent to which the material selection was responsible for the failures. They all agreed that Maraging 200 was known to be subject to hydrogen embrittlement (a phenomenon that results in cracking of some metals after exposure to atomic hydrogen), and that the cold temperatures and high water pressures might have exacerbated that susceptibility. But were the tine failures during the ascent due to the material selection? Or were the problems caused by unplanned-for events that occurred during the bottom operations?

The Lockheed designers contended that the Maraging 200 would have been an entirely satisfactory material selection if the procedures for driving the tines under the target had been less aggressive, and if the tines hadn't been exposed to compressive and twisting loads while sitting on the ocean bottom for twenty hours waiting for completion of heave compensator repairs.

## Tine Instrumentation

Another contributing factor to the breaking of the beams and davits was the failure of many of the pressure gauges and position sensors on the tines. They were supposed to provide feedback to the capture vehicle operators while the tines were being driven down through the soil and under the target. These failures were traced to rusting of the sensor connectors and wires that were encapsulated in pressurized boxes mounted on the tines. These welded connector boxes had been thoroughly checked with helium gas during construction to ensure that they were airtight. Helium testing has been used for years for many air, water, and space applications to ensure the airtight integrity of welded containers, and Lockheed was confident in the suitability of this test for the capture vehicle application. What they hadn't considered, the Tiger Team argued, was the effect of high pressure on the integrity of the welded seams of the pressure vessels. The CV was experiencing water pressures as high as 7,500 psi—hundreds of times higher than the pressure at which the helium test had been performed. Under these pressures, water molecules apparently managed to penetrate the welds of the electrical boxes, resulting in corrosion and ultimate failure of the wires and contacts within.

## Tine Operation Procedures

Review of the instrumentation logs of the pressure sensors on the CV tines suggested that the ocean bottom on which the target was resting was significantly harder than estimated. One of the objectives of the first *Glomar II* mission in the winter of 1970 was to get core samples from the soil at the target site. Data on the density, composition, and hardness of the soil were a high priority as an input to tine design and development of the tine actuation procedures. Unfortunately, the payload lowered from the *Glomar II* broke before those samples could be collected. The design of the tines and the development of operational guidelines had to rely on estimated soil characteristics. After the mission, Lockheed members of the Tiger Team suggested that the control center operators should have driven the tines through the soil at a slower rate, allowing the water jetting from the ends of the davits more time to wash away the sand and sediment. This could have resulted in less stress on the beams and davits, possibly avoiding the fractures that occurred. Unfortunately, there were no sensors on the beams and davits that directly measured stress and could have indicated to the capture vehicle operators that they were trying to drive the tines too quickly. The only tine instrumentation the operators had during bottom ops was the actuator pressure gauges and position indicators—a number of which had already failed.

### Leaking Beam and Davit Actuator Seals

During the bottom operations, it was noted that some of the hydraulic actuator seals on the beams and davits were leaking, causing some of the tines to change position. Although some leaking of the beam actuation cylinders had been noted during the descent of the claw, postmission analysis suggested that the integrity of the seals on the actuators might have been further compromised while the tines were being driven through the hard ocean bottom, forcing mud and sand into the actuator seals. The seals continued to leak during ascent, resulting in altered load distribution levels between the tines. Some of those tines might have become overloaded, resulting in their ultimate failure.

### Leaking Breakout Leg Seals

The number 3 breakout leg on the capture vehicle was leaking badly during the extended time on the bottom while the heave compensator system was being repaired. The leaking breakout leg was cited as a possible cause for the cracking of some of the beams and davits during bottom ops. Since the CV was resting on the bottom for over twenty hours while the heave compensator was being repaired, a leaking breakout leg could have caused a change in the roll and/or pitch attitude of the CV, along with resultant twisting loads being put into the beams. Lockheed had not designed the box-section beams and davits to absorb large twisting (or torsional) loads. It was believed that such loads would be minimal during normal bottom operations. Even if twisting had not occurred, a leaking breakout leg could have resulted in redistribution of the load on the tines, possibly causing stress levels higher than planned or observed.

———

The Tiger Team's list of capture vehicle design factors that might have contributed to the loss of part of the target was all valid, but the team apparently didn't recognize that all of those problems might have been operationally insignificant were it not for the failure of the heave compensator system immediately after the first breakout of the target had been completed.

As a result of the heave compensator failure, the claw and the target had to be lowered back onto the ocean bottom, and the heave compensator itself had to be lowered 7.5 feet down to the snubbers. Lowering the claw back into the soil put higher compression loads on the tines—loads they were not designed to absorb. Lowering the heave compensator down to the snubbers effectively took it out of play. For nearly twenty hours, until the repairs were completed, all the heave motion of the *HGE* was transferred directly into the pipe string. During this time, the CV's bridle was being subjected to varying tensions of perhaps ±400,000 pounds resulting from the heave motion of the ship and tidal variations.

Furthermore, the ocean bottom under the target wasn't level. It pitched downward at an angle of about nine to eleven degrees. The disturbed soil was muddy and unstable. Any downhill sliding of the capture vehicle and the target would have put significant twisting loads on the tines—well outside of the design specification.

Although in hindsight the Maraging 200 steel might not have been the best choice for construction of the tines, it's problematical whether any other choice of steel would have survived the unplanned-for conditions that the CV had to endure for nearly twenty hours without similar fracture problems.

Lockheed took most of the Tiger Team heat for the breakaway incident. Global Marine and Western Gear should have shared that heat equally.

———

The Tiger Team report also included the views of some who felt that partial responsibility for the tine failures should be borne by the personnel directing the operation of the capture vehicle. Some of these control center operators had improvised work-around procedures necessitated by failed sensors and instrumentation. When the report was given to John Parangosky for approval, he refused to sign it or issue it as written. He was unwilling to have blame assigned to the crew by anyone who wasn't actually on the ship observing the nature and timing of the failures and the improvisation of the work-arounds. To my knowledge, those parts of the report that were critical of the capture vehicle operators were never released. At least, I never saw them. Quite possibly (probably?) I was one of the crew members fingered for not adhering completely to the written operational procedures.

This episode was another illustration of Parangosky's complex personality. He would fire one of his own people without hesitation if he felt that he wasn't trying hard enough. But he refused to accept criticism of his team by outsiders. This characteristic was one of the reasons that his staff—though pushed hard and sometimes verbally abused by Parangosky—were all intensely loyal to him. They knew that he would be loyal to them, too.

While the Tiger Team was completing its analyses, other elements of the AZORIAN program had determined that the lost portion of the *K-129* submarine apparently had more structural integrity than many submarine experts believed possible. The part of the target that had been lost during ascent had survived the fall back to the ocean bottom essentially intact. Furthermore, the position and attitude of the structure were such that only slight modifications to the claw's beam and davit configurations would be required to enable it to recover the *new* target.

According to authors Varner and Collier, "Lockheed reduced the number of arms [tines] from eight to five. For the second attempt, there would be three claw arms on one side and two on the other. The side with two was designed to fit around the conning tower, with an added long beam pointed aft that curved under the missile area."[18]

So we knew we had a target and we knew exactly where it was. At least those prerequisites for a 1975 mission had been met. But was it feasible to modify, refurbish, and test all the components of the recovery system in time? The schedule was very tight but appeared to be doable. Just.

# 7

## MATADOR

### Still Alive in '75?

John Parangosky and Carl Duckett knew it would be a serious challenge to persuade the administration and the Congress that it made sense to attempt another recovery mission in the summer of 1975. President Nixon, who had been a big supporter of the AZO-RIAN mission, had resigned in disgrace during the 1974 mission. President Gerald Ford was still somewhat of an unknown quantity. Although he'd given his approval to initiate the capture of the target in 1974—even while the Soviet *SB-10* tug was standing by observing—it wasn't clear that he'd be willing to back another CIA recovery attempt in 1975.

Some of the original team of AZORIAN supporters were still in place. Henry Kissinger remained as President Ford's secretary of state. Although Kissinger was never counted as a strong supporter of the *K-129* recovery effort, he had deferred to CIA directors Richard Helms and William Colby and had introduced no obstacles. Senator John Stennis (Democrat, Mississippi) was still the chairman of the Committee on Armed Services. Senator Stennis had been a strong supporter of the 1974 mission, and his support of the 1975 mission was still solid. Dr. David Potter was still the undersecretary of the Navy. Dave Potter had been a strong advocate for the program prior to the first mission and continued to believe that a second recovery effort was both technically feasible and potentially of great intelligence value.

On the other hand, there were some new players in the administration, and not all of them were on the side of the CIA. John

Warner, who had been a supportive undersecretary of the Navy, and later (May 1972) secretary of the Navy, had resigned. He had been replaced by Admiral J. William Middendorf II. So far as Parangosky and Duckett knew, Middendorf was still neutral.

Admiral Thomas Moorer had retired. In his previous job as chief of naval operations, Moorer had initially been a strong advocate of the CIA's plan to recover the largest part of the *K-129* that was still in one piece. As chairman of the Joint Chiefs of Staff (1970–1974), however, Admiral Moorer had lost his enthusiasm for the CIA's recovery plan, realizing that the costs were climbing and the intelligence was getting older. Would the partial success of the first mission rekindle his enthusiasm for the program?

Moorer's replacement, Admiral Elmo Zumwalt, had been a constant and outspoken critic of the CIA's program until his retirement in July 1974. Zumwalt's replacement, Admiral James L. Holloway, was less outspoken but could hardly be considered a friend of the program. Rear Admiral Bobby Ray Inman, the new director of naval intelligence, believed that AZORIAN was siphoning money away from Navy programs that were, in his opinion, far more valuable than the CIA's effort to recover part of the *K-129*. Inman and other high-ranking naval officers were trying mightily to persuade the secretary of the Navy (W. J. Middendorf) and the undersecretary (Dr. David Potter) to turn the program off. They were also lobbying Congress in hopes of exciting some new opposition there. The U.S. Intelligence Board (USIB) never wavered, though. It reaffirmed the potential value of the intelligence that could be gained from recovery of the *K-129*.

When all the smoke had cleared, the CIA still retained the endorsement of the administration and Congress. DCI Colby was given a go-ahead to proceed with plans for another mission to recover the remaining portion of the original target in 1975. For security reasons, the code name AZORIAN was dropped. The new mission would be called MATADOR.

---

When told that he had approval to attempt a second mission, John Parangosky was pleased, but he had some reservations. He had received the report from the Tiger Team and had talked to many of the *HGE* crew. He knew that the 1974 mission had been fraught with electronic and mechanical failures. The potential for catastrophic damage to the ship and the crew had been very real. If he was going to attempt another mission in 1975, he wanted to be absolutely certain that the design failures could be corrected, and corrected in time to meet the summertime "weather window."

It was already October. That meant we had, at the most, eight months to accomplish the needed redesign, refurbish all major and secondary systems on the ship and the capture vehicle, and complete a thorough and comprehensive integrated systems test of the entire recovery system. We had completed most of the postmission analysis, and we knew what had to be done.

## Redesign for the MATADOR Mission

Although the entire recovery system was going to have to be checked out, repaired, and in some cases redesigned, the most extensive and time-challenging changes were those that would have to be made to the capture vehicle. The tines on the claw would have to be completely reconfigured. The new MATADOR target was, of course, smaller than the AZORIAN target. It was also lying on the ocean bottom in a different attitude and configuration, and the seafloor had different slope characteristics in the new location.

Replacing the tines was the major task facing the Lockheed engineers. Although there was never a consensus that the Maraging 200 steel had been the major factor in the breakaway incident (Lockheed continued to protest that operator error was the most significant factor), all the metallurgists agreed that there were better materials available. Furthermore, since the beams and davits would have to be redesigned anyway in order to accommodate the new target for the 1975 mission, it made sense to use a tougher, less brittle steel. The choice was HY-100, the same steel used in the lifting yokes of the heavy lift system. We would have to order 300 tons of HY-100 steel for the tines. To make matters worse, the workers at Bethlehem Steel—Lockheed's primary supplier—were on strike.

Some problems were easier to solve. Lockheed came up with a simple solution to the leaking pressurized connector boxes that caused many of the pressure and position sensors on the capture vehicle tines to fail. They replaced the pressure vessels with pressure-compensated boxes filled with oil. Since there would be no differential pressure between the connector boxes and the outside water, the problems resulting from seawater leaking into the boxes and corroding the wires and electronics disappeared. The redesign went further, though. In addition to the pressure and position sensors used on the tines for the 1974 mission, Lockheed incorporated strain gauges on both the beams and the davits. For MATADOR, the CV operators would know exactly what stresses the tines were experiencing at all times.

As previously mentioned, bottom operations for the AZORIAN mission had to be put on hold for about twenty hours while the heave compensator system was being repaired. During this waiting time, one of the breakout legs was observed by the Lockheed operators to be leaking excessively, causing the capture vehicle and the target to continuously shift their position/attitude while resting on the bottom. For MATADOR, the seals between the cylinders and pistons of the breakout legs would be redesigned to reduce leakage. The nylon spacers that separated the pistons from the cylinders were also increased in size to reduce any tendency for the piston to cant within the cylinder.

The CCTV cameras and sonars on the capture vehicle had performed reliably during the 1974 mission. No major modifications were needed. But additional cameras with pan/tilt capability were added to enhance the operators' ability to assess the status of the capture vehicle and the target during bottom operations.

The hydraulic motors that powered the CV's positioning propellers had held up surprisingly well during the 1974 mission. Those motors were originally designed to be used with hydraulic oil—not the seawater that was used for the recovery mission. To reduce internal friction in the motors, Lockheed had coated the internal parts with a graphite compound and had used a lubricity additive in the seawater that was being pumped down the lift pipe. Amazingly, the motors showed very little internal wear. Lockheed was able to use the same motors for the MATADOR CV by replacing bearings and recoating the interior surfaces with the graphite compound.

———

Required modifications to the *HGE* and its systems to meet MATADOR requirements were minimal. Although the ship's systems had experienced their share of failures during the mission, the problems had all been repairable. Metallurgists were called in to look at the pump room and the forty-eight hydraulic pumps used to power the heavy lift system—focusing on why some of the pumps disintegrated during the mission. Vibration was the suspected culprit, and the recommended fix was a redesign of the shock mounts for the pumps.

The basic designs of the principal elements of the recovery systems (e.g., heavy lift, heave compensator, pipe handling, etc.) seemed to be generally satisfactory. Still, system reliability had been a continuing and disturbing problem during the AZORIAN mission. Some of the reliability problems were due to the learning curve for the operators. Other problems were caused by erratic automatic control systems. Global Marine and Western

Gear believed that tweaking some of the control systems would increase the reliability of the heavy lift, heave compensator, and pipe-handling systems while speeding up the operational tempo significantly. The whole crew hoped they were right.

## Under Pressure to Get It Right

The CIA recognized that the schedule for MATADOR was going to be challenging. In order to expedite the process, more authority for contractor direction was transferred to the WCPO in El Segundo. Shifting more management responsibility to the West Coast did not mean that there was less interest or program oversight from the East Coast, however. Management review meetings (MRMs) were held at least once a month, with John Parangosky and most members of the Lauderdale panel always in attendance.

The MRMs would usually last all day, the conference room filled with cigarette smoke. By afternoon, most of us were fading fast. It was during these afternoon briefing sessions that I really came to admire Curtis Crooke's talent for dozing off without being detected. Crooke was the absolute master of covert napping. Who hasn't had the humiliating experience of falling asleep in a meeting? For most of us, it starts with just closing your eyes (smoke-filled conference rooms encouraged that). Then your chin drops, your lower jaw may gape open, sometimes you start to snore. Worse yet is waking up. When you wake, your head may snap up with whiplash velocity. Then, you surreptitiously look around to see if anyone has noticed that you were asleep. Of course they have! The kindest of them will just pretend they didn't notice. Some of the others may choose to snicker at your discomfiture.

None of that happened to R. Curtis Crooke, though. He could shut his eyes and lower his head as though he were musing on an important issue. He'd *muse* like that for ten minutes or so. When he awoke, there were no sudden movements. He'd remain motionless for a moment or two. Then he'd open his eyes and slowly raise his head. Perhaps, he'd ask a question just to show that he was paying attention. I was in awe.

———

The members of the oversight panel hardly ever napped, however. They had a very strong voice in the decisions that were being made on the program and enjoyed getting into some of the technical details. One member of the team insisted that Lockheed attempt to duplicate the failure (leakage during bottom operations) of the seals on the beam and davit actuators.

Another took a strong hand in the decision to go with HY-100 steel for the beams and davits for the MATADOR mission. After reviewing the Tiger Team conclusion that twisting loads were probably imposed on the tines during bottom ops, the oversight panel ordered an analysis to determine whether any *other* choice of steel (notably HY-100) might also have cracked. The program office welcomed their interest. They were all strong supporters of both AZORIAN and MATADOR and they wanted to ensure that their reputations as skilled technical managers would be sustained.

———

Most of the senior CIA crew signed up to return for MATADOR. Dale Neuwirth would still be our mission director, Dr. Jack Sparkman would be his deputy. Dr. Earnest Ruggles would be the director for exploitation, and I would be the director of recovery systems. There was no question in our minds about wanting to go back and finish the job we'd started.

Almost all of the Global Marine people responsible for running the ship, including captains, mates, cooks, and bakers, were ready to go, as were the mining crew that included the foremen, crane operators, pipe handlers, welders, and roughnecks. Most of these Global Marine employees had been with the company for years and were used to life aboard drilling rigs operating all over the world.

It was my job to make sure we'd have a team of managers and engineers that could operate those parts of the recovery system built by Global Marine, Lockheed, Western Gear, and Honeywell. The AZORIAN mission had had some tense moments. A number of the engineers and technicians decided that they'd had enough seagoing adventure and opted out.

There had also been some hard feelings that evolved from the many system problems and failures we experienced during the mission. A few of these hard feelings developed during the mission itself, but the extended Tiger Team analyses that followed the mission also resulted in lots of finger pointing and blame placing. The Lockheed team was probably the most distressed. They felt they had been unfairly targeted as the weak link in the chain because of their choice of Maraging 200 steel for the capture vehicle tines, some of which failed during the recovery. Their resentment was arguably justified. After all, in terms of *numbers* of problems and failures, Global Marine and Western Gear had the major share. They were lucky, though, in that they were able to repair their systems during the mission. On the other hand, once the capture vehicle was undocked, Lockheed had to live with whatever failures occurred during the weeks that the claw was underwater.

These feelings manifested themselves during the crew selection process for MATADOR. The engineers from Global Marine weren't much of a problem. All of these men had already spent some time at sea. After all, they chose to work for Global Marine because they were attracted to that kind of work. Almost all of the Global engineering crew elected to return for the second mission. A couple of them didn't. Perhaps more clearly than others, they recognized the thin line between problems and disaster that had been strained, but not quite crossed, during the 1974 mission. They didn't want to push their luck.

Other engineers were available to take their place, though. Most important, the key Global engineers involved in the design of the heavy lift, heave compensation, gimbals, pipe-handling, and lifting pipe systems all elected to return for the MATADOR mission. Knowing that people like Sherm Wetmore, Jim McNary, John Owen, and Leon Blurton would be with us in 1975 was reassuring.

The Lockheed and Honeywell crew selection was a different kind of problem. Most of the LMSC and Honeywell engineers and technicians had never been to sea before. The experience had been unnerving to some of them and gave them a renewed appreciation of the pleasures and security that go with a family life—on land. Some of the LMSC technical people had also been stung by the finger pointing of the postmission analysis efforts. Ott Schick, the Lockheed program manager, was especially upset because the senior Lockheed engineer onboard the ship was not given complete authority over the control center operations. With some justification, he believed it was unfair to hold LMSC responsible for capture vehicle problems that occurred while its operation was being directed by someone other than a Lockheed manager. His point was certainly valid, although I had no second thoughts about the choice I'd made for the director of the capture vehicle control center.

It looked to me like I was facing defection of most of the Lockheed crew unless I could do something to reassure them or recover their confidence. I asked Ott—who was not only the program manager but also the clear leader of the LMSC team—if he'd consider going on the ship to head up the Lockheed crew for MATADOR. At first, he demurred. Although he and I had a mutual respect for each other, we had argued frequently over CV design details and CIA program management style. Why would he want to come on the ship and work for me? When I explained to him that I needed the strongest Lockheed leader that I could find, he began to come around. Ultimately, he agreed to become part of the crew with full responsibility for maintenance of the capture vehicle as well as control of all CV operations from the control center. And, fortunately and predictably, most of the LMSC engineers also decided to return under his management aegis.

We weren't so lucky with the Western Gear team responsible for operating the heavy lift and heave compensator systems. The WG engineers had to operate their systems from the heavy lift control room located in the port wing wall section of the ship. This area of the ship was subject to intense shaking and vibration during docking and undocking operations. And, although the control room was above the water level, it wasn't by much. It was easy for someone in the control room to be convinced, during especially violent docking or undocking ops, that he was about to be involved in a replay of an old World War II submarine movie, complete with shaking, loud acoustic noises reminiscent of depth charges, and spouts of water leaking through the seams. The heavy lift control room had a clean record for structural integrity during all test and mission operations, but it could be frightening.

Tom Fry, the chief Western Gear engineer onboard the ship, was the guy I was pursuing. He, his deputy Chuck Porter, and his Global Marine counterparts had done a superb job keeping the powerful but erratic heavy lift and heave compensator systems running under sometimes frightening circumstances during the 1974 mission. Tom and his Western Gear crew had had to leave the cramped and noisy wing wall control room on more than one occasion—coming out on the main deck just to get some fresh air and recover their composure. Tom didn't want to come back for MATADOR. We kept raising the ante we'd be willing to pay for his services. Didn't matter. He was unshakable in his determination to stay on dry land. We eventually had to settle for another Western Gear engineer who, I was sure, would be very competent. I knew that I'd miss Tom's calm, composed presence, though.[1]

———

In the meantime, the Deep Ocean Mining Program continued to remain involved in ocean mining conferences and activities. Global's Manfred Krutein and Paul Reeve, the general manager of Summa's Ocean Mining Division, traveled to several international seminars on ocean mining to show a Summa presence and assure the mining community that the DOMP was still going strong.

Krutein was finding it difficult, though, to answer all the questions directed at him about the design of the DOMP mining concept. Some of the engineers in the ocean mining community pointed out that the six-inch inner diameter of the pipe string wasn't large enough to pump up meaningful quantities of nodule slurry from the bottom. Krutein had to agree with them, but he countered that the first experiments of the DOMP were only to prove the feasibility of ocean mining techniques, not to attempt collection of commercially viable quantities of nodules. Furthermore, he continued, Summa had never declared just what their preferred technique for bringing nodules to the surface might be. An obvious option might be, he hinted, to entirely fill a nodule collection vehicle while on the bottom and then raise the entire load into the ship's well for subsequent transport to a processing facility. That approach, though not favored by most ocean mining experts, certainly matched the actual operations of the *HGE* more closely. No one had enough ocean mining experience to say that the approach made no sense. The experts were left wondering if the secretive (and perhaps irrational?) Howard Hughes knew something that they didn't, or if he might just be trying to confuse and mislead them in order to protect the results of his mining experiments. The cover story was still working.

———

Throughout this whole process of redesign, repair, and selection of a MATADOR mission crew, the CIA also had some major security issues that wouldn't go away. The FBI and the Los Angeles Police Department still hadn't discovered who was responsible for the June burglary of the Hughes business office on Romaine Street. We had learned from Summa officials that the sensitive document had not been marked with any classification indicators. The optimists among us were hoping that the burglars might not have recognized the memo as something of value.

That wishful thinking was soon challenged by events. Several months after the burglary, a ransom demand was received by Summa. Someone claiming to know the burglars promised that he could deliver *all* the files and documents that had been taken from the safes in exchange for $100,000.

Summa Corporation was skeptical. Bill Gay, acting for Howard Hughes, refused to pay any ransom. After all, he argued, it wasn't even known for sure if the handwritten note on AZORIAN had even been in the Hughes safes. And if it had been in the safes, how would we know that the burglars had not already copied and disseminated the notes? With no assurance that the thieves hadn't already made copies of the document—and perhaps offered them up for sale to other parties—the agency elected to pay the ransom. The money was left in an alley, as directed by the intermediary. The cash was never seen again. Neither were any of the files from the burglarized safes or the handwritten note that was causing us so much concern.

## AZORIAN Blown

On Friday, February 7, 1975, the *Los Angeles Times* newspaper featured a five-inch-tall headline in its late final edition: "U.S. REPORTED AFTER RUSS SUB." Taking up the rest of the front page were photographs of a Russian submarine (not a Golf II–class) and an overhead shot of the *Hughes Glomar Explorer* at the Long Beach pier. The feature article was titled, "Sunken Ship Deal by CIA, Hughes Told."[2] The report went on to claim that "Howard Hughes contracted with the Central Intelligence Agency to raise a sunken Russian nuclear submarine from the North Atlantic, according to reports circulating among local law enforcement officers."

DCI William Colby had gotten a hint of the impending story late Friday.[3] In a late afternoon meeting in the White House with Dr. Kissinger, Secretary of Defense James Schlesinger, Joint Chiefs of Staff chairman General David Jones, and presidential assistant Donald Rumsfeld, he told the group, "I hate to raise this, but the *Los Angeles Times* just asked whether we had raised a piece of a Soviet submarine. We have called [the Office of Security] to try to kill it." He added, "It doesn't seem to be a Washington leak."[4]

After the meeting, Colby immediately telephoned Steve Craig (WCPO security chief) on the HY-2 secure voice phone that was kept in the vaulted Harvey Wallbanger area. Colby told Craig and Bob James to get in touch immediately with the editor of the *Los Angeles Times*, Bill Thomas, and "tell him anything he needs to know about the program to stop publication of the story." Colby said that he would personally call Thomas as soon as he hung up to request that Thomas publish nothing on the story until Craig and James arrived. Colby wouldn't be able to give any details to Thomas because there was no secure voice capability in the *Times* offices, but he hoped that Thomas would agree to hold the story until he could be personally briefed. Colby instructed Craig and James to "leave right now. By the time you get there I will have already told him that you're coming."

Following Colby's orders, Craig and James briefed Thomas on the AZORIAN program, emphasizing the need to keep the story quiet until the midsummer mission had been completed. The editor called in the staff investigative reporter who was writing the story so that he could be briefed as well. When the reporter heard the purpose of the visit from CIA security officials, he blanched. The Final Edition of the *Los Angeles Times,* he explained, had just been put on the streets an hour ago—with the submarine story on the front page.

Bill Thomas was genuinely sorry for what had happened. He hadn't given much credence to the story himself and hadn't even considered that the publication might endanger the success of a CIA mission. The best that he could offer, given the circumstances, was to move the story to the back pages of Saturday's paper and then drop it altogether after that. That helped somewhat, but a lot of damage had already been done.

Most of the *Times* story dealt with details and rumored implications of the June 1974 robbery of the Hughes offices. Our CIA security people had briefed the Los Angeles Police Department (LAPD) detectives investigating the robbery on some details of the AZORIAN program and our reasons for concern,[5] although they were not briefed on the identity or location of the target object. There was some suspicion that the source of the *Times* story might actually be someone from the LAPD. The source, whoever it was, guessed wrong in assuming that the intended target was in the North Atlantic. The *Times* staff writers surmised that the likely target was either "a nuclear powered attack submarine of the Soviet November class which the Pentagon believes sank off Spain in April, 1970" or "another nuclear submarine which foundered in March 1972 about 900 miles northeast of Newfoundland."

Of course, the big question for us was "What will the Soviets believe?" Will they note the contradiction between the known location of the *HGE* in the summer of 1974 (after all, they were there) and discount the *Times* story completely? Or will they begin to wonder more about what the *Explorer* was actually doing during July and August while the Soviet tug, *SB-10*, observed its operations at (very) close hand?

Although one might initially assume that the Soviets would immediately put the known facts together and conclude that the *HGE* had been salvaging their submarine, there was also some reason to believe that they might be reluctant to accept such a recovery attempt as fact. After all, acknowledgment that the CIA had recovered part of a Soviet submarine—and right under the noses of Soviet intelligence ships—would suggest serious failures of the KGB's intelligence apparatus. Acceptance of the recovery story would put the careers of a number of intelligence and naval officers in serious jeopardy. Perhaps, more significantly, it could prove to be a humiliating situation for Chairman Leonid Brezhnev. Many in the CIA, including Director Bill Colby, believed that there might be some—albeit small—chance that the Soviets would prefer to ignore the allegations in the *Times* and hope that the story about the recovery of one of their submarines would simply "go away."[6]

———

There are numerous examples of intelligence agencies and individuals who have refused to acknowledge an uncomfortable truth that ran contrary to what they wanted to believe. Former CIA officer Tennent Bagley relates many such cases dating from the eighteenth century to the present in his book *Spy Wars*.[7] Bagley writes at length of the almost incredible reluctance of Britain's MI-6 to acknowledge the perfidy of one of its most senior officers, Kim Philby, in spite of mountains of evidence that strongly suggested he was a Soviet spy. After many years of service to the Soviet Union, Philby had risen to become head of MI-6's Washington bureau. His cover began to crumble, though, when two of his fellow conspirators, Guy Burgess and Donald Maclean, fled to the Soviet Union in 1953. Philby was dropped from MI-6 but was still allowed to travel abroad—with security clearances—for many years thereafter. Finally, in 1962 the noose began to tighten and Kim Philby fled to the Soviet Union, where he lived until his death in 1988.

———

The CIA didn't expect the attempted recovery of the *K-129* to remain a secret forever. It hoped, though, that the natural reluctance of the Soviet Union to acknowledge such an event—especially after the Soviet navy had rejected as "impossible" reports suggesting that such an attempt might be made by the United States—would provide enough time to complete a second mission attempt in 1975.[8]

Seymour Hersh, the investigative reporter from the *New York Times* who had agreed to hold off publication until after the 1974 mission had been completed, was still keeping a public silence. It was unclear, however, whether Hersh or his source had talked openly to other members of the media since his discussion with Colby. We know that after Hersh talked to Colby, other columnists and reporters began to show up, one by one, at the director's office for a full briefing in exchange for their temporary silence.

In the next couple of weeks, Colby spoke to editors and publishers of the *New York Times* and the *Washington Post* newspapers, along with the editors of *Parade*, *Newsweek*, *U.S. News and World Report*, and *TIME* magazines. He even spoke to senior executives of some of the major radio and television networks. His story was consistent and truthful. He told them that the CIA had recovered a portion of a Soviet submarine and that recovery of another major portion was planned for the summer of 1975.[9] He asked for their help in keeping the story under wraps until the mission had been completed. The reporters, editors, and publishers all agreed, albeit sometimes reluctantly, to sit on the story for the time being.

Of course, these news people continued with renewed energy the compilation of facts for the stories they were writing for eventual publication.

They had agreed not to publish, but they were all doing research, pulling together whatever details about the program they could find. In a short time, the story became common knowledge within the news media. The CIA crossed its fingers, hoped for the best, and watched for any Soviet reactions that might provide a clue as to what its security people were thinking.

———

The CIA's wistful optimism that the program security might hold didn't survive for very long. On March 18, columnist and TV personality Jack Anderson presented a special report on the *HGE* program during his syndicated radio show. Anderson had been briefed previously by the CIA and told about the sensitivity of the mission. His rationale for breaking the story was that "everyone" knew about the *HGE*. Sooner or later, someone was bound to publish the facts. And he wanted to be first. In a reluctant defense of Anderson's action, Colby later acknowledged in his memoir, "I have to admit that it [the *Glomar* program] was becoming the subject of chatter around the Press Club bar."[10]

The White House was uncertain how to respond to Anderson's story. The next morning, March 19, Colby met in the White House with President Ford, Secretary of Defense James Schlesinger, counselor to the president John Marsh Jr., assistant to the president Donald Rumsfeld, and Lieutenant General Brent Scowcroft.

President Ford put it simply: "Now where do we go?"

Schlesinger favored an acknowledgment of the bare facts of the mission, pointing out that "no comment" would be taken as a confirmation anyway. "If we move now we can take the high ground—if not we will be pilloried."

Colby disagreed. He said, "I go back to the U-2. I think we should not put the Soviet Union under such pressure to respond."[11]

Colby prevailed—at least for the time being. The president decided to say nothing until something was heard from the Soviets.

———

The other news media didn't take long to get their stories out, too. The *New York Times* published Seymour Hersh's version within a couple of days, followed immediately by the *Washington Post*. Although all of the stories essentially compromised the fact that the CIA—with the help of Howard Hughes—had attempted the recovery of a Soviet Golf II–class submarine, there were some important differences.

Even though Colby had given the same story to each magazine and newspaper, the staff writers differed in their understanding of the recovery method and the actual results of the recovery attempt. Colby had been consistent in claiming that the CIA had only recovered the forward one-third of the submarine, but some of the news reports speculated that Colby had only intended to deceive them about the *real* results. Speculation on the actual recovery results ranged from "nothing" to "the entire submarine."

Admittedly, the CIA was grasping at straws by this time, but we still dared to hope that the natural reluctance of the Soviets to acknowledge the weaknesses in their intelligence capabilities might work in our favor. Perhaps the inconsistencies in the public reports on the program would provide at least temporary confusion for the Soviets, allowing us to complete the MATADOR mission before the Soviets could get their facts straight and their act together.

William Colby, in his memoir, *Honorable Men*, wrote that he believed there was still a "fair chance" that the Soviets would not be convinced by the stories in the *Los Angeles Times* and the *New York Times*. He felt that there were so many contradictions and errors in the two stories that neither would seem credible to the Soviets. In fact, the *LA Times* story referred to operations in the North Atlantic—rather than the Pacific—where the *Explorer* had actually been. It seemed to Colby that if the CIA stuck to its ocean mining cover story, the opportunity for completing the MATADOR mission in 1975 might still be alive.[12]

After several weeks, we had still heard no reaction from the Soviets. We figured there were three possible explanations: One, they may have been uncertain about just what the HGE was up to in 1974. Recovery of one of their subs might have seemed like such a difficult (even impossible) challenge that they discounted that hypothesis. After all, the *K-129* was 330 feet long and the Soviets had no way of knowing that the submarine had broken into several pieces. Two, the Soviets had accepted the fact of our recovery of part of the *K-129* but were unwilling to publicly declare the fact. Certainly, they would have been embarrassed to have to acknowledge such a CIA coup taking place directly under their noses. Their reluctance to have the truth exposed to their own people might have encouraged them to remain silent. Three, the Soviets knew what had happened in the summer of 1974 but were waiting to see what the CIA plans for the future might be before protesting. To me the third option seemed most likely, but we couldn't be sure—and we didn't want to arbitrarily give up on the possibility of completing the mission objectives. We continued preparations for MATADOR.

## Enter: Brezhnev; Exit: MATADOR

If some of us thought that Soviet embarrassment about what the CIA had accomplished in 1974 would be so great that they'd be willing to just stand by and observe while we attempted a second recovery attempt in 1975, we were badly mistaken.

Anatoly Dobrynin was the Soviet ambassador to the United States at that time. In his memoir published in 1995, Dobrynin wrote that a few months after Gerald Ford replaced Richard Nixon as president, someone slipped a note under the door of the Soviet embassy saying, "Certain authorities of the United States are taking measures to raise the Soviet submarine sunk in the Pacific Ocean." The note was signed "Well-wisher." Dobrynin reported the incident to Moscow, but apparently the Soviet navy did not believe it possible to raise a submarine from such a depth and declined to follow up on Dobrynin's alert.[13]

Months later, on March 29, 1975, Dobrynin hand-delivered a note to Secretary of State Henry Kissinger, who also served as the president's national security adviser. The note was classified SECRET/SENSITIVE/EYES ONLY. It read:

> Moscow paid attention to the reports in foreign press, including the American press, regarding the fact that certain U.S. services have conducted for some time the work of raising the Soviet submarine that sunk in 1968 in the open sea in the area northwest of Hawaii. According to those reports, the operation has been carried out by a special U.S. ship, the Glomar Explorer. It was reported, in particular, that a part of the submarine has been recovered some time ago with the bodies of the crew members, that were thrown out into the sea.
>
> It goes without saying that we cannot be indifferent to any operation of raising any parts and property of the submarine belonging to the USSR.
>
> Special concern is caused by the fact that the bodies of the crew members of the sunken submarine, according to the press reports, were recovered and then thrown back into the sea. The matters related to the submarine and the dead seamen are the prerogatives of the Soviet Union alone.
>
> We expect from the U.S. side explanations with regard to the above mentioned reports, including complete information about the bodies of the crew members of the sunken Soviet submarine and also information on the discontinuance of any operations connected with the submarine.[14]

According to Dobrynin, Secretary of State Kissinger replied (after some hesitation), "This whole problem has already caused extensive debate inside the government." Kissinger declined to elaborate, saying he needed more information. Four days later, on April 2, 1975, Henry Kissinger sent the following memorandum to President Gerald Ford. The subject was "Soviet Query on Submarine Salvage." The memorandum was also classified SECRET/SENSITIVE/EYES ONLY. It read:

> Dobrynin gave me March 29 the note at Tab A which complains about the activities of the Glomar Explorer, and specifically about the disposition of the bodies of the Soviet sailors. The note, however, refers only to press reports.
>
> We could offer a quasi-confirmation and supply the names of the three bodies that were identified. This, however, would be extremely risky; any official, written confirmation by me would challenge the Soviets. Even if they did not react at present, they would have it in reserve and could spring it at any time. Moreover, there is no explanation that would assuage them. In particular, we cannot argue the legality or legitimacy of the operation without starting a polemic, and the Soviets cannot possibly concede its legality as their note indicates.
>
> Therefore, I intend to make orally to Dobrynin the points at Tab B which indicate that we do not confirm, deny or otherwise comment on alleged intelligence activities and that there will be no official U.S. position on this matter. This conforms to your standing instruction not to comment.[15]

Tab B of Kissinger's memorandum to the president included the substance of what Kissinger proposed to orally deliver to Dobrynin. Tab B read:

> The United States has issued no official comment on the matters related to the vessel Glomar Explorer. It is the policy of this government not to confirm, deny, or otherwise comment on alleged intelligence activities. This is a practice followed by all governments, including the USSR. Regardless of press speculation, there will be no official position on this matter.

Several days later, according to Dobrynin, Kissinger assured him that no work on the Soviet submarine recovery program was under way at the time, nor would it be in the future. More information was given to Dobrynin in a written message from Kissinger's deputy, Lieutenant General Brent Scowcroft. The written message acknowledged that the United States had recovered the bodies of six Soviet seamen, had identified three of them, and had buried them at sea with full military honors.[16] No details were provided regarding any intelligence value that may have come from the mission.

If Kissinger's reassurances and Scowcroft's acknowledgments to Dobrynin convinced the Soviet ambassador that the United States had canceled any plans for a future recovery attempt, he was wrong. The WCPO continued its preparations for a June mission without interruption. On May 5, the *Explorer* sailed to Catalina Island, where the redesigned capture vehicle was transferred into the well of the ship. On May 31, we sailed out of Long Beach for an integrated systems test of the refurbished recovery system, returning to Pier E on June 11 with all technical objectives having been met. We were ready to go.

In the meantime, the debate back in Washington over whether to continue or cancel MATADOR continued from early April until mid-June. I didn't know the details regarding which of the political high rollers were pro-mission and which ones were against, nor what arguments they were using. (Parangosky brushed off my questions with "Your job is to get the ship ready. Headquarters will deal with the political issues.") But, I had a pretty good idea. I was confident that William Colby was still hoping that the Soviets were confused by the inconsistent and sometimes illogical facts and conclusions reported by the U.S. media. He was betting that the Soviets wouldn't dare risk the embarrassment and the international diplomatic repercussions that would result from interference with a commercial ship (the *Explorer*) unless they were absolutely positive that it was truly engaged in the recovery of one of their submarines.

Carl Duckett, the CIA's director of science and technology, would likely have been another strong proponent for mission continuation. Carl's desire to recover the target was so strong and arguably irrational during the 1974 recovery operation that he demanded repeatedly to be connected to the ship on an open telephone line so he could order the crew to attempt recovery of the target portion that had fallen away. Only the persistent calming arguments of John Parangosky prevented Duckett from making the call, which, had it been made, would have compromised the mission and put both the ship and the crew at risk.

I had no reason to believe that Duckett was any less dedicated to the idea of recovering the target, regardless of risk, than he had been during the 1974 mission. His enthusiasm was infectious and stimulating; however, his logic may have fallen victim to his recognized problem with alcoholism.

Arguments for cancelling the MATADOR mission would almost certainly have come from the State Department and the Navy. Kissinger and the State

Department had a lot at stake with the ongoing U.S.-Soviet negotiations on détente, SALT II. What would happen to those talks if the United States attempted a confrontational recovery of part of one of their submarines—especially after the United States had at least informally acknowledged the 1974 recovery attempt to Ambassador Dobrynin? The Navy, for its part, might have been desperate to prevent a possible situation in which it would have to respond to Soviet interference with a commercial ship flying an American flag. And, what if the Soviets boarded and commandeered the *Explorer*? What then? These unsavory possibilities existed for the 1974 mission, too, but they seemed much more likely if the 1975 MATADOR mission were to be attempted.

––––––

The debate over the fate of the MATADOR mission finally came to a head in late June, about one week before we were scheduled to depart Pier E for the mission. I received a phone call from John Parangosky on the infamously unintelligible HY-2 secure telephone. I knew the call must be important, and I could guess what the probable subject was. Parangosky told me that "highest authority" had ordered the CIA to terminate all plans for the MATADOR mission. Secure cables were in the process of being sent to our contractors. I was told to notify the ship's crew immediately. We didn't talk long. Parangosky gave me the essential ingredients of the tacit agreement that had been worked out with the Soviets. It was simple. The United States, on its part, would say nothing publicly or officially about the mission. The Soviets would not formally protest the CIA's 1974 actions.

I asked Parangosky what argument or event had swung the vote to cancellation. He replied, "The Russians. They told us that if we try it, they'll stop us." I guess that said it all. Before we hung up, he also reminded me to acknowledge the source of the decision only as "highest authority." That was standard procedure for covert operations like ours. The president was always given the flexibility for plausible denial of his knowledge or involvement in the operation.

––––––

I called down to the ship and requested that all hands be available for a meeting in the mess room in a couple of hours. On the way down from the Summa offices in El Segundo to Pier E in Long Beach, I tried to come up with the right words to use. I knew the *Explorer* crew was eager to begin the MATADOR mission. We had completed the IST only a week earlier, and they looked forward to successfully concluding the job that had been left unfinished last year. They wouldn't be happy. Many would be resentful.

When I got to the ship, the crew was waiting in the mess room. I gave them my prepared speech as best I could. I explained that the CIA had full confidence in the ability of the crew to pull off the mission. The agency deeply appreciated the hard work that they'd put into preparation and training and the dedication to the program that they had displayed. But, I added, senior officials in the U.S. government had determined that continuation of the MATADOR mission would pose unacceptable risks for the ship and the crew. These senior officials had ordered us to terminate the mission.

> "Who are these senior officials?" one foreman asked.
> "The highest authority," I replied.
> "Who's that? JP?" he persisted.
> "No," I said, "higher than that."
> "Are you talking about Colby?" another asked.
> "No, higher than Colby," I responded.
> "That doesn't leave much question, I guess."
> "No, it doesn't," I agreed.

The letdown those men felt was excruciating. For most of them, AZORIAN had been by far the most exciting work they'd ever had in their lives. To have it end so abruptly, and so close to mission departure, was hard to accept. Watching and listening to them made me suddenly aware of how much the mission had meant to me, too. I knew, even then, that in all probability I would never again be involved in a program with so much challenge and excitement.

## Winding Down

Once the program was terminated, the excitement died. Everything from that point on was anticlimactic. Nevertheless, there were still a number of things to be done. As with the end of all large programs, things had to be cleaned up.

### John Parangosky Retires

Parangosky had been planning to retire for several months. He was fifty-five years old, and the CIA had opened up a window of opportunity for employees to retire with greater benefits than would normally have been received.

This window was set to close before the program was terminated, so Parangosky elected to retire in the spring of 1975 and continue to work pro bono for the program until its completion. With the termination of MATADOR, he felt that it was time to really call it quits. Doug Conrad, Parangosky's deputy for six years, took over management of the headquarters office as the program closed down.

*Clementine Returns to Redwood City*

Shortly after the mission cancellation, Clementine was carried by the *HGE* to Isthmus Cove for the final transfer operation. For the last time, the *HMB-1* was submerged into 160 feet of water and the sliding roof was opened. The *HGE* maneuvered itself over the *HMB-1*, opened the well gates, and lowered the CV down onto the massive support blocks in the barge. The operation was effortless, with no hitches. Over the last couple of years we had developed the transfer operation into a routine procedure. The barge, with Clementine inside, was towed back to Redwood City. It was torn apart there and those parts that were not sight-sensitive were sold for salvage. The seawater-driven propellers, used to hold the CV in position over the *K-129* target, were left out in a field in plain view where they were quickly covered with rust. There was little demand for large hydraulic motors that had been powered by seawater.

———

Although the final transfer of the capture vehicle from the *HGE* into the *HMB-1* went quickly and efficiently, it didn't escape the notice of conspiracy theorists. A gentleman named Chuck Kenworthy, president of Quest Corporation, believed that the two giant vessels working in the waters off Catalina were, in fact, hunting for treasure—treasure that he claimed rightfully belonged to him. In an article in the *San Mateo Times* on October 18, 1975, it was disclosed that Kenworthy had sent a letter to the State Lands Commission alleging that the Summa Corporation had "secretly snatched a $30 million cache of gold from a sunken Spanish galleon."

Kenworthy had a current, valid state permit giving him exclusive exploration rights in the area around Santa Catalina—precisely where the transfer operations had been conducted. Kenworthy said, "We believe the *Glomar* gobbled up a $30 million treasure, half of it belonging to the State of California, and half of it belonging to me. The state's been ripped off, and I've been ripped off. They have violated the sovereignty of the state." A Summa spokesman had no comment on the charges but claimed that the *Glomar* "conducted only sea tests, and did not engage in any salvage operation."[17]

## Tax Assessments and Ultimatums

Adding to the agency's problems, Los Angeles county tax assessors had levied large tax bills against the Summa Corporation earlier in the year, and the San Mateo County tax assessor was trying to collect additional taxes from Lockheed for the *HMB-1*.

Philip Watson, the Los Angeles County tax assessor, had been trying for several months to collect taxes from Summa for the *HGE*. CIA representatives had told Watson in secret session that the ship really belonged to the CIA—not Summa—and therefore no taxes were owed. At the same time, though, the CIA was publicly denying having anything to do with the *Hughes Glomar Explorer*. Watson felt that he was getting "jerked around," and as the battle escalated over the liability for taxes due on the large ship floating at Pier E, the tax amount kept getting higher. The CIA did not want to publicly admit that the ship was theirs, but Watson had to put *something* down in the public record regarding ownership of the *Hughes Glomar Explorer*.

Finally, in frustration Watson "closed down" Pier E. The gates were locked and guarded. No one was to be allowed access to the pier or the ship. (This "no access" order wasn't strictly enforced. Los Angeles County still permitted "named" people from Global Marine and the Summa Corporation to visit the ship as needed.) The fences and gates were festooned with signs indicating a "Notice of County Tax Collector's Sale." The notice declared that the Summa Corporation owed $4,658,882.07 in taxes and penalties for the "vessel known as the GLOMAR EXPLORER." That number included a seizure fee of $3.00 and a mileage fee of $17.50 (twenty-five miles at $0.70 per mile). The notice went on to say that the Los Angeles tax collector would hold a public auction on August 27, 1975, to sell the *Hughes Glomar Explorer* to the highest bidder.

Watson's action eventually forced a compromise. CIA agreed to acknowledge that the *HGE* belonged to the "U.S. government" (not the CIA). This seemed to satisfy all parties. The problem was put to rest. The CIA and Summa escaped the tax bill.

Lockheed was not so lucky. LMSC got trapped by its efforts to protect the cover story of the program. The Coast Guard documentation for the *HMB-1* indicated that the barge was built for "ocean research" rather than "salvage." As it happened, the assessment rate for these two purposes was different. With all the media coverage about the real mission of the *HMB-1*, the tax assessor of San Mateo County decided that LMSC had attempted to evade taxes by paying the lower rate applicable for an ocean research vessel. Although LMSC's lawyers and the tax assessors of San Mateo County argued back and forth, Lockheed eventually had to pay the larger assessment (plus penalties) for a "Salvage" barge.[18]

In the fall of 1975, the *Hughes Glomar Explorer* was a ship with an infamous history but no future. The government (now the acknowledged owner of the ship) was trying hard to find a buyer. My deputy, Norm Nelson, and I were both busy giving tours of the ship to curious government officials as well as potential corporate purchasers. John Wayne, famous movie actor, actually sailed into Long Beach Harbor and tied up to the *HGE* in his private yacht, the *Wild Goose*. Wayne, a personal friend of Curtis Crooke, was also given a courtesy tour of the ship.

When no eager buyers surfaced, the agency authorized Global Marine to produce a motion picture extolling the potential value of the *Hughes Glomar Explorer* for research and development and ocean exploration. The film, narrated by TV actor Richard Anderson,[19] combined footage taken aboard the ship at Pier E with actual video taken from the recovery mission. Some footage exposing Clementine in the well of the ship was quickly edited out by security so that only part of the deck of the still-recognizable Clementine could be seen above water.[20] Even with the aggressive marketing by the government, however, there were no ready buyers for the *Glomar Explorer*. Apparently, no one had a requirement for a ship capable of lifting up to 14 million pounds.

Impressed by what he had seen during his tour of the *Explorer*, John Wayne sent a telegram to President Ford on September 29, 1976, seeking to intercede on behalf of the ship. He wrote:[21]

DEAR MR PRESIDENT,

I KNOW THAT TIMES ARE RIGHT NOW HECTIC BUT THERE IS SOMETHING THAT DE-
MANDS YOUR IMMEDIATE ATTENTION THE GLOMAR PROJECT, WHICH IS TO THE EARTH
WHAT NASA IS TO SPACE. PLEASE REVIEW THE ADVICE OF YOUR NATIONAL ADVISORY
COMMITTEE ON THE OCEANS AND THE ATMOSPHERE AND DON T ALLOW BOOKKEEP-
ERS TO SCRAP A TREMENDOUS VEHICLE, THE CUTTING TORCHES ARE IMMINENTLY IN
HAND. THERE ARE CORPORATIONS THAT WILL LEASE THE GLOMAR AND KEEP IT IN
CONDITION AND SAVE THE GOVERNMENT SPENDING MILLIONS TO SCRAP ONE OF THE
MOST IMAGINATIVE VEHICLES OF ALL TIME. I IMPLORE YOU TO HALT THE IMMEDIATE
DESTROYING OF THIS SHIPS SYSTEM THE VALUE OF WHOSE TREMENDOUS CAPABILITIES
HAS STILL NOT BEEN ASCERTAINED.

Within five days, on October 4, 1976, President Ford responded to Wayne's telegram with a personal letter. He wrote:[22]

Dear Duke:

I have your telegram on the Glomar "Explorer," and I would like to assure you that there are no plans afoot to scrap the vessel.

As you know, we were, regretfully, unable to find an immediate use for the "Explorer." Nevertheless, we are hopeful that organizations such as the National Science Foundation may be able to utilize its unique capabilities in the years ahead.

Given present circumstances and our strong desire to preserve the "Explorer" for the future, we have decided to inactivate the ship and place it in reserve in the Suisun Bay anchorage north of San Francisco. Unfortunately, the derrick will have to be removed so that the vessel will be able to pass under the Bay bridges, but that is the only use of the cutting torch planned.

I very much appreciate having your views on the "Explorer," and I know that we both look forward to the day when it again sets sail.

With best regards,

[*signed*]

We still had about eighty-five personnel working in the CIA's WCPO in El Segundo. The "Summa Corporation" sign on the door had become a curiosity for the other inhabitants of the building. Suddenly, the people working on the fifth floor were objects of intense curiosity. Some program office employees preferred to take the steps, rather than ride the crowded elevators whose doors opened right across the hall from the entrance to the Summa offices.

Most of the program office employees were still officially employed by MRI, Lockheed, Honeywell, or Global Marine. Over the space of about two months, all of these people were returned to their home offices. Every couple of weeks we'd have a *departure ceremony* to honor (and to *roast*) the departees. These were emotional times. It was difficult to break away from a mission that had demanded—and received—such hard work and dedication.

The remaining people in the program office were all occupied trying to clean up the registry and accounting for classified documents. We tried, but accounting for all the documents in that office was truly a mission impossible. Many of the documents used in the WCPO were unclassified, having been written to be consistent with the DOMP cover story. "Capture vehicle" had been replaced by "mining machine." "Target site" had been replaced by "nodule collection site." My own title on the ship, "director of recovery systems," had been replaced by "mining superintendent." With these substitutions, the documents could often be treated as unclassified and were not recorded and controlled by the JENNIFER Document Control System. Now, however, with the real meaning of those terms exposed to the public, the documents had to be considered classified (or at least sensitive). Trying to recover all the copies of these documents to determine whether they should be treated as classified or not was time-consuming and frustrating. I can honestly say that we did our best. Still, our final accounting for documents wasn't a pretty sight.

In October of 1975, I returned to Washington for a new assignment—one in which I could use my real name.

## The Failure and the Success of AZORIAN

The CIA's bold attempt to recover the largest portion of the broken *K-129* from ocean bottom was only partially successful. Only a thirty-eight-foot section of the bow was brought up into the well of the *Hughes Glomar Explorer*. Although not a complete failure, the mission could not in any way be considered an unqualified operational success. Some significant information was learned from this analysis, but the parts of the submarine that the intelligence community most wanted to analyze—the remaining nuclear missile and the hardware and documentation that would have been located in the sail of the submarine—were all lost when the major piece of the target broke away during the ascent.

If the AZORIAN mission had not been compromised in early 1975, the strategic gain of the United States would have been limited to the value of that intelligence obtained from the bow section of the sub. Worth the reported $350–$500 million cost of the program? Probably not. The AZORIAN program would have had to be classified as an intelligence failure.

However, the program *was* compromised and the Soviets learned that the United States had recovered at least some part—they had no way of knowing just how much—of the *K-129*. That changed the game in a major way. Having learned of the recovery operation, the Soviet Union was forced to assume that the United States might have recovered *all* of its submarine—including the nuclear missiles, cryptographic gear, codebooks, ship's logs, and all the other valuable artifacts that the CIA had hoped to gather.

Details of the intelligence gained from the recovery mission were given the highest possible degree of security protection by the CIA. Significantly, the intelligence *not* gained from the analysis was given equivalent security protection. The objective of the intelligence community was to maximize the Soviet uncertainty about how much the United States had actually learned from the recovery operation. This tactic effectively put our Cold War adversary in a position where it had to assume that the United States might have managed to learn everything about the *K-129* and the weapons it carried, thereby causing the greatest confusion and expense for the Soviet Union.

Total uncertainty about the extent of the intelligence compromises forced the Soviet navy—the submarine forces, in particular—to make substantive changes to their operational procedures. Route selections, reporting protocols, and test schedules would all have to be altered. The Soviets would also have to modify or develop new cryptographic hardware and issue new codebooks. This situation was an unexpected windfall for the U.S. Navy and the CIA, and it put increased emphasis on providing the highest possible security protection to the details of the *Glomar Explorer's* mission.

The CIA, with the help of many reporters and authors who inadvertently perpetuated the confusion regarding the AZORIAN mission, was remarkably successful for many years in protecting the actual program details and results. This security wall was intentionally lowered in 1992, when DCI Robert Gates chose to acknowledge to Boris Yeltsin, president of the Russian Federation, that the CIA had recovered only the forward bow section of the *K-129*, along with the remains of six Soviet sailors. Until that time, however, the Soviet Union was plagued with the uncertainty regarding the intelligence haul of the *Hughes Glomar Explorer*. Perhaps the real success of the AZORIAN program should be measured by the confusion—and resultant expenses—that our onetime adversary was forced to endure for so many years.

———

The AZORIAN program was arguably the most technologically significant collection program ever undertaken by the CIA's Directorate of Science and Technology during the Cold War period. I don't mean to denigrate in any way the magnificent technical achievements represented by the overhead reconnaissance satellites developed and launched by the CIA (as Program B of the NRO) during that same Cold War period, or the reconnaissance aircraft that were developed and operated under the aegis of Program D of the National Reconnaisance Office. I've had the privilege of working on some of those programs, both satellites and aircraft, and the engineering achievements associated with those programs are breathtaking.

AZORIAN, though, represented something unique and unmatched by any other CIA program. AZORIAN was an attempt to do something that was completely unprecedented in marine engineering. It was undertaken by CIA officers who, for the most part, had no previous experience in the marine environment. And yet they succeeded in generating an engineering concept and delivering a complete recovery system in less than four years. After five years they had used the system operationally to attempt a mission so radical and bizarre that the Soviet navy, when first alerted to a possible U.S. attempt to recover their sunken submarine, discounted the report, rejecting the notion as absurd.

Two other features of the AZORIAN program stand out as unique. First, some of the same engineers who designed, developed, and tested the recovery system actually manned the ship during the mission. Second, the whole operation, with a total cost speculated to be anywhere from $350 million to $500 million, was done without compromising the U.S. government's (or the CIA's) hand in the operation. The development and execution of the security plan, including the DOMP cover story, may be even more impressive than the technology achievements.

Many adjectives have been used to characterize the *Hughes Glomar Explorer* program over the past thirty-five years. Its supporters have called it bold, brassy, courageous, innovative, ingenious, and historic. Its detractors have described it as crazy, politically inspired, irresponsible, wasteful, and illegal. Some critics have used colorful hyperbole such as "a colossal boondoggle," the "*Glomar* caprice," and a "$500 million sand castle." No one can deny, though, that the AZORIAN program was a breathtaking engineering tour de force that attempted a mission called "impossible" by the Navy— and nearly succeeded in meeting all of its objectives.

In 2006 the American Society of Mechanical Engineers declared the *Hughes Glomar Explorer* to be a "National Historic Mechanical Engineering Landmark." Curtis Crooke was the keynote speaker at the award ceremony. An unclassified brochure was created for the event that fully described all of the operating elements of the recovery system and gave deserved credit to all of the contractors who participated in the development and operation of the system. The ASME gave the CIA an opportunity to send representatives to the award ceremony, but the invitation was declined.

Historically, the CIA has shown a great deal of pride in its many significant programs of technical espionage. Expansive histories of the U-2 and OXCART reconnaissance aircraft are available on the CIA's website for historians to read. A definitive history of the first satellite reconnaissance program, CORONA, has also been officially released within the last few years. Yet the CIA has said very little about AZORIAN. The history released in January 2010 was heavily redacted and raised more questions than it delivered answers. Why? Obviously, the CIA believes that there are still AZORIAN details that are sensitive enough to demand the protection of continued classification.

I'd love to see the agency show more pride in what they managed to accomplish with the *Hughes Glomar Explorer* in 1974. I'd like to see some *official* public release of the details of the incredible design, with credit given to the contractor and government men and women who dedicated years of their lives to the achievement of the CIA's goals.

I don't, however, expect that to happen. I have great faith and respect for the men and women in the CIA's office of security. I feel confident that their reasons for keeping all records of the AZORIAN program classified at such a high level, even after thirty-eight years, are well intended. It's unfortunate, however, that the government's focus on protecting the history of the program may forever preclude the official recognition of those managers, planners, designers, engineers, and sailors who conceived and executed this bold program in the middle of the Cold War era.

The AZORIAN program did not achieve the ambitious goals set by Bill Colby, Carl Duckett, John Parangosky, and the dedicated CIA and contractor team members. Perhaps those goals were, as the Navy suggested, absurdly optimistic to begin with. Perhaps the mission was truly impossible. Nevertheless, the dedication and passion of the AZORIAN team who persisted in trying to successfully complete the mission under the most adverse circumstances until there was nothing more they could physically do are unparalleled. As Jack Porter, the ship's security officer and unofficial chief philosopher, put it, "What man could do, we did!"

# Epilogue

## AZORIAN Fallout on the CIA

The AZORIAN program was one of the largest and most technically ambitious programs ever undertaken by the CIA. The sheer technical hubris of attempting to recover a submarine from a seabed three miles under the surface was only matched by the ingenious development of a brazen commercial cover story that was carried off successfully in front of the whole world. As often happens in history, however, the boldest ventures tend to affect everything they come in contact with—and not always positively. And so it was with AZORIAN.

One of the most far-reaching effects of the *Glomar Explorer* program was the reaction of some members of Congress who were already intent on curbing what they considered the excesses of the intelligence community. Although there were many supporters of the CIA's efforts to recover the *K-129*, others believed it to be a major intelligence failure and an irresponsible waste of money.

Senator Frank Church, in particular, was an outspoken critic of the program and of the intelligence community. In 1975 Senator Church was chair of a Senate committee called the United States Senate Select Committee to Study Governmental Operations with Respect to Intelligence Activities—more commonly known as the Church Committee. This committee, the predecessor to today's Senate Select Committee on Intelligence, was formed after revelations stemming from rumored intelligence activities (including attempted assassinations, meddling with the stability of foreign governments, and illegal surveillance of U.S. citizens) raised questions regarding the methods being used by some members of the intelligence community—particularly the CIA and the FBI. Church, persuaded that the CIA had recovered nothing of value from the *K-129* submarine, was outraged at the cost of the program, reportedly saying, "No wonder we are going broke!" He also suggested that the CIA needed to be subjected to a "cost-benefit analysis."

President Gerald Ford wrote in his memoir, "The Church probe was sensational and irresponsible—Church made no secret of his presidential ambitions—and it was having a devastating impact on morale at the CIA. Director Bill Colby, Kissinger and Scowcroft all told me that the agency was losing good people and that the employees who remained were increasingly inhibited in supplying opinions and analyses."[1]

To be sure, the AZORIAN program was not the only—and probably not the most egregious—of the intelligence community offenses that inspired Church to refer to the CIA as a "rogue elephant." However, it was a very expensive program and it provided a high-profile example of what he referred to as CIA "misconduct." As a result of the Church Committee's efforts, Congress was given unprecedented oversight authorities over the entire intelligence community. The House Permanent Select Committee on Intelligence (HPSCI) and the Senate Select Committee on Intelligence (SSCI) were formed largely as a result of his efforts.

These committees serve a very important function for the American people. They serve as a safeguard to ensure that the intelligence community operates within the limits of its chartered authorities and approved budgets. However, there is a real cost associated with this added protection for the American people. The oversight committees have often been accused of having their own political agenda. There have also been suggestions that discussions and debate about sensitive intelligence programs in congressional forums—even those as restricted in numbers as the HPSCI and SSCI—have led to public exposure of U.S. espionage programs whose success depended largely on their covertness.

The value to the country of alert congressional oversight over the intelligence community is indisputable. However, the resulting risks to program security sometimes restrict the ability of the community members to perform some highly sensitive missions. I do not believe that a program like AZORIAN could be successfully undertaken in the current oversight environment. Is that a bad thing or a good thing? It depends on your perspective.

————

The same environment of distrust that led to the formation of new oversight committees to scrutinize the actions of the intelligence community also contributed to the career terminations of the senior officers in charge of the AZORIAN program. Within a year of the public exposure of AZO-RIAN/MATADOR, William Colby, Carl Duckett, and John Parangosky had all resigned from the agency.

CIA director William Colby was asked to resign by President Gerald Ford on November 2, 1975. Although Colby stayed on as director until his replacement, George H. W. Bush, could be sworn in on January 30, 1976, he was the most prominent casualty associated with the failed mission to recover the *K-129*.

Carl Duckett probably recognized and accepted his program as a failure on that fateful day in August 1974 when he was told that part of the target had broken away and fallen to the ocean bottom. Upon receiving the report from the ship, he was nearly irrational, insisting that he be allowed to call the ship on an open telephone line so he could order the crew to return the capture vehicle to the seabed to recover the lost portion of the target.

Carl Duckett's CIA career never recovered after the AZORIAN failure. He had a recognized problem with alcohol abuse that apparently worsened as he received one disappointment after another. When Colby was removed as DCI by President Gerald Ford, Duckett had good reason to expect that he would be promoted to director. Instead, Ford selected George H. W. Bush. George Bush had been alerted to Duckett's problems with alcohol but valued his political acumen. He reportedly tried to counsel and encourage Duckett, but nevertheless declined to appoint him as his deputy. After a serious security transgression in March 1976, Carl Duckett's resignation from the CIA was accepted by Director Bush.

---

Years later, in 1979, former AZORIAN security officers Steve Craig and Bob James had lunch with William Colby to discuss an issue totally unrelated to the *Glomar Explorer* program. When asked about Carl Duckett's problems with alcohol abuse, Colby reflected that "Carl, soused, was smarter than most of my staff when sober!"

---

John Parangosky could also see that the breakaway event during the recovery mission would probably lead to the failure of his program. He knew as well as Duckett that the security on the program would probably not hold together for a follow-on attempt to recover the remainder of the target. Nevertheless, he continued efforts to ready the recovery system for another mission.

When the AZORIAN program was exposed by Jack Anderson in March 1975, Parangosky knew the handwriting was on the wall. He submitted his retirement papers. He stayed on in a pro bono capacity until the MATADOR program was officially declared dead and then returned to private life, ending a brilliant CIA career of twenty-seven years.

Parangosky was recognized in 2000 by Keith Hall, then director of the NRO, as one of forty national reconnaissance pioneers for his work on both satellite and aircraft reconnaissance systems. After his death in 2004, the NRO published an "In Memoriam" tribute to him in its unclassified journal, *National Reconnaissance: The Discipline and Practice*.[2] The tribute lauded Parangosky's roles in the developments of the U-2 and A-12 (OXCART) aircraft and the CORONA reconnaissance satellite, in addition to his management of the AZORIAN program.

———

In spite of the criticism that the CIA received from Congress for their management of the submarine recovery effort, the men and women of the agency were justifiably proud of what had been achieved—and perhaps even prouder of what had been *attempted*.

The AZORIAN program certainly received mixed reviews from the media and from other government agencies. When AZORIAN was initially exposed in 1975, the American and international press were almost uniformly impressed with the boldness and ingenuity of the operation. Even those who thought the mission to be politically irresponsible had to applaud the bravura of the CIA's program team. Though the agency had tried to suppress publication of all the articles, commentary, and books about the program, the publicity provided a big boost to the morale of the CIA that, according to many critics, was being outclassed by the Soviet KGB in the Cold War intelligence battles.

## International Relationships

*SALT Stays on Track*

One of the major State Department concerns about the AZORIAN mission was the impact that the program might have on diplomatic relations between the United States and the Soviet Union if the mission were to be compromised. In 1975 the United States and the Soviet Union were negotiating an expansion of the Strategic Arms Limitation Treaty (SALT I) signed in 1972. It was in the middle of these intense negotiations that the CIA's attempt to recover the *K-129*—in plain view of more than one Soviet ship monitoring the operation—became public knowledge. This was both an affront and an embarrassment to Leonid Brezhnev, the general secretary of the Communist Party of the Soviet Union. The *K-129* was a ship of state. It belonged to the Soviet Union and was not subject to salvage law.

The CIA and the backers of the program all knew that. They had been convinced, however, that they could carry out the mission without the security being compromised. And, quite possibly, they were inclined to continue with the illegal mission because it was just so damned exciting. They wanted to believe the risks were minimal, because they wanted so badly to do the mission. Of course, the mission *was* compromised and the government was in the position of having egregiously offended the Soviet general secretary—and having possibly torpedoed the chances for a SALT II Treaty.

In 1960, following the Soviet shoot-down of an American U-2 spy plane along with its pilot, Francis Gary Powers, party chairman Nikita Krushchev angrily denounced the United States in the United Nations forum and broke off détente negotiations with the United States. Would Brezhnev do the same? DCI William Colby and National Security Adviser Henry Kissinger thought there might be a way to avoid a similar reaction.

There was a significant difference in the two situations. In 1960 the Soviets had all the bragging rights. They had the wreckage of the U-2 aircraft (along with the onboard camera), and they also had the pilot—alive and well. In 1975, however, the situation was entirely different. Sure, the Soviets held the legal high ground, but the United States had part of their submarine—recovered within plain view of Soviet surveillance ships. The bragging rights belonged to the United States.

William Colby and Henry Kissinger believed that the 1960 debacle with Krushchev did not necessarily have to be repeated. When Powers was shot down, President Eisenhower publicly took responsibility for approving that and previous U-2 espionage missions. This put Khrushchev on the spot. He couldn't possibly just ignore the U.S. transgression when the president was publicly taking credit for it. Kissinger and Colby realized that Khrushchev had been, in effect, forced to respond to the U-2 incident. They therefore advised President Ford to make no comment at all regarding the recovery of the *K-129*. In fact, Kissinger sent an oral message to the Soviet ambassador, Anatoly Dobrynin, stating explicitly that the United States would have no comment to make on the incident. The result? Brezhnev was free to simply ignore the incident—neither confirming nor denying that it ever happened—and proceed with the SALT II negotiations, a very high priority for him. Dobrynin later wrote, "What mattered most to Leonid Brezhnev was better relations with America."[3] Face was saved for both sides.

In 1979, SALT II was signed by both President Jimmy Carter and Chairman Brezhnev. Subsequent international events (including the Soviet Union's invasion of Afghanistan) impeded ratification by the U.S. Senate, but the provisions of the treaty were honored by both countries for many years.

*Law of the Sea Fades*

In 1973 the United Nations convened the Third United Nations Conference on the Law of the Sea (UNCLOS III) in New York. This conference, which continued through 1982, aimed to resolve and codify an international agreement on how the world's nations could use, and share, the natural resources of the oceans. At the time that UNCLOS was convened, there was some interest in ocean mining, but it was not the driving consideration for the members of the conference. The most critical concerns included decline of fish stocks and other renewable sources, effects of sewage and chemicals on human health, and alteration and destruction of marine habitats and ecosystems.

That changed rapidly when it was announced that Howard Hughes was convinced that ocean mining could soon become an economically attractive venture, and that he was sponsoring a Deep Ocean Mining Program to explore the feasibility of profitably mining manganese nodules from the ocean bottom. All of a sudden, ocean mining became the hottest topic at the conference. Many of the participating countries began to look hard at how they could profit most from this new and potentially lucrative field of endeavor. Although most experts felt that Hughes's expectations were wildly optimistic, they were awed at the financial investment that he was willing to make to back up his conviction. They didn't want to be left behind in the race to recover the oceans' mineral treasures.

The Summa Corporation participated in UNCLOS III in a minor way, primarily to maintain credibility of the DOMP cover story. Paul Reeve, the general manager of Summa's Ocean Mining Division, communicated regularly with other members of the conference, occasionally making small presentations on Summa's progress in certain technology areas. None of these presentations were intended to be misleading, but the DOMP probably influenced a few companies to invest large sums of money unwisely. Several of those companies, and consortiums of companies, were persuaded to start their own ocean mining research programs. Although the invested dollars were small in comparison to the cost of the DOMP, they consumed a significant amount of the funding available for research at those corporations.

It was a sudden shock to the conference and its member nations when the DOMP was revealed, in the spring of 1975, as nothing but a cover story for a CIA program aimed at the recovery of a sunken Soviet submarine. The credibility of the U.S. representation at UNCLOS III was, of course, seriously damaged.

The conference lasted until 1982, and an agreement was opened for signature by the member countries on December 10 of that year. The United States signed the convention, but the Senate has never ratified it. One of the sticking points has been Section XI of the convention, which establishes an international seabed authority to authorize seabed exploration and mining and to distribute the mining royalties. Conservatives in the Senate believed this provision would have been restrictive to free enterprise. Resolution of the final issues of the convention may drag on for many years, but the United States has accepted many of the convention's provisions and has been quite comfortable in honoring them as though they were international law.

## Legal Issues

*Mission Exposure Hurts Investors*

Shortly after the CIA's attempt to recover the *K-129* became public in 1975, the lawsuits started coming to Langley. Some were personal injury suits, easily handled out of court. Grievances more difficult to adjudicate included those alleging that the CIA had not followed approved contracting practices in selecting its AZORIAN contractor team or had infringed on one or more patents related to undersea search techniques. Perhaps the most serious of the CIA's legal issues evolving from AZORIAN resulted from the outrage of Global Marine stockholders who, believing that they were partial owners of a company at the forefront of an exciting and potentially lucrative ocean mining industry, suddenly found that Howard Hughes's Deep Ocean Mining Program was only a cover story.

Global Marine's economic fortunes had been affected very strongly (and positively) by the Summa relationship. Global stock had been quite volatile over the years prior to the AZORIAN program. Global Marine was a very highly leveraged company whose apparent value to investors went up and down depending on the world market for oil and the need for, or interest in, offshore oil exploration. When investors perceived Global Marine to have a prominent role in a major new offshore industry—deep ocean mining—with heavy financial involvement from Howard Hughes, the price of Global Marine stock took off. Lockheed and Honeywell stock values were also affected but to a lesser degree. Global Marine was perceived (rightly or wrongly) to be the lead player in the Summa DOMP, and the dollars ostensibly coming in from Summa were clearly a major part of Global Marine's total income.

When the DOMP was exposed as merely a CIA cover story, stockholders rushed to sell their Global Marine stock. Many of those stockholders were left with large losses. Understandably, they cried "foul!" and looked for ways to recover their losses. The Securities Exchange Commission (SEC) was furious. The SEC looked at this manipulation of a free market—even though unintended—as a serious breach of trust.

There were two main problem areas: First, Global Marine stockholders had been told that the company was working on an ocean mining program (it wasn't). Second, they'd been told that Global Marine's sponsor was Howard Hughes's Summa Corporation (it wasn't). The SEC was looking for both admission of wrongdoings from the CIA and penalties for Global Marine.

Walt Logan from the headquarters program office participated in the trial.[4] Logan was a lawyer as well as one of Parangosky's most trusted officers. In response to the charge that the DOMP cover story was a lie, Logan argued that the government actually *did* collect manganese nodules on each of the Global Marine–sponsored missions. In fact, when the *Glomar II* sailed in 1970, the ship collected a small quantity of manganese nodules that were brought back and stored. When the *Seascope* sailed in 1972, it dredged over a ton of nodules. (Most of them were subsequently encased in plastic cubes and given as gifts to executives and engineers working in the ocean mining area to enhance the credibility of the cover.) This might appear to be a thin defense, but the SEC couldn't claim that the DOMP cover story was an outright lie.

The CIA further maintained that Global Marine was not guilty of withholding information from stockholders. Since the information was classified by the U.S. government, Global was restricted by security constraints from making the real nature of their activity public, and therefore should be held harmless of any wrongdoing. Logan sought advice from the office of legal counsel, that part of the Justice Department that provides legal assistance to government offices. The assistant attorney general for the office of legal counsel at the time was Antonin Scalia, currently a justice of the Supreme Court. Scalia did not get involved in the case, but he gave Logan encouragement that his argument had some merit. Logan took heart from the encouragement and he kept persevering, hoping that the SEC would eventually tire and drop the charges against Global Marine.

Ultimately, the case was settled without any punitive damages. Global Marine agreed to notify its stockholders that they were not actually involved in ocean mining, and that their sponsor was the U.S. government, not the Summa Corporation. But no further information was provided relative to the activities that were actually pursued. When all the shouting was over, the CIA earned the displeasure of the SEC, but nothing more.

Would any CIA program manager attempt to employ a cover story like the DOMP for a major covert program in today's environment? I can't answer that, but I'm confident that the risks would be considered very carefully before any approvals were given to proceed with such a plan.

*Willard Bascom vs. CIA*

The Securities Exchange Commission was not the only organization upset with the CIA. In 1962, noted marine engineer and author Willard Bascom had made a proposal to both the CIA and the Air Force to develop a capability for raising Soviet test missiles from the ocean depths.[5] The scheme included the use of a sophisticated search capability that Bascom had patented. The proposal even provided a white-world explanation for the intended recovery efforts. He suggested that the recovery ship be given the ostensible scientific mission of drilling into deep ocean sediment—sort of an extension of the original Mohole Project. Bascom claimed the CIA found the proposal interesting, but nevertheless turned it down.

In 1976, after the AZORIAN mission had been exposed, Willard Bascom sued the CIA for the theft of intellectual property and patent infringement. He demanded $100 million in compensation. The case was tried in April 1977 before the court of claims in Washington, D.C. That court is responsible for hearing all cases of patent infringement against the U.S. government. The *Washington Post* reported that the trial was the most secret ever heard by the court of claims.[6] Presiding Judge Francis Browne had placed a gag order (he described it as a protective order) on all prospective witnesses a year earlier. He also included all secretaries, stenographers, and typists who might have access to trial testimony under the gag order, as well as all the documents produced in the trial. According to the *Washington Post:*

The trial was held in a closed courtroom whose location was not posted on the court's bulletin board. Dates and times of the trial were not posted either. Witnesses came to the trial one at a time, leaving by a different door so they would not be seen by the next witness.

There was no bailiff in the case. The stenographer tape-recorded the testimony. The only people outside of Judge Browne and the lawyers for each side who heard the whole case were two "observers," believed to be employees of the CIA.

Two groups of witnesses testified. One group included people who knew Bascom, his work and his proposals to raise the missiles back in 1962. This group is identified in documents in the court's public record. The second witness group was made up of people involved in the Glomar Explorer project to recover the submarine. Their names are nowhere in the public record.

Among other things, Bascom claimed that the *Hughes Glomar Explorer* had used his patented technique for underwater search to find the *K-129*. Bascom's search scheme proposed the use of a sensor platform attached to ordinary drill string. The platform would be lowered to the bottom and towed by a surface ship in a controlled search pattern to look for missile debris or archaeological artifacts.

Not knowing that the CIA already knew the location of the *K-129* submarine to within a hundred feet or so, Bascom concluded that the CIA would have been searching for the target with sensors attached to the end of a large pipe string—the same technique described in his proposal to the CIA and NASA twelve years earlier. That, he maintained, would be an infringement of his patent. In fact, the actual search for the target by the *HGE* was simply a process of lowering the CV at the known location until either the side-looking search sonars or the closed-circuit TVs were able to make acoustic or visual contact.

As the director for recovery operations on the ship, I was selected as a government witness to refute the charges that the CIA had infringed on Bascom's patent. Although, as the *Washington Post* reported, the proceedings of the trial were kept secret, I certainly don't remember entering the court by one door and exiting by another (also reported by the *Post*) to avoid being seen by other witnesses. In fact, Willard Bascom, his lawyer (George Wise), and I were told to wait in the same room until it was time for the case to be heard. Since I was a great admirer of Bascom, and he was truly impressed by what the CIA had accomplished, we spent some pleasant time together talking about ocean engineering in general, his previous accomplishments with the Mohole Project, and the recovery of sunken ships of archaeological interest. We did not, however, discuss or refer to the case about to be heard by the court.

Bascom's claims were rejected by the U.S. Court of Claims. He appealed to the U.S. Court of Appeals and lost again. Ultimately, he petitioned the Supreme Court to hear the case, but it declined to do so.

## Maintaining AZORIAN Secrets

*Authors and Memoirs*

The security for the AZORIAN program was remarkably effective from its beginning in 1969 until its calamitous breakdown early in 1975. Even after the disclosure of the 1974 recovery mission and the cancellation of the follow-on MATADOR mission, the government persisted in holding the program details very closely.

Despite its efforts, however, the CIA was unable to prevent the disclosure of many program details by a handful of authors publishing their own versions of the AZORIAN history and their personal involvement. Former CIA director William Colby and former president Gerald Ford both described their own participation in the *Glomar Explorer* program in published personal memoirs.

Colby described his efforts to discourage the media from exposing the *Glomar* mission until it was completed.[7] He also discussed the problems encountered in the recovery operation and the loss of most of the target object. Before publication of his memoir, a senior CIA official, Ernest "Zeke" Zellmer, tried to persuade Colby to remove the discussion about the mission success (or lack thereof). Colby reluctantly agreed to take out the offensive information, but it was too late to change the French edition of his memoir. It was already in publication.

President Gerald Ford reflected in his memoir that he was asked to approve the final raising of the *K-129* into the well of the *Hughes Glomar Explorer*, even though a Soviet surveillance ship was standing close by, observing the ship's operations.[8] There was concern that the Soviet trawler might attempt to stop the recovery. Ford decided that we had come too far to turn back. He gave the approval to proceed. He also referred to the loss of part of the submarine during the ascent to the surface.

———

There's an interesting historical footnote regarding President Ford's recollections about approving the recovery. Ford states in his memoir that he was asked to approve the final raising of the *K-129* on the "second morning of my presidency." Since Ford was sworn in as president on August 9, 1974, his decision would have been made on either August 10 or 11. In fact, the *Glomar Explorer* had already completed the recovery and left the target site on August 8. Approval for beginning the final ascent would have to have been given no later than July 30, ten days before Ford was even sworn in.

Why the discrepancy in the dates? The CIA has nothing to say on the matter.

However, I believe it's quite possible that the agency actually requested Ford's approval to continue the mission while he was still vice president, preferring to ask for his permission rather than that of President Nixon, who might well have been too distracted by his own personal problems to make a responsible decision. In writing his memoir in 1979, President Ford could have chosen to disguise the fact that he was, in fact, assuming the role of "highest authority" while still vice president. He might well have concluded that no one would ever be able to challenge the dates anyway.

## The Glomar Response

During this same time period, hundreds of requests for information on the AZORIAN program were coming in from Congress. These questions went to the intelligence community staff for distribution to the appropriate agency. The intelligence community staff member who was redirecting all these questions was Walt Logan, formerly the chief of the Commercial Operations Division within the AZORIAN program office. Logan, a CIA veteran, was a skilled lawyer who had spent many years working for the office of security. This legal training and security experience made him a natural choice for this new responsibility.

Ultimately, however, the questions from Congress were joined by a huge number of queries from private (*ostensibly* private, at least) citizens through the FOIA channels signed into law by President Lyndon Johnson in 1966. As the workload grew, so did Logan's staff, and it was ultimately transferred to the office of the CIA's general counsel.

The FOIA requests posed a dilemma for the CIA. The tacit agreement reached by the Soviet and U.S. governments was that both sides would maintain a public silence about the *K-129* recovery attempt.[9] For that reason, FOIA requests for information on such things as cryptographic equipment and codebooks caused a special problem. If the government acknowledged the information existed—even if it didn't release the information because of classification—it would be declaring publicly that the AZORIAN mission had, indeed, recovered information or hardware relating to those subjects. That could be interpreted by the Soviets as flaunting the success of the mission. For the *HGE* program, it wasn't sufficient to just protect information by classification. Instead, the very existence of the recovered information/material had to be protected.

The intelligence community had a second problem with FOIA requests, independent of the understanding with the Soviets. The intelligence community wanted to protect not only what we had learned from the recovery mission; it also wanted to deny the Soviet Union any knowledge about what we had *not* learned from the mission. If, for example, the government were to respond to a hypothetical FOIA request for information on plutonium levels in the recovered wreckage of the *K-129*, a reply to the effect that no information existed on that subject would suggest that, in fact, no missile warheads or other missile parts had been recovered, giving the Soviets some assurance that the state of their missile technology was still protected. The intelligence community didn't want to provide any assurances of that kind. It preferred to leave the Soviet Union with maximum uncertainty regarding what the United States had—and had not—learned about their submarines, missiles, torpedoes, codes, equipment, and operational procedures. The Soviets would be confronted with the need to rethink all their procedures and equipment designs under the assumption that they may have been compromised to the United States.

Walt Logan and his team developed a stock answer to be used for all FOIA requests relative to the *Hughes Glomar Explorer* mission. The response, which came to be known as the *"Glomar* response," was that the agency would refuse to confirm or deny even the existence of any records relevant to the FOIA request. As Walt Logan jokingly described it to me, "We'd tell the requestor that we could neither confirm nor deny the existence of any records responsive to the request, but if we *did* have any such records, they would be classified. So, either way, they're screwed!"

The *Glomar* response was first judicially recognized in the national security context in 1976.[10] However, the "Glomarization" principle has been used for other programs since that time. Under guidelines provided to FOIA attorneys in 1998 from the assistant solicitor, Branch of General Legal Services, Division of General Law, "A 'Glomar' response can be justified only when the confirmation or denial of the existence of responsive records would, in and of itself, reveal exempt information."

Today, thirty-eight years after the AZORIAN mission, the *Glomar* response is still being used for many FOIA requests relevant to that program. A recent (May 12, 2008) request to the Office of Naval Intelligence for photographs taken of the wreck of a Soviet Golf-class submarine from the USS *Halibut* got the following response:

> Please be advised that a search for records conducted by our Maritime
> Intelligence Directorate, Special Programs Department, produced no docu-
> ments responsive to your request, in that ONI [Office of Naval Intelligence]
> can neither confirm nor deny the existence or non-existence of the documents
> you requested.

The CIA has historically been very effective in resisting attempts to get information on the AZORIAN program through FOIA channels. In a landmark FOIA case that extended from 1975 to 1981, *Military Audit Project v. William Casey, Director of Central Intelligence,*[11] the CIA successfully defended its right to continue classification of almost all aspects of the AZORIAN program—even facts that had been previously disclosed to the public by authors, investigative reporters, and former government officials. The case was finally closed on May 4, 1981, in the United States Court of Appeals, District of Columbia Circuit.

In 2007, however, the CIA received an FOIA request for information on the AZORIAN program that it couldn't ignore or answer with the *Glomar* response. The request came from the National Security Archive, associated with George Washington University in Washington, D.C. While searching through declassified documents of another intelligence agency, the National Security Archive had found a reference to an internally generated CIA history of the *Explorer* program. The National Security Archive submitted a request for that document, "Project AZORIAN: The Story of the *Hughes Glomar Explorer,*" through FOIA channels.

This created a real problem for the agency. It couldn't reply with the *Glomar* response because existence of that history had been officially (even though inadvertently) acknowledged in an unclassified government document. The CIA was stuck. They had to respond. In January 2010, the agency replied to the National Security Archive with a censored version of the CIA's own program history. And, although heavily redacted, the FOIA release contained much information that the CIA had treated as classified up to that time—including a large number of program facts that had been redacted from my own unpublished manuscript.

Adding to the CIA's security challenges from authors and FOIA requestors is the erosion of the sense of urgency to protect AZORIAN information. By the 1990s, the security indoctrination that had been given to AZORIAN contractors and crew members was beginning to fade away in their memories. Increasingly, personnel were taking the opportunity to relate their program participation in lectures, seminars, oral histories, and technical articles. Today, many former crew members and government officials are surprised when told that the agency still considers their old program to be sensitive and highly classified.

*Cold War Thaw*

Perhaps the most significant *official* acknowledgment of facts related to AZORIAN was made by DCI Robert Gates in 1992. On October 16 of that year, Gates visited Russia and personally delivered to Boris Yeltsin, president of the Russian Federation, artifacts recovered from the *K-129*. He also delivered a video recording of the at-sea burial—on September 4, 1974—of the six Soviet sailors recovered with the submarine. Delivering the materials and artifacts to Yeltsin so soon after the end of the Cold War was spelled out in his memoir as "a gesture of intent, a symbol of a new era."[12] Gates had hoped that the gesture would persuade the Russian government to reciprocate with some information about American pilots lost over the Soviet Union years before. Whether or not the gesture helped establish greater cooperation between the two nations for sharing information on Cold War casualties has been a subject of speculation. The Russians may have appreciated receiving the tape of the burial, but they chose not to make its existence public at the time.

The information about the AZORIAN program provided to Yeltsin by Gates was remarkably forthcoming and revealing. The text follows:

In the summer of 1974, the Glomar Explorer recovered a section of the Soviet submarine PL-722. This submarine had sunk in March 1968 in the North Pacific Ocean. The remains of six Soviet crewmen were discovered in the forward compartment of the submarine.

Three crewmen were found with personal identification: Viktor Lokhov, Vladimir Kostyushko, and Valentin Nosachev. The other three crewmen carried no personal identification and could not be identified. The three identified crewmen were all 20 years of age when they died; the ages of the unidentified crewmen could not be determined. No personal effects were recovered with the bodies. The ship's surgeon listed the cause of death for all sailors as "Explosion and crushing injuries incurred while working on duty vessel." No autopsy was performed.

In anticipation that human remains would be recovered, the Glomar Explorer was prepared to bury the dead. From the time of their recovery from the submarine's hulk until the burial ceremony, the remains were handled with the utmost care and respect. A heavy steel box, 8 × 8 × 4 feet in dimension, was chosen for the burial ceremony and six individual shelves were installed to support the bodies.

On the appointed day, September 4, 1974, two rehearsals were held to ensure that the actual ceremony would proceed smoothly and with the appropriate dignity. A six-person Honor Guard was selected from among the volunteers. Immediately prior to the ceremony, the Honor Guard transported each body to the burial vault individually. During transportation, a Soviet Naval Ensign, carried for this purpose by the Glomar Explorer, was draped over each body. The same ensign shrouded each body.

After all bodies were placed in the burial vault, together with a representative portion of the vessel on which they served and perished, the ensign was mounted alongside the US National Flag behind the vault.

The ceremony, attended by some 75 of the ship's company, began with the National Anthems of the United States and of the Soviet Union. It continued with what was thought to be the closest ceremony approaching the actual Soviet Navy burial at sea ceremony. In addition, the US Navy ceremony for the burial of the dead at sea followed. An interpreter translated the Soviet Service and the US Navy Service into Russian.

After the vault doors had been bolted shut, the vault was slowly hoisted over the side while the Committal and Benediction were read and the US Navy Hymn was played. At 1921 local time, during the final light of evening twilight, the vault, now completely flooded, was released into a calm sea and fell free to the ocean floor.

The burial site is located approximately 90 miles southwest of the Island of Hawaii at Latitude 18-29.0 N, Longitude 157-34.0 W. The Soviet Naval Ensign used has been stored since the ceremony and is being presented to the Russian Government as a symbol of the US Government's respect both for the six sailors and for the service they rendered to their nation.

Boris Yeltsin, after the Gates visit in 1992, commissioned a group of scientists to inventory Russian nuclear materials lost or dumped at sea. The Russian report was prepared at President Yeltsin's request by a team of forty-six experts led by Dr. Aleksei V. Yablokov, his top environmental adviser.[13] The report was made available to the International Atomic Energy Agency (IAEA), a United Nations group that monitors nuclear affairs. The September 2001 issue of the IAEA report contains the information provided by the Russian Federation on the exact location and the amount of nuclear material still aboard the *K-129*.[14] It also contains the following notes:

On March 6, 1968 the diesel submarine K-129, which carried two torpedoes with nuclear warheads and three ICBM Rockets, was lost in Pacific Ocean approximately 1230 miles from Kamchatka, near the Hawaiian Islands. In August 1974 the bow part (three compartments of this submarine with nuclear warheads) were raised by RV "Glomar Explorer."

The source for the information was listed as "INTERNATIONAL MARITIME ORGANIZATION, *Facts and Problems Related to Radioactive Waste Disposal in Seas Adjacent to the Territory of the Russian Federation*, Office of the President of the Russian Federation, Moscow, 1993."

On March 30, 2004, the U.S. State Department declassified some of the 1975 correspondence between Soviet ambassador Anatoly Dobrynin and U.S. secretary of state Henry Kissinger. Those letters, discussed earlier in this book, had resided in the Gerald R. Ford presidential library as classified documents for over twenty-five years. They were arguably the most sensitive written records still remaining from the diplomatic exchanges between the Soviet Union and the United States when the fact of the AZORIAN mission was uncovered.

## Some Mysteries Still Remain

Almost all details of the *Hughes Glomar Explorer* program have been revealed to the general public and to the Russian government. There are, however, three program-related subjects that are—at least for now—still protected. The first category includes the actual intelligence that was gleaned from the exploitation of the recovered portion of the *K-129*—how much the United States learned (and *didn't* learn) about Soviet submarine design and construction, cryptographic equipment and codes, missile warhead design, built-in safeguards to prevent unauthorized/inadvertent firing of the missiles, crew training procedures, and other such subjects. The second category relates to what the intelligence community knows about the real cause of the *K-129* loss. The third category is the contingency plans that would have been followed had a foreign government actually captured the *Hughes Glomar Explorer* and its crew and started steaming toward a foreign port.

*What Did We Learn?*

All of the artifacts and documents removed from the *K-129* during the exploitation phase of the mission were preserved, tagged, and stored in vans. When the *HGE* returned to Long Beach, the exploitation vans were removed from the ship and transported to a remote, secure government facility in the southwestern United States. Trained analysts and submarine experts descended on the exploitation site and worked for many months to glean all possible intelligence from the salvaged portions of the sub. The intelligence gained from the analysis has always been given the highest possible degree of security protection by the government. Significantly, the intelligence *not* gained from the analysis has always been given equivalent security protection. As discussed earlier, the objective of the intelligence community was to maximize the Soviet uncertainty about how much the intelligence community had actually learned, putting our Cold War adversary in a position where it had to assume that the United States might have managed to learn *everything* about the K-129 and the weapons it carried—causing the greatest confusion and expense for the Soviets in their response to the CIA's recovery of their submarine.

Of course, the CIA's motivation to protect information about the actual intelligence value of the AZORIAN mission was also inspired by the desire to withhold from critics of the program any information that might provide evidence that the recovery mission had been an intelligence failure. (For someone determined to minimize the CIA achievement, of course, no accounting of the intelligence value of the mission would be likely to change his mind.)

The CIA has not been completely successful in concealing the actual inventory of artifacts and documents removed from the K-129. Researchers seeking information on the AZORIAN program have managed to acquire some of those lists. So far as I am aware, however, the intelligence community *has* been successful in protecting the details of what was—and what was not—learned from those artifacts and documents. It's hard to keep anything secret for thirty-eight years. It might also be said that intelligence information that's over thirty-eight years old may not be worth the trouble it takes to protect it.

*What Really Happened to the* K-129?
Another aspect of the AZORIAN story that continues to attract the interest of both authors and readers—as well as the Soviet navy—is the real cause of the *K-129* loss.

Soviet/Russian officials and veterans have consistently claimed that the *K-129* sank as the result of an accidental collision with a U.S. submarine. In most cases they cite the USS *Swordfish* as the other party to the accident. They may, or may not, believe their own public assertions. Research on this hypothesis suggests that the *Swordfish* is an unlikely candidate for the collision theory. A photograph of the U.S. sub appeared in a Japanese newspaper in Yokosuka, Japan, seven days after the loss of the *K-129*. The *Swordfish* showed no sign of any damage other than a bent periscope (incurred, according to the Navy, from trying to surface through an ice floe)—certainly not the kind of damage that would be associated with a collision resulting in the loss of another ship.

According to Roger Schumacher, the U.S. deputy director supporting the U.S.-Russia Joint Commission on POW/MIAs (USRJC), the United States turned over the deck logs of both the *Swordfish* and the *Halibut* submarines to the Russians in 1995. This was in response to repeated requests from

Russian officials working on the USRJC. However, even this action failed to dissuade them from their conviction that a U.S. sub was responsible for the loss of the *K-129*.

As recently as May 2007, in an interview with filmmaker and author Michael White, Soviet rear admiral Viktor Dygalo spoke of his belief that the *K-129* had collided with a U.S. sub. He said, "That is my conviction, and I will always stick to it and defend it in front of anybody." In the September 10, 2007, edition of *Pravda Online*, retired captain first rank Pavel Dementiev was quoted as saying, "There is just one version—that [*K-129*] collided with an American submarine."

———

If the Russians seem to be uniformly convinced that the *K-129* sank as the result of a collision with the USS *Swordfish*, the same cannot be said for the large number of creative authors who have written about the *Hughes Glomar Explorer* and its mission. Some authors' accounts of the *K-129*'s loss lean toward rather pedestrian causes. In *Blind Man's Bluff*, for instance, Sherry Sontag and Christopher Drew suggest that the *K-129* probably sank as the result of an explosion fueled by a buildup of hydrogen gas from battery-charging operations while the submarine was on the surface.[15]

Other authors, however, have come up with more exciting (if not more plausible) explanations. In *The Silent War*, John Craven suggests that the *K-129* was possibly a rogue submarine—operating outside of Soviet navy command channels—that met its end while attempting to launch a nuclear missile at Hawaii.[16] In *Red Star Rogue*, Kenneth Sewell advances that same hypothesis (although with much more certainty) while embellishing the story with an enticing conspiracy theory suggesting that the Soviet rogue submarine was actually trying to start a war between the United States and China.[17] In *Scorpion Down*, Ed Offley suggests that the *K-129* sank as the result of a collision with a U.S. submarine, most probably the USS *Swordfish*.[18] More recently, authors Norman Polmar and Michael White claim that the most likely cause of the submarine loss was an unintended ignition of two of the sub's missile tubes during a mock firing exercise.[19]

Some of these hypotheses are ridiculous. Others have enough credibility to make them interesting and worthy of further investigation. In an attempt to get additional facts that might help explain the loss, historians are seeking the hydroacoustic records from the *K-129*'s sinking. These acoustic signals, picked up by U.S. underwater hydrophone arrays operating at six different locations in the Pacific Ocean, were analyzed in 1968 to determine the time and location of the *K-129*'s loss. Once the analysts determined the origin of the acoustic signals and concluded that they most probably originated from a sinking submarine, they turned over all records to the Office of Naval Intelligence in Washington.[20] It's unclear whether the Navy ever did any additional analysis of the signals to uncover the cause of the accident. It seems reasonable to assume, though, that these records might hold the keys to the puzzle of the *K-129*'s demise. Unfortunately, all formal requests to the Navy and CIA for information on *K-129* imagery and acoustic signals have received the *Glomar* response.

———

The CIA will not permit me to publish any information that I have relating to the cause of the loss. However, I *can* state that I find inconsistencies between every one of the hypotheses that have been presented by AZORIAN authors and my own personal knowledge of the target's condition and its contents. None of the proposed scenarios convincingly explain *all* of the existing data and facts relevant to the loss of the *K-129*.

I don't know what caused the loss of the *K-129*, but I believe there is a fairly strong likelihood that the truth, if exposed, could still be politically embarrassing to the governments of the United States and the Russian Federation. The list of people who actually know the cause of the *K-129*'s loss is very small—and that list is getting smaller every year. I suspect that if I knew the truth, I would choose not to publish it.

## The Armageddon Contingency Plan

Prior to the start of the AZORIAN mission, rumors were circulating through the ship's crew that the CIA had a secret contingency plan for use in the event that the *HGE* was captured and boarded by a foreign military force. The story was that the CIA had implanted explosives in the four corners of the well. These demolition charges would be remotely detonated to sink the ship if it were boarded and headed toward a foreign port. The rumor was completely false. The CIA had no plans, under any conditions, to destroy its ship and endanger the lives of the crew.

That said, what *would* the government have done if the Soviets had captured the *Explorer* and steamed off toward a Soviet port? When President Gerald Ford approved the final raising of the *K-129* target—in full view of the Soviet *SB-10* that was monitoring the *HGE*'s operations—he must have had some assurance that the United States had a plan in place to respond to a hostile takeover.

Permitting a foreign government to sail the *Explorer*—along with its crew (some of whom were CIA employees) and all the evidence aboard the ship—to a foreign country would have been very unpalatable in view of having so recently endured the same excruciatingly embarrassing situation when the USS *Pueblo* was taken to North Korea. On the other hand, would the U.S. Navy have dared to engage a Soviet boarding party in a firefight to rescue the *HGE* and its crew? Possibly precipitating an escalation of violence leading to a major conflict with the Soviet Union? Not likely.

In *Project AZORIAN,* Michael White and Norman Polmar claim that an unofficial plan was in place for such a contingency.[21] They suggest that the Navy had equipped one of their submarines at Pearl Harbor, the USS *Tautog,* with Mark 14 and 16 torpedoes that were optimally effective against surface ships. In the event of a Soviet boarding of the *HGE,* the submerged *Tautog* would intercept the *Explorer* and sink it, along with all the evidence of espionage—and along with the loss of many of the crew. Did such a plan—even if informal—really exist?

When I addressed this question to the former director of the joint organization under whose auspices the AZORIAN program was executed, Ernest Zellmer, he assured me he'd never heard of such a plan. Further, he felt confident that William Colby had also been unaware of any such plan— and in any event would have never approved its implementation.

Whether or not this Armageddon contingency plan ever existed, I believe its implementation would have been a political and diplomatic disaster for the president and the country. If called upon to execute the plan, the *Tautog* would have been attacking a commercial ship with both U.S. civilians and Soviet sailors onboard, risking the lives of all.

The operation could not have been done covertly, either. The Soviets would know that a U.S. submarine had been responsible for the attack, and any Soviet submarines in the vicinity (remember, the target location was frequently used as a "crossroads" for Soviet submarines transiting to and from their patrol areas) would be called into the area immediately to lend assistance for recovery of survivors. And, what would the *Tautog* do? Stay submerged while American and Soviet sailors—many no doubt wounded—drifted in small lifeboats (if they were lucky) waiting for rescue? No. Humanitarian concerns would dictate that the *Tautog* assist in the rescue efforts, thereby exposing themselves as the attacker of an American commercial ship.

Would the contingency plan described by Polmar and White have avoided the type of political and diplomatic problems created by the capture of the *Pueblo*? Possibly, but in preventing that kind of embarrassment, the *Tautog* would have created a frightening situation with the potential for escalation into an armed conflict between the opposing navies of the United States and the Soviet Union. If that was the ultimate contingency plan for a hypothetical Soviet capture of the *Glomar Explorer*, it was a very poorly conceived one.

Was there another contingency plan that President Ford and other senior administration officials knew about? Were the president and his advisers so confident about the overriding Soviet desire for détente that they ruled out the possibility of a diplomatically inflammatory boarding of the *Explorer* by Soviet sailors? Or is it realistic to assume that the faith of the entire U.S. government was vested in the ability of a few members of the *HGE* crew to ward off a foreign warship with fire hoses, sawed-off shotguns, and vodka?

I can say this much with certainty: I knew nothing of any contingency plan that called for the destruction of the *Hughes Glomar Explorer*, nor do I believe that any other crew member knew of such a plan. None of us were crazy enough to have volunteered for that mission under those circumstances—none of us would have been on the ship if we had thought that death by intentional friendly fire was the ultimate contingency plan.

Still, sometimes I wonder.

# Appendix A

## *Perceptions Management and Disinformation*

Perceptions management, or PM, is an integral part of any cover story. PM is essentially the art of getting people who are not cleared on the program—the *outsiders*—to believe what you *want* them to believe about your program. In the case of AZORIAN, the CIA wanted everyone outside the program to believe that the *Hughes Glomar Explorer* was a prototype ocean mining ship being developed by Howard Hughes. It's easy to simply declare to the white world that the *HGE* was a mining ship and that Lockheed was building a mining machine. That's a cover story. But, how do you convince observers that your cover story is really true? That's where perceptions management comes in.

A perceptions management plan tries to control observables to create a false (and preferred) impression as to what the real objectives of the program are. Program observables that are consistent with the cover story are emphasized. Program details that might be inconsistent with the cover story are hidden from view. Sometimes, however, it may be necessary to explicitly and publicly disseminate *false* information to create the desired perceptions about the nature of the program. That practice is often referred to as *disinformation*, and it can become very controversial.

PM can easily approach that thin line between what is and what is not ethical and/or legal. The employment of cover stories and the creation of observables to lead uncleared observers to believe something that is not true must be managed with great care. There are few, if any, hard and fast rules applicable to PM planning, but there are some guidelines that are commonly used.

The guidelines for using perceptions management as part of a strategic deception are obviously different during times of peace and times of war. During a time of war, the priority is clearly focused on ensuring that the country's security interests prevail. Legal and ethical issues are of secondary consideration. Anthony Cave Brown's masterpiece, *Bodyguard of Lies*,[1] describes in exquisite detail the months of preparation and planning that went into perceptions management operations prior to the D-day invasion of Europe in World War II. General Dwight D. Eisenhower and his command went to great lengths to create observables that would reinforce the perception that the Allied invasion would come ashore at Pas-de-Calais rather than Normandy. The overall perceptions management effort, monumental in its scope, knowingly sacrificed ships, aircraft, and even lives in order to preserve the element of surprise for the eventual landing at Normandy.

During a time of peace, these guidelines for PM planning change. An intelligence objective, no matter how important, is not usually considered justification for the same sacrifices that would be used to protect the welfare of the country during a war. For an espionage program in peacetime, the PM planner must consider very carefully all of the risks associated with the execution of the plan.[2]

First, he must consider the downside risks if the PM plan is compromised as nothing more than a deception. Will the exposure of the plan cause serious embarrassment to the sponsoring agency, the administration, or the U.S. government? Will any ongoing treaty negotiations be impacted? Will it affect U.S. credibility with its allies?

Second, he must consider potential problems that may result if the PM plan is successful and is *not* compromised. Will the successful deceptions intrinsic to the plan have an adverse effect on any corporations or individuals? For example, could the PM plan result in a corporation investing capital in a new line of business that looks attractive *only* because of the PM deceptions? Or, could it induce an individual stockholder to buy stock in a company that he feels, on the basis of PM deceptions, may stand to make large future profits?

Some of the toughest judgment calls a program manager may have to make relate to the use of perceptions management to protect the nature of his program and its mission. Broadly, it can probably be said that any plan to disseminate false information to mislead people about the nature of the program should only be undertaken after full consideration has been given to (1) the likelihood that the use of disinformation might be discovered and the false information will be identified as such; (2) the impact that compromise of the disinformation program will have on the United States, the administration, the government agency, and the program itself; and (3) the impacts that a *successful* PM plan might have on organizations and private individuals. Not an easy call—and one that doesn't adapt easily to overly simplistic rules or guidelines.

———

My personal views on the guidelines for cover stories and perceptions management are sometimes at variance with what might be called mainstream thinking. In recent years, some program managers have suggested arbitrary rules to define what is acceptable and what is not acceptable for a PM plan or a cover story. Two of the frequently suggested rules are (1) the cover story must be true, and (2) you cannot lie.[3] If these constraints were taken literally and enforced, I don't believe the U.S. government would ever be able to manage any covert acquisitions or perform any covert operations.

The first constraint, "the story must be true," makes no sense at all. To come up with a *true* cover story, you'd have to compromise your mission. Some legal analysts contend that if there is just *some* truth to the cover story, then the story can be called "true." That is a very fine line of legality. Too clever, in my opinion. If having some truth in your cover story helps you maintain the credibility of the cover, fine. But it would be naive to let yourself be convinced that a small element of truth in your cover story makes the story "true," thereby absolving you of any legal responsibility for undesired consequences that might result from your PM plan.

The second constraint, "you cannot lie," deserves a little more consideration. One might logically conclude that an "untrue" cover story would be the same as lying. There are some significant differences, however, in various classes of lying. I believe that if the lie does no harm, it's acceptable. If there is a potential for a perceptions management lie to do harm (to an individual, corporation, government office, or country), then the need for its use should be carefully reviewed before using it.

———

Since there are no hard rules for strategic deception, the program manager generally must decide for himself what program protection and perceptions management techniques are justifiable on the basis of legal, ethical, and policy considerations.[4] All of these risks must be weighed against the value of the proposed covert mission and the importance of the PM deception to the success of the mission. Questions on legality of the PM plan may go up to the general counsel of the sponsoring agency. In rare cases, the questions may go all the way to the Office of the Attorney General of the United States.

As stated earlier, the security objectives for the AZORIAN program were much more demanding than those for most classified government programs. If the mission of the *Hughes Glomar Explorer* had been compromised, the option to proceed with the operation would have been closed off. Failure of the cover story was simply not acceptable. For this program, it was apparent that ingenuity, ethics, and legality would have to be pushed to the limit.

# Appendix B

## *The Docking Problem*

Of all the hydrodynamic analyses that were completed during the design phase of the *Hughes Glomar Explorer*, those pertaining to the docking system were the most complex and frustrating. The problem we were trying to solve was how best to *capture* a large body—swinging at the end of a string of pipe about 110 feet below the ship—so it could be raised, under control, into the well of the ship. The problem was of course complicated by the fact that the ship would be rolling and pitching in response to the seaway, with motions largely independent of those of the large subsea body (i.e., the claw, with or without the target in its grasp). It was the task of the docking legs—the large truss structures at either end of the well that could be lowered 110 feet below the ship—to somehow capture the claw and bring its motions into sync with those of the ship.

The relative motions between the extended docking legs and the capture vehicle were significant, as might be expected. As the surface ship rolled and pitched, the rig floor (and the top of the pipe) stayed almost level, but it moved laterally with roll and longitudinally with pitch. With the rig floor perhaps 130 feet above the roll center of the ship, a roll angle of three degrees would move the top of the pipe laterally about 7 feet. This motion induced a side-to-side swinging motion to the capture vehicle at the lower end of the lifting pipe. Note that a roll to port, for example, would induce a CV motion to port, at the same time swinging the bottoms of the extended docking legs—below the ship's roll center—to starboard. Pitching motions of the surface ship similarly induced relative fore and aft motions between the docking legs and the capture vehicle.

To make things more complicated, the motions of the CV and the bottom of the docking legs were uncorrelated. That is, the natural resonant periods for the giant claw swinging on the end of the pipe were not the same as the roll or pitch resonant periods for the *HGE*, so the relative motions between the docking legs and the CV would go in and out of phase—sometimes moving together, sometimes moving 180 degrees out of phase with each other.

Consider this: During a typical docking operation in favorable sea conditions, the relative fore-and-aft distance between the CV support pins and the docking legs might vary over a range of, say, ten feet. The average period for this back-and-forth motion might typically be about nine seconds. The maximum relative velocity between the CV and the docking legs under these conditions would be three to four feet a second. How much energy would have to be dissipated if the capture vehicle impacted on the docking leg at that speed? To figure that, you have to take into account the total effective mass of the capture vehicle—the sum of its mass in air, the entrained mass of all the water inside the structure, and the added mass of the water surrounding and moving in sync with the structure. The pound-mass of the CV, by itself, was about 4 million pounds. The *entrained* water and *added mass* water probably raised the effective mass of the CV to about 10 million pounds.[1] With those assumptions, the kinetic energy of the capture vehicle impacting a docking leg at four feet per second would be about 2.5 million foot-pounds. To put it in perspective, that figure is equivalent to the kinetic energy of a greyhound bus traveling at over forty miles per hour. And the docking legs had to absorb that energy over and over until the relative motion of the CV was contained and brought into sync with the motion of the docking legs. The *Hughes Glomar Explorer* was a large, strong vessel, but those docking impacts caused the entire ship to shake and vibrate.

————

During the *HGE* design phase, both the program office and Global Marine invested a lot of time and money trying to estimate the magnitudes of those relative motions. It was referred to as the three-body dynamics problem—the three bodies being the surface ship, the pipe string, and the mining machine. Computer processing power was very limited during those years. (Remember, IBM didn't produce its first PC until 1982!) The applicable equations were mostly nonlinear and couldn't be handled easily by closed-form solutions or deterministic equations. Accordingly, we put more confidence in what we could learn from model testing.

Although Global Marine used several model basins during the design phase of the *HGE,* most of the model testing for the ship and for the three-body problem was handled under an unclassified Global Marine contract with the David Taylor Model Basin (DTMB) in Carderock, Maryland. Because of the unique nature of the three-body problem, DTMB had several senior people at the model basin supporting the program. The value of the help they provided was inestimable. The scientist responsible for coordinating the DTMB support for Global Marine was the head of hydrodynamics, Jacques Hadler.

In trying to set up valid model tests for the three-body problem, Jacques was faced with a dilemma—whether to scale the model using Reynolds numbers or Froude numbers. Without going into technical details, when using scaled models that will be operating in a homogeneous viscosity (e.g., aircraft or automobiles operating in air), the scaling laws dictated by Reynolds numbers are conventionally used. When using scaled models that will be operating in a medium affected by gravity (e.g., ships operating in a seaway), the scaling laws dictated by Froude numbers are conventionally used. For the three-body problem with a station-keeping ship and an appendage swinging below the ship, the proper use of the two scaling constants could only be estimated. Jacques put together a heavily instrumented test rig and took data for a number of sea state conditions. Then he took on the unenviable task of trying to interpret the measured data so as to correct for the errors resulting from using combinations of the Froude and Reynolds scaling laws. To his everlasting credit, Hadler's analysis of these data gave us a pretty good idea about the magnitudes of the relative motions to be expected between the docking legs and the mining machine, but it didn't do a very good job of predicting which relative motions (vertical, lateral, or fore and aft) would be dominant. It should also be added that the tests didn't prepare us intellectually or emotionally for the physical shock and vibration that would be imparted to the ship from the impacts between the capture vehicle and the docking legs.

———

Here's how the docking procedure was supposed to go:

- When the capture vehicle had been lifted to within a couple of hundred feet of the surface by the pipe string, the docking legs were lowered and tilted out so that the keyholes would be as far away from the ends of the CV as possible.
- The heavy lift system continued to raise the capture vehicle until the docking pins were about level with the centers of the upper (and

wider) keyhole sections. The heave compensator system would have already been tightened up (by removing air bottles from the plenum, stiffening the pneumatic spring) as much as possible to reduce relative heave motion between the legs and the CV.

- At this point, the upper part of the pipe string was removed from the heavy lift yokes and placed on the parking brake, permitting the capture vehicle to be adjusted in yaw until it was aligned longitudinally with the ship.
- Then, the keyholes at the bottom of the docking legs were moved laterally until they were roughly centered with the average lateral position of the capture vehicle support pins. The CV and the docking legs were now aligned at the optimum position to begin the capture process.

If the ship and the capture vehicle were both stationary (not a real-world situation), the next step would be to simply close the docking legs until they contacted the CV, with the support pins more or less in the center of the keyhole. Then, the docking legs could be raised and the sloping sides of the keyholes would guide the support pins to the forty-eight-inch-wide slots at the base of the keyholes. Once the support pins had settled into the bottom of the keyhole slots, the capture vehicle would have been captured by the docking legs, eliminating all relative motion. The CV (perhaps with the target) could then be raised into the well of the ship and the gates closed. That's the way it would work if there were no relative motion!

Unfortunately, there was usually plenty of relative motion between the legs and the CV. Deciding just when to start closing the docking legs to capture the support pins was the real moment of truth. From the control room, one could monitor the time-amplitude history of the relative motions. Normally, we would have periods of low-amplitude relative motion followed by periods of high-amplitude motion. The period for these cycles could range from a couple of minutes to perhaps five minutes. Of course, it would have been great if the engagement of the docking legs and the support pins could have been completed instantly during a period of low relative motion, but the legs couldn't be moved fast enough to do that. Once we began tilting the docking legs inward, we just had to cross our fingers and hope that we'd be in a relatively quiet period when the engagement of the support pins and the docking legs actually took place.

The excitement began when the contacts between the docking legs and the capture vehicle started. As stated earlier, the force of the impacts was huge. The entire ship would shake and vibrate as though it were a bell being rung. Everyone on the ship pretty much stopped whatever they might be doing and just waited until the mating was completed. This usually took between five and ten minutes—assuming we didn't have to abort the operation, which happened more than once. When the docking was completed, the entire crew breathed a sigh of relief.

It's an amazing testimony to the engineering and design skills of John Graham and his team that they were able to build a docking system capable of withstanding these impact forces. No one had ever tried to design an at-sea docking system for such massive bodies. To have gotten it right on the first try, without the benefit of today's CAD/CAM capabilities, is simply incredible.

# Acknowledgments

It has taken me five years to write a manuscript and develop it into a book satisfying both the high standards of my publisher and the security concerns of the Central Intelligence Agency. During those long, often frustrating years, I've had the pleasure of working with some wonderfully talented people who have made it possible for me to publish this story.

Curtis Crooke, the former president of Global Marine Development and a man with great engineering imagination, provided invaluable insights into the offshore oil drilling technology and how it influenced the design of the recovery concept. Sherm Wetmore and Dr. Hank Van Calcar—both senior engineers on the *Hughes Glomar Explorer* during the recovery mission—were able to fill the gaps in my memory related to the events that occurred during the summer of 1974. Oscar "Ott" Schick, Lockheed's program manager for AZORIAN, provided his unique understanding of the creative engineering efforts that guided the design and operation of both the claw and the gigantic transfer barge, the *HMB-1*. Ott continued to respond to my barrage of questions even when he knew that he had but a short time to live. It was extremely important to him that Lockheed's part of the story be accurately presented.

I received an immense amount of help and encouragement from film producer and author Michael White, an indefatigable researcher willing to share much of the unclassified information he had collected for his film, *Project AZORIAN*. The film stands far above any other visual account of this exciting program.

I owe a huge debt of gratitude to those government and contractor personnel who served on the AZORIAN program with me, some of whom were with me on the ship. They provided personal stories I had not heard and corrected my imperfect recollections when necessary. For reasons of security, I'm not permitted to mention the real names of most of the CIA personnel, or of the other government employees who served on the *Hughes Glomar Explorer*. But they know who they are. They all show up in the book—albeit most of them with pseudonyms—and I could not have pulled this story together without their enthusiastic support.

My two-year encounter with the CIA's Publications Review Board— trying to get its permission to publish the manuscript—would never have been successful without the aid of a small group of people who provided suggestions and guidance while I attempted to steer through the bureaucracy. These mentors include Jeffrey K. Harris, former director of the National Reconnaissance Office; Joyce Pratt, former CIA comptroller; and Bob Wallace, former CIA official and author of several books about the agency and its tradecraft. I also want to express my appreciation to Mark Zaid, my legal counsel. His extensive experience in handling cases similar to mine was critically important in the development of documents and letters supporting my legal right to publish this story.

I am indeed lucky to be teamed with the University of Kansas Press and its editor in chief, Michael Briggs. Mike had the insight to recognize that my book was more than just another collection of previously published facts about AZORIAN, and the patience to advise and guide me throughout the editing process. He and his entire staff of assistant editors and reviewers provided the outstanding support that is so important for a first-time author.

Finally, I am enormously grateful for the understanding and dedication of my wife, Candy. As a participant in the *Hughes Glomar Explorer* program, Candy's proofreading and editing skills were informed, sorely needed, and deeply appreciated. Without her unfailing patience and constant encouragement, I doubt that I could have maintained my determination to publish this story of an incredible Cold War espionage program.

# Glossary

| | |
|---|---|
| AGI | NATO designation for a Soviet ship used for intelligence purposes. |
| ASK | Automatic station keeping. |
| ASME | American Society of Mechanical Engineers. |
| beam | Vertical segment of a capture vehicle tine. |
| black world | Slang expression for the community of people with security accesses to classified programs. |
| breakout legs | Hydraulically driven legs on the capture vehicle used to break the target loose from the ocean bottom. |
| CC-23 | Soviet submarine tender used as an AGI during the *Glomar II* mission. |
| *Chazhma* | Soviet missile-tracking ship that encountered the *Hughes Glomar Explorer* during the AZORIAN mission. |
| claw | Alternative name for the capture vehicle. |
| Clementine | Nickname given to the capture vehicle. |
| COD | Commercial Operations Division, an AZORIAN program office group focusing on maintaining the cover story. |
| cookie cutters | Vertical plates at the base of the breakout legs to stabilize the capture vehicle while resting on the sea bottom. |
| CORONA | Classified code name for the NRO's first reconnaissance satellite system. |
| cover story | Innocent explanation for classified activity. |
| *CUSS I* | Early drilling ship built and used by Global Marine, Inc. |
| *CUSS II* | Original name of the *Glomar II* drilling ship. |
| CV | Capture vehicle. |
| davit | Horizontal element of a capture vehicle tine. |
| DCI | Director of Central Intelligence. |

| | |
|---|---|
| DDL | Digital data link. |
| deep sound channel | Water depth where speed of sound is at a minimum. |
| DIRNSA | Director of National Security Agency. |
| DOMP | Deep Ocean Mining Project. |
| double (pipe) | Two thirty-foot sections of lifting pipe screwed together into a sixty-foot section. |
| drill string | Pipe used for offshore oil drilling. |
| DSDP | Deep Sea Drilling Project sponsored by the National Science Foundation. |
| DSSV | Deep Submergence Surveillance Vehicle, a Navy program. |
| effective mass | Sum of dry mass, entrained mass, and added mass. |
| elevator/subspinner | Segment of the pipe-handling system that raised the pipe double up to the top of the derrick and then lowered it into the top of the pipe string and torqued it up. |
| EM cable | Electromechanical cable. |
| FBI | Federal Bureau of Investigation. |
| Froude number | Scaling factor used to interpret surface ship model testing results. |
| G.M. | Metacentric height. |
| *Gidrograf* | Soviet AGI involved with the *Glomar II* missions. |
| *Glomar Challenger* | Global Marine ship involved with deep-sea drilling experiments. |
| *Glomar II* | Global Marine ship used by CIA to support the DOMP cover story. |
| GMDI | Global Marine Development Inc. |
| *Halibut* | U.S. Navy submarine. |
| Harvey Wallbanger | Euphemism for a secret entrance into the West Coast program office. |
| heave compensator | Large air-oil spring used to support the *HGE* derrick and isolate ship heave motions from the lifting pipe. |
| heavy lift system | Hydraulic system used to raise/lower lifting pipe on the *Hughes Glomar Explorer.* |
| *HGE* | *Hughes Glomar Explorer.* |
| *HMB-1* | *Hughes Mining Barge–I.* |
| HY-2 | Early-generation secure voice communications system used by the government in the 1970s. |
| innocent text | Secret writing technique. |
| IST | Integrated systems test. |
| IT | Innocent text. |
| JENNIFER | Classified code name of the security system used for the AZORIAN program. |
| *K-129* | Soviet submarine that sank in 1968 in the central North Pacific. |
| ksi | Kilo-pounds per square inch. |
| kts | Knots (nautical miles per hour). |
| LAPD | Los Angeles Police Department. |

| | |
|---|---|
| LBS | Long baseline position reference system. |
| LLL | Lawrence Livermore Laboratories. |
| LMSC | Lockheed Missiles and Space Company |
| MATADOR | Classified code name for the planned 1975 target recovery mission. |
| metacentric height | Measure related to the righting moment of a ship. |
| mining vehicle | White-world euphemism for the capture vehicle. |
| Moho | Mohorovicic discontinuity. |
| Mohole | Project to drill through the Earth's crust to the Mohorovicic discontinuity. |
| MRI | Mechanics Research Inc. |
| MV | Mining vehicle. |
| nm | Nautical mile. |
| NSA | National Security Agency. |
| ONI | Office of Naval Intelligence. |
| OPSEC | Acronym for Operational Security. |
| OXCART | Classified code name for the CIA's A-12 aircraft development program. |
| parking brake | Stationary, rotatable, support structure for the lifting pipe when not supported by the heavy lift yokes. |
| pipe string | A series, or "string," of pipe segments screwed together. |
| PM | Perceptions management. |
| psi | Pounds per square inch. |
| *Pueblo* | U.S. Navy intelligence collection ship captured by North Korea in 1968. |
| Reynolds number | Scaling factor used for model testing in a homogenous fluid. |
| rogue wave | Wave with much greater height than average for existing sea state. |
| SALT II | Acronym for the second Strategic Arms Limitation Treaty. |
| *SB-10* | Soviet AGI used to monitor *Glomar Explorer* recovery operations in 1974. |
| SBS | Short baseline position reference system. |
| *Seascope* | Converted Navy minesweeper used for nodule exploration in 1972. |
| SEAL | Acronym for versatile Navy diver group operating in sea, air, and land. |
| SEC | Securities Exchange Commission. |
| snubbers | Flexible dampers at top and bottom of heave compensator travel. |
| sonar, profiling | Downward-looking sonars used to profile area directly below the capture vehicle. |
| sonar, side-looking | Capture vehicle sonars used for search. |
| SOSUS | Acronym for Sound Surveillance System. |
| strongback | Large box structure making up the hull of the capture vehicle. |
| Summa | Corporate name given to Howard Hughes's business activities in 1972. |

| | |
|---|---|
| target | Shortened form of target object, the portion of the *K-129* to be recovered. |
| target object | Portion of the *K-129* that the CIA attempted to recover. |
| Tiger Team | Panel of experts pulled together to assess a specific problem. |
| tines | Clawlike arms used to encircle and contain the target before raising. |
| TO | Target object. |
| TPRS | Transponder Position Reference System. |
| transfer boom | Transfer cart railway extending from main deck to rig floor. |
| transfer cart | Cart used to transfer pipe doubles along the transfer boom from main deck to rig floor. |
| transfer crane | Crane used to transfer pipe doubles from pipe storage hold to transfer cart. |
| UNCLOS III | United Nations Convention on Law of the Sea. |
| WCPO | CIA's West Coast program office, operating under the cover of Summa Corporation. |
| white world | All people without accessed to a classified program such as AZORIAN. |

# Notes

### Preface

1. CIA, *Project AZORIAN: The Story of the Hughes Glomar Explorer* (Washington, DC: FOIA Response, 2010), 37; CIA, Office of Public Affairs and Agency Information, news release on DCI Robert Gates's visit to Moscow in October 1992, released November 10, 1992.

2. CIA, *Project AZORIAN*, 1.

3. Robert M. Gates, *From the Shadows: The Ultimate Insider's Story of Five Presidents and How They Won the Cold War* (New York: Simon & Schuster, 2007), 553–554.

### Chapter 1. Genesis

1. International Atomic Energy Agency, *Technical Document 1242, Appendix 1.3, Accidents Resulting in Actual or Potential Release to the Marine Environment* (September 2001), 24.

2. CIA, *Project AZORIAN: The Story of the Hughes Glomar Explorer* (Washington, DC: FOIA Response, 2010), 2, 4.

3. Norman Polmar and Michael White, *Project AZORIAN: The CIA and the Raising of the K-129* (Annapolis, MD: Naval Institute Press, 2010), 31–33.

4. Sherry Sontag and Christopher Drew, *Blind Man's Bluff: The Untold Story of American Submarine Espionage* (New York: PublicAffairs, 1998), 78–80.

5. Polmar and White, *Project AZORIAN*, 45–46.

6. Ibid., 46.

7. Sontag and Drew, *Blind Man's Bluff*, 79–80.

8. Ibid., 60–61.

9. Ibid., 81.

10. William J. Broad, *The Universe Below: Discovering the Secrets of the Deep Sea* (New York: Simon & Schuster, 1998), 79.

11. Sontag and Drew, *Blind Man's Bluff*, 83.

12. John Craven, *The Silent War: The Cold War Battle Beneath the Sea* (New York: Simon & Schuster, 2001), 108–111.

13. Craven, *The Silent War*, 113–114; Norman Polmar, *Ship and Aircraft of the U.S. Fleet*, 18th ed. (Annapolis: Naval Institute Press, 2004), 95–96.

14. Sontag and Drew, *Blind Man's Bluff*, 84.

15. Ibid., 305.

16. CIA, *Project AZORIAN*, 4.

17. On February 10, 1964, DCI John McCone wrote to his deputy, General Marshall Carter: "Two subjects on which we must reach an agreed policy decision are (a) the surfacing of the Ox, and (b) the management of NRO. With reference to the former, I reviewed the 'visibility' of the Ox on Friday. I find that Drs. Wheelon and Maxey are agreed that the improved Soviet radar capability makes the Ox visible both to the long range search radar and the radars associated with the surface-to-air missile systems. Therefore, it is impossible to fly the Ox over the Soviet Union without detection."

18. CIA, *Project AZORIAN*, 4.

19. Richard Helms, *A Look over My Shoulder: A Life in the Central Intelligence Agency* (New York: Random House, 2003), 395.

20. Sontag and Drew, *Blind Man's Bluff*, 83.

21. Willard Bascom, *The Crest of the Wave: Adventures in Oceanography* (New York: Doubleday, 1990), 264.

22. Curtis Crooke told this story in his speech at the ASME award ceremony on July 20, 2006, naming the *Hughes Glomar Explorer* as a National Historic Mechanical Engineering Landmark.

23. Craven, *The Silent War*, 115–127.

24. Associated Press, "Russia Clears 9-Year British Naval Mystery; London Did Not Know Fate of Lost Submarine," *New York Times*, August 18, 1928.

25. William Colby, *Honorable Men: My Life in the CIA* (New York: Simon & Schuster, 1978), 296.

26. Sontag and Drew, *Blind Man's Bluff*, 84.

27. Ibid., 305.

28. CIA, *Project AZORIAN*, 9–12.

## Chapter 2. The Magic Trick

1. US Air Force, *Program Protection Planning: US Air Force Pamphlet 63-1701* (Washington, DC: Air Force e-publishing, 2003), http://www.e-publishing.af.mil.

2. A program *observable* is any piece of information on a program that can be viewed by people *outside* the program. Examples include the identity of the sponsor (government or commercial), the backgrounds/expertise of contractor personnel assigned to the program, existence of special security precautions at contractor plants, etc.

3. Richard A. Sampson, "The Hughes Glomar Explorer Project," *Journal of the OPSEC Professional Society*, 2nd ed. (1995): 42.

4. Manfred Krutein, who died in 2002, wrote a book that discussed his involvement with the AZORIAN program. Coauthored with his wife, Eva, *Amerika? America!* was published in 1997 by Amador Publishers.

5. Interestingly, in an interview given years after the HGE program was completed, former secretary of defense Melvin Laird alluded to his own role in the program. He confirmed that he had favored the program largely because of the potential for the system to be used to rescue crew from sunken U.S. submarines. He also indicated that he had talked personally to Howard Hughes about the program at that time.

6. The CIA has never officially acknowledged that LMSC was involved in the *Hughes Glomar Explorer* program, even though Lockheed negotiated a number of unclassified contracts for design and fabrication of equipment for AZORIAN. Most notably, Lockheed openly con-

tracted with National Steel and Shipbuilding (NASSCO) in San Diego for the construction of the *Hughes Mining Barge* (*HMB-1*), the submersible barge in which the capture vehicle was built.

The CIA's gratuitous (and not entirely welcome) protection of Lockheed's involvement continues to this day. Interestingly, that protection was never extended to Global Marine or Hughes Tool Co., both of whom also had direct contracts with the CIA. I remind the reader that my alleging that Lockheed was involved in the AZORIAN program does not represent an official CIA confirmation of that fact.

7. CIA, *Project Azorian*, 5.

## Chapter 3. Living the Lie

1. The Soviet government agreed to participate in negotiations to reduce aggressive at-sea actions in October 1971. The agreement was eventually signed in May 1972.

2. Eva Krutein and Manfred Krutein, *Amerika? America! From Immigration to Espionage* (Albuquerque: Amador Publishers, 1997), 192, 193.

## Chapter 4. Final Design

1. Dr. Hank Van Calcar, "Precision Subsea Navigation System," *Navigation* 17, no. 2 (Spring 1970): 149–157.

2. In the mid-1980s, the Defense Advanced Research Projects Agency (DARPA) contracted with Lockheed to build a stealthy ship. This ship, the *Sea Shadow*, was actually built in the *HMB-1*. Initially, the *Sea Shadow* underwent testing only at night, but in 1993 it was disclosed to the world.

## Chapter 5. Getting Ready

1. Richard Helms, *A Look over My Shoulder: A Life in the Central Intelligence Agency* (New York: Random House, 2003), 403.

2. William Colby, *Honorable Men: My Life in the CIA* (New York: Simon & Schuster, 1978), 303–306; Helms, *A Look over My Shoulder*, 396–408.

3. Memorandum of Conversation, President's meeting with Dr. Kissinger, Secretary Schlesinger, Director Colby, and Adm. Moorer, January 22, 1974, folder: January 22, 1974, box 3, National Security Adviser—Memoranda of Conversations, Gerald R. Ford Library, 5.

4. In *The Silent War*, John Craven humorously describes a meeting with some AZORIAN people in a bar at Isthmus Cove (221–222). He apparently had the impression that they were engaged in some kind of covert activity. In actual fact, however, the white-world activity in which the *HGE* was involved was the transfer of the Hughes mining machine from the *HMB-1* into the well of the ship—all very straightforward and consistent with the DOMP cover story.

5. Associated Press, "Russia Clears 9-Year British Naval Mystery; London Did Not Know Fate of Lost Submarine," *New York Times*, August 18, 1928.

6. William Colby, as quoted in Sontag and Drew, *Blind Man's Bluff*, 316–317.

7. Colby, *Honorable Men*, 373.

8. Ibid., 414.

9. Sherry Sontag and Christopher Drew, *Blind Man's Bluff: The Untold Story of American Submarine Espionage* (New York: PublicAffairs, 1998), 316–317.

## Chapter 6. The Recovery Mission

1. CIA, *Project AZORIAN: The Story of the* Hughes Glomar Explorer (Washington, DC: FOIA Response, 2010), 37.

2. Harry Jackson, in an oral history interview conducted by the Naval Institute, reported that the fight between the captain and the injured messman occurred in the wardroom of the *Bel Hudson* after a heavy drinking session and, perhaps, some competition for women who were present.

3. CIA, *Project AZORIAN*, 39–40.

4. In this case, the unclassified ship's log refers to the mining machine as the NCV (nodule collection vehicle).

5. William Colby, *30 Ans de CIA* (Paris: Simon & Schuster, 1978), 331–335.

6. CIA, *Project AZORIAN*, 47.

7. Ibid., 43.

8. CIA, *Project AZORIAN*, 46.

9. Eva Krutein and Manfred Krutein, *Amerika? America! From Immigration to Espionage* (Albuquerque: Amador Publishing, 1997), 248.

10. CIA, *Project AZORIAN*, 48.

11. Gerald Ford, *A Time to Heal* (New York: Harper & Row, 1979), 136. In an interview by ABC News in Washington, November 13, 1992, Colby said, "It was helpful. I wouldn't say it was as useful as if we had totally succeeded of course! I mean we would have been much better off, but we did get certain things out of it."

12. Bear in mind that the AZORIAN oversight panel chaired by Carl Duckett's deputy, Lloyd Lauderdale, had assessed that the ship and crew were not really prepared for the mission in summer of 1974. But, given the high risk of program exposure, they determined that we couldn't wait until 1975. Their advice to the program office was "Take a stab at it," recognizing that the probability of success was low.

13. William Colby, *Honorable Men: My Life in the CIA* (New York: Simon & Schuster, 1978), 413–414; William Colby, in a January 13, 1992, interview with ABC News, said, "and we hope to be able to go back again—next summer—and finish the job that we partially finished the previous summer."

14. Krutein and Krutein, *Amerika? America!*, 248–249.

15. Ibid., 251.

16. Sherry Sontag and Christopher Drew, *Blind Man's Bluff: The Untold Story of American Submarine Espionage* (New York: PublicAffairs, 1998), 197.

17. Roy Varner and Wayne Collier, *A Matter of Risk: The Incredible Inside Story of the CIA's Hughes Glomar Explorer Mission to Raise a Russian Submarine* (New York: Random House, 1978), 191.

18. Varner and Collier, *A Matter of Risk*, 194.

## Chapter 7. MATADOR

1. So far as I know, Tom never went to sea again. In fact, he quit his engineering job at Western Gear and by the time I left the program had reportedly become a full-time ski instructor at a prestigious West Coast resort.

2. William Farr and Jerry Cohen, "Sunken Ship Deal by CIA, Hughes Told," *Los Angeles Times*, February 7, 1975.

3. William Colby, *Honorable Men: My Life in the CIA* (New York: Simon & Schuster, 1978), 414.

4. Memorandum of Conversation, President's meeting with Dr. Kissinger, Secretary Schlesinger, Director Colby, Gen. David Jones, Donald Rumsfeld, February 7, 1975, folder: 2/7/75 Ford, Kissinger, Schlesinger, Colby, General David Jones, Rumsfeld, box 9, Gerald R. Ford Library, 2.

5. Colby, *Honorable Men*, 414.

6. Colby, *Honorable Men*, 415.

7. Tennent H. Bagley, *Spy Wars: Moles, Mysteries, and Deadly Games* (New Haven: Yale University Press, 2007).

8. Interview with Rear Adm. Viktor Dygalo, conducted by Michael White, May 15, 2007.

9. Colby, *Honorable Men*, 416, 417.

10. Ibid.

11. Memorandum of Conversation, President's meeting with Secretary Schlesinger, Philip Buchen, John Marsh, Amb. Rumsfeld, Lt. Gen. Scowcroft, and Director Colby, March 19, 1975, folder: 3/19/75 Ford, Schlesinger, Colby, Buchen, Marsh, Rumsfeld, box 10, Gerald R. Ford Library.

12. Colby, *Honorable Men,* 415.

13. Anatoly Dobrynin, *In Confidence: Moscow's Ambassador to America's Six Cold War Presidents* (New York: Times Books, 1995), 357.

14. Note from Amb. Anatoly Dobrynin to Dr. Henry Kissinger, March 29, 1975, folder: Glomar Explorer, box 1, Staff Assistant Peter Rodman Files, Gerald R. Ford Library.

15. Memorandum from Secretary Kissinger to President Ford, April 2, 1975, folder: Glomar Explorer, box 1, Staff Assistant Peter Rodman Files, Gerald R. Ford Library.

16. Dobrynin, *In Confidence, 358.*

17. Associated Press, "Did Hughes' Spy Ship Pirate Gold Treasure?" *San Mateo Times*, October 18, 1975.

18. Varner and Collier, *A Matter of Risk*, 219.

19. Richard Anderson is probably most famously remembered for his role as "Oscar," the doctor who created the biomechanical hero in the TV series *The Six Million Dollar Man*.

20. The film has survived and was shown in its entirety in 2006 at a *Hughes Glomar Explorer* award ceremony sponsored by the American Society of Mechanical Engineers.

21. Telegram from John Wayne to President Ford, September 29, 1976, folder: White House Central File; Wayne, John, box 3353, Gerald R. Ford Library.

22. President Ford to John Wayne, October 4, 1976, folder: White House Central File; Wayne, John, box 3353, Gerald R. Ford Library.

### Epilogue

1. Gerald Ford, *A Time to Heal* (New York: Harper & Row, 1979), 265.

2. "In Memoriam: John Parangosky, National Reconnaissance Pioneer," *National Reconnaissance: Journal of the Discipline and Practice* (2005-U1): 67.

3. Anatoly Dobrynin, *In Confidence: Moscow's Ambassador to America's Six Cold War Presidents* (New York: Times Books, 1995), 134–135.

4. Walt Logan had been chief of the program's Commercial Operations Division before transferring to the Intelligence Community Staff and finally back to the office of security when MATADOR was terminated.

5. Willard Bascom, *The Crest of the Wave: Adventures in Oceanography* (New York: Doubleday, 1990), 241–242.

6. Thomas O'Toole, "Glomar Roots Go Back to 1962 Scheme," *Washington Post*, May 22, 1977.

7. William Colby, *Honorable Men: My Life in the CIA* (New York: Simon & Schuster, 1978), 414–417.

8. Gerald R. Ford, *A Time to Heal* (New York: Harper and Row, 1979), 135–136.

9. Colby, *Honorable Men*, 417.

10. *Phillipi v. CIA*, 546 F.2d 1009 (US Court of Appeals, DC, 1976).

11. *MAP v. Casey*, 656 F.2d 724 (US Court of Appeals, DC, 1981).

12. Robert M. Gates, *From the Shadows: The Ultimate Insider's Story of Five Presidents and How They Won the Cold War* (New York: Simon & Schuster, 2007), 553.

13. William J. Broad, "Russia Says U.S. Got Sub's Atom Arms," *New York Times*, June 20, 1993.

14. International Atomic Energy Agency, Attachment E, *Inventory of Accidents and Losses at Sea Involving Radioactive Material*, IAEA-TECDOC-1242, Appendix I.3, 21–24.

15. Sherry Sontag and Christopher Drew, *Blind Man's Bluff: The Untold Story of American Submarine Espionage* (New York: PublicAffairs, 1998), 81.

16. John Craven, *The Silent War: The Cold War Battle Beneath the Sea* (New York: Simon & Schuster, 2001), 206, 217.

17. Kenneth Sewell, *Red Star Rogue: The Untold Story of a Soviet Submarine's Nuclear Strike Attempt on the U.S.* (New York: Simon & Schuster, 2005).

18. Ed Offley, *Scorpion Down: Sunk by the Soviets, Buried by the Pentagon: The Untold Story of the USS Scorpion* (New York: Basic Books, 2007).

19. Norman Polmar and Michael White, *Project AZORIAN: The CIA and the Raising of the K-129* (Annapolis, MD: Naval Institute Press, 2010).

20. Craven, *The Silent War*, 204–206.

21. Polmar and White, *Project AZORIAN*, 106.

## Appendix A. Perceptions Management and Disinformation

1. Anthony Cave Brown, *Bodyguard of Lies* (New York: Harper & Row, 1975).

2. Carolyn Pumphrey and Antullio Echevarria II, "Strategic Deception in Modern Democracies: Ethical, Legal, and Policy Challenges," Conference Brief, Strategic Studies Institute, U.S. Army War College, and Triangle Institute for Security Studies, 2003, pp. 2–3.

3. John Craven, *The Silent War: The Cold War Battle Beneath the Sea* (New York: Simon & Schuster, 2001), 219, 220.

4. Pumphrey and Echevarria, "Strategic Deception," 1.

## Appendix B. The Docking Problem

1. Entrained water is the water contained within the structure of a body, increasing the effective mass of the body. The expression "added mass" refers to the mass of water external to the structure of an underwater body that essentially moves in sync with it, increasing the effective mass of the body. The calculation of added mass is dependent upon a number of variables, such as velocity and drag coefficient.

# Bibliography

Alpern, David M. "CIA's Mission Impossible." *Newsweek*, March 31, 1975.

ASME. *Hughes Glomar Explorer, an ASME Historic Mechanical Engineering Landmark.* Brochure prepared for the award ceremony in Galveston, TX, July 20, 2006.

Associated Press. "Russia Clears 9-Year British Naval Mystery; London Did Not Know Fate of Lost Submarine." *New York Times,* August 18, 1928.

Bagley, Tennent H. *Spy Wars: Moles, Mysteries and Deadly Games.* New Haven: Yale University Press, 2007.

Barlett, Donald, and James Steele. *Howard Hughes: His Life and Madness.* New York: W. W. Norton, 1979.

Bascom, Willard. *Crest of the Wave: Adventures in Oceanography.* New York: Doubleday, 1990.

Broad, William J. "Russia Says U.S. Got Sub's Atom Arms," *New York Times,* June 20, 1993.

———. *The Universe Below: Discovering the Secrets of the Deep Sea.* New York: Simon & Schuster, 1998.

Brown, Anthony Cave. *Bodyguard of Lies.* New York: Harper & Row, 1975.

Burleson, Clyde W. *The Jennifer Project.* Englewood Cliffs, NJ: Prentice-Hall, 1977.

Central Intelligence Agency. Memorandum from Director of Central Intelligence McCone to the Deputy Director of Central Intelligence (Marshall Carter), DCI (McCone) Files, DCI McCone Memoranda, March 1, 1962.

———. Office of Public Affairs and Agency Information. News release on DCI Robert Gates's visit to Moscow in October 1992. Released November 10, 1992.

———. *Project AZORIAN: The Story of the Hughes Glomar Explorer.* Washington, DC, FOIA response, 2010.

Colby, William. *Honorable Men: My Life in the CIA.* New York: Simon & Schuster, 1978.

———. *30 Ans de CIA.* Paris: Simon & Schuster, 1978.

———. Interview by ABC News in Washington, November 13, 1992.

Craven, John P., Dr. *The Silent War: The Cold War Battle Beneath the Sea.* New York: Simon & Schuster, 2001.

Dobrynin, Anatoly. *In Confidence.* New York: Times Books, 1995.

Earley, Pete. *Family of Spies: Inside the John Walker Spy Ring.* New York: Bantam Books, 1988.

Farr, William, and Jerry Cohen. "Sunken Ship Deal by CIA, Hughes Told." *Los Angeles Times,* February 7, 1975.

Ford, Gerald R. *A Time to Heal.* New York: Harper & Row, 1979.

Gates, Robert M. *From the Shadows: The Ultimate Insider's Story of Five Presidents and How They Won the Cold War.* New York: Simon & Schuster, 2007.

Global Marine Development. Deck logs of the *Hughes Glomar Explorer.* July 1, 1974–August 31, 1974.

———. *The Glomar Explorer: Deep Ocean Working Vessel, Technical Description and Specification.* Newport Beach, CA: Global Marine, 1975.

International Atomic Energy Agency. *Technical Document 1242, Appendix 1.3, Accidents Resulting in Actual or Potential Release to the Marine Environment.* September 2001.

Jackson, Harry. Oral interview conducted by the Naval Institute, September 3, 1998.

Krutein, Eva, and Manfred Krutein. *America? America! From Immigration to Espionage.* Albuquerque, NM: Amador Publishers, 1997.

Offley, Ed. *Scorpion Down: Sunk by the Soviets, Buried by the Pentagon: The Untold Story of the USS Scorpion.* New York: Basic Books, 2007.

Polmar, Norman. *Naval Institute Guide to the Soviet Navy.* 5th ed. Annapolis, MD: Naval Institute Press, 1991.

———. *Ships and Aircraft of the U.S. Fleet.* 18th ed. Annapolis, MD: Naval Institute Press, 2004.

Polmar, Norman, and Michael White. *Project AZORIAN: The CIA and the Raising of the* K-129. Annapolis, MD: Naval Institute Press, 2010.

Pumphrey, Carolyn, and Antullio Echevarria II. "Strategic Deception in Modern Democracies: Ethical, Legal, and Policy Challenges." Conference brief, Strategic Studies Institute, U.S. Army War College, and Triangle Institute for Security Studies, 2003.

Reed, W. Craig. *Red November: Inside the Secret U.S.-Soviet Submarine War.* New York: HarperCollins, 2010.

Richelson, Jeffrey T. *The Wizards of Langley: Inside the CIA's Directorate of Science and Technology.* Boulder, CO: Westview Press, 2002.

Sampson, Richard A. "The Hughes Glomar Explorer Project." *Journal of the OPSEC Professional Society,* 2nd ed. (1995): 39–46.

Sewell, Kenneth, and Clint Richmond. *Red Star Rogue: The Untold Story of a Soviet Submarine's Nuclear Strike Attempt on the U.S.* New York: Simon & Schuster, 2005.

Sontag, Sherry, and Christopher Drew. *Blind Man's Bluff: The Untold Story of American Submarine Espionage.* New York: PublicAffairs, 1998.

Sutton, Roger J. *Secure Communications: Applications and Management.* London: John Wiley & Sons, 2002.

U.S. Air Force. *Program Protection Planning: US Air Force Pamphlet 63-1701.* Washington, DC: Air Force e-publishing, 2003. http:///www.e-publishing.af.mil.

Van Calcar, Henry. "Precision Subsea Navigation System." *Navigation* 17 (Spring 1970).

Varner, Roy, and Wayne Collier. *A Matter of Risk: The Incredible Inside Story of the CIA's Hughes Glomar Explorer Mission to Raise a Russian Submarine.* New York: Random House, 1978.

Wallace, Robert, and H. Keith Melton. *Spycraft: The Secret History of the CIA's Spytechs from Communism to Al-Qaeda.* New York: Dutton, 2008.

Wetmore, Sherman. "The Global Marine Story." *Global Marine News*, August 1989.

———. *Hughes Glomar Explorer*. Speech given at Offshore Energy Center during ASME Historic Mechanical Engineering Landmark Award, Galveston, TX, July 2006.

Whitman, Edward C. "SOSUS: The 'Secret Weapon' of Undersea Surveillance." *Undersea Warfare* 7, no. 2 (Winter 2005).

Wirtz, James J., and Loch K. Johnson. *Strategic Intelligence: Windows into a Secret World. An Anthology*. Westport, CT: Greenwood Publishing, 2006.

# Index